THE ORIGINS OF THE FRENCH REVOLUTIONARY WARS

ORIGINS OF MODERN WARS
General editor: *Harry Hearder*

Titles already published:

THE ORIGINS OF THE FIRST WORLD WAR
   James Joll
THE ORIGINS OF THE ARAB-ISRAELI WARS
   Ritchie Ovendale
THE ORIGINS OF THE RUSSO-JAPANESE WAR
   Ian Nish
THE ORIGINS OF THE FRENCH REVOLUTIONARY WARS
   T. C. W. Blanning

THE ORIGINS OF
THE FRENCH
REVOLUTIONARY WARS

T. C. W. Blanning

LONGMAN
London and New York

LONGMAN GROUP LIMITED
Longman House, Burnt Mill, Harlow
Essex CM20 2JE, England
Associated companies throughout the world

*Published in the United States of America
by Longman Inc., New York*

© Longman Group Limited 1986

First published 1986

BRITISH LIBRARY CATALOGUING IN PUBLICATION DATA

Blanning, T.C.W.
The origins of the French Revolutionary wars.
—(Origins of modern wars)
1. France—Politics and government—1789–1900
I. Title
944. 04   DC148

ISBN 0-582-49051-0

LIBRARY OF CONGRESS CATALOGING IN PUBLICATION DATA

Blanning, T. C. W.
The origins of the French revolutionary wars.

(Origins of modern wars)
Bibliography: p.
Includes index.
1. First Coalition, War of the, 1792–1797—Causes.
2. Second Coalition, War of the, 1798–1801—Causes.
I. Title. II. Series.
DC220.B63   1986   944.04   85–6936
ISBN 0–582–49051–0

Set in 10/11pt Linoterm Times
Produced by Longman Group (FE) Limited
Printed in Hong Kong

CONTENTS

EDITOR'S FOREWORD

The third volume to be published in this series, Dr Blanning's *The Origins of the French Revolutionary Wars*, is the first in a chronological sense. It starts with a penetrating study of the causes of wars in general. Dr Blanning reminds his readers in Chapter 1 that 'political intercourse between most states in most periods is conducted peacefully'. War, then, is an aberration but an aberration of such importance that a study of the causes of specific wars will always be a vital task for historians. To look more closely at one aspect of the question, it should be asked why two countries can repeatedly go to war with each other over long periods, and then reach a point at which further war between them becomes unlikely, and eventually almost inconceivable.

The war whose origins Dr Blanning examines was most persistently fought by France on the one hand and Britain on the other. It was in one sense the culmination of centuries of intermittent warfare between the two countries. Yet after 1815 France and Britain always patched up crises between them without resorting to war. The two countries were allies against Russia in 1854. Very soon after the Crimean War there was still the possibility of armed conflict over several issues, and something of a naval race developed between them. Yet peace was kept. The last time when it was conceivable that France and Britain might go to war with each other was during the Fashoda crisis in 1898, when large sectors of public opinion in both countries were eager for war, but the governments were too wise to fight over a distant corner of East Africa. In the twentieth century it has become increasingly unthinkable that France and Britain should go to war with each other, so that in the present volume Dr Blanning is considering, among much else, the causes of the last war between the two Western countries – a war fought a century ago.

There are other examples of two countries whose relations have reached a point beyond which war seems inconceivable. The U.S.A. and Canada is an obvious one; France and West Germany since 1945 is another. To explain such happy developments in terms of a common enemy or membership of a supra-national organization is too facile and sometimes wholly unconvincing. Any answer to the question must surely take into consideration political, diplomatic and economic factors, but it must also go deeper and consider psychological factors – changes in national mentality, or what public opinion will permit the government to do.

Professor Joll in his *Origins of the First World War* stressed the role played by the miscalculations of the political leaders, in causing war. Dr Blanning, in his Chapter 3, shows that the French revolutionary government in 1792 mistakenly believed that a war against Austria would lead to widespread revolutionary outbreaks in Belgium and Germany. On the other hand the Austrians and Prussians mistakenly believed that a war against a revolutionary rabble could be easily won. Blanning also reminds us that not all citizens of a country, or even members of the ruling circle, want war for the same reason. This was especially true of France in 1792. At the outbreak of any war there will be a group of people who want to preserve peace, and other groups who want war, or fear that it cannot be avoided, for various and sometimes contradictory reasons. A statement like 'French motives for war were . . .' must therefore almost always be a simplification, but simplifications are sometimes needed in the narration of history.

In his Conclusion Blanning considers the role of ideology. Again, it is easy to over-simplify and to classify one war as an ideological one, and another as a war of interests. In practice, ideological and strategic or *Realpolitik* factors become hopelessly entangled. Dr Blanning deals convincingly with this theme in his Introduction and Conclusion and the illustrations he provides from the 1790s underline the point.

In his chapter on the origins of the War of the Second Coalition, Dr Blanning has an interesting passage in which he says 'war had become a way of life, even a matter of necessity for the Directory', and he quotes Sorel: 'War alone assured the existence of the Directory, and war could be sustained only by war itself.' This is grimly reminiscent of Eisenhower's frank comment that the industrial-military complex needs continual re-armament, in order to sustain its enormous profits and prestige. Whether an indefinitely continued policy of massive armaments must lead ultimately to war is an open question, but Eisenhower, in his last days, saw the enormous danger in such a policy. The French government of the Directorate in the 1790s depended for its survival not only on the retention of a large army, but on the waging of war itself. It is difficult to feel sorry for the Directorate when Napoleon took over. As Dr Blanning suggests there was a certain poetic justice in the fact that 'a regime which had lived by the sword should be executed by its most successful general'. But Napoleon's authority was, of course, to be less brief, and, so far as the destruction of human life was concerned, far more terrible.

HARRY HEARDER

PREFACE

Although at one time or another I have worked in the relevant archives in London, Paris, Vienna and elsewhere, this book does not claim to be based on extensive archival research. Reworking the mountains of material sifted so painstakingly by nineteenth-century scholars such as Ranke and Sybel would be a task to last at least one lifetime. What I have tried to do is to read all the printed sources and secondary works I could find in an attempt to unravel the origins of the 'first of modern wars'. As will be explained in Chapter 2, most of those works derive from the last century. In recent decades, the history of international relations, so far as the French Revolution is concerned at least, has been not so much neglected as ignored. If it were known at all, Ranke's observation that the French Revolution should be studied as one part of international relations, rather than the other way round, would excite only incomprehension or derision from most historians of the period. In a later work I intend to argue that Ranke's dictum is not as foolish as it may sound and that 'history from below', despite the brilliance of some of its exponents (most notably Richard Cobb), is not the *only* valid approach. In the meantime, it is hoped that this present book will suggest that there is still something to be gained from the study of international relations in the revolutionary period.

In preparing this book I have accumulated numerous debts of gratitude, not least to several generations of undergraduates with whom I have argued about the general and specific issues raised in it. I am particularly grateful to the following for the opportunity to expose an early draft of Chapter 1 to public discussion and criticism: the Irish History Students Association, the Stubbs Society, Oxford, and the history societies of Queen's University, Belfast, Churchill College, King's College, Trinity College and Sidney Sussex College, Cambridge. Of the various libraries I have used, I am particularly indebted to the University Library, Cambridge; the British Library, London; the Bibliothèque Nationale, Paris; the Nationalbibliothek, Vienna; and the library of the Institut für Europäische Geschichte, Mainz. Last but not least, I must thank the editor of this series, Professor Harry Hearder, and Professor Derek Beales for reading and commenting on a first draft.

T. C. W. BLANNING
Cambridge, January 1985

Chapter 1

THE ORIGINS OF GREAT WARS

They spent the rest of the hour discussing violence in the modern world. On the whole, the bricklayers seemed to think it was a good thing.

'I mean what's the point of going out on a Saturday night and getting pissed if you can't have a bit of a barney at the same time? Got to get rid of your aggression somehow', said an unusually articulate bricklayer, 'I mean it's natural isn't it?'

'So you think man is a naturally aggressive animal', said Wilt.

'Course he is. That's history for you, all them wars and things. It's only bloody poofters don't like violence.'

(Tom Sharpe, *Wilt*)[1]

PSYCHOLOGICAL EXPLANATIONS OF WAR

The problem with which the day-release bricklayers were wrestling at the Fenland College of Arts and Technology has exercised many minds from many disciplines in every age, and never more intensively than at present. A recent bibliography, disconcertingly but perhaps appropriately sponsored by the Mental Health Research Institute of the University of Michigan, lists about 2,500 authors.[2] The destructive potential of the nuclear bomb, although used in anger only twice during the forty-odd years since its invention, has made war *per se* a subject on which only one opinion is possible. While there is much furious debate on how best to avoid it, deterrence theorists vie with unilateralists in the vehemence of their condemnation. Long gone are the days when such robust theorists as Heinrich von Treitschke extolled 'the greatness of war', 'the sublimity of war', 'the moral majesty of war' and derided the notion of perpetual peace as 'not only impossible but immoral as well'.[3] Treitschke, of course, lived at a time when wars were short, when casualties were light and – most important of all – when the God of Victories smiled on the 'right' side. Tens of millions of deaths in twentieth-century conflicts – and the prospect of untold millions more to come – have lent a new urgency to the investigation of the origins and nature of war, so that it can be better avoided in future.

To the fore in this exercise have been psychologists. As they have plumbed the depths of the human psyche, they have been able to trawl up what seem to be the really fundamental causes of war. Far, far removed from the diplomatic historian's surface-world of tainted mushrooms or railway timetables, down past the structures of the social scientist and the economist's forces of production, the psychologists' bathyscope keeps going until it touches rock-bottom. Needless to say, the fantastic creatures they find there vary considerably in shape and dimension. What the observers have in common, however, is an angle of vision which is both individualistic (because the starting-point is always the individual human psyche) and abstract (because human nature is always regarded as timeless and universal).

In 1932, under the auspices of the League of Nations, Sigmund Freud exchanged letters with Albert Einstein on the causes of war, without alas being able to rise above the level of tentative superficiality.[4] More representative of the genre is E. F. M. Durbin and John Bowlby's *Personal Aggressiveness and War,* first published on the eve of the Second World War but still influential and still cited with respect.[5] At the core of their analysis lie man's aggressive impulses. Punished and prevented in childhood by parents and in adulthood by the state, his ensuing frustration is resolved by three unconscious mechanisms. The first is 'transformation', by which the hostility is transferred from the immediate repressing agent to some more distant collective target: Jews, Communists, Fascists, Germans, Argentinians, or whoever have the best credentials at the time. But just as a child's relationship with his parents is an ambivalent mixture of love and hatred, so is transformation accompanied by a second, more positive mechanism: 'displacement'. By this means, familial loves and hatreds are transferred to some greater entity such as a church, a political party or, above all, a state: 'These various kinds of groups can attract absolute loyalty and canalise torrents of hatred and murder – through the mechanism of displacement.'[6] A third crucial mechanism is 'projection', by which the individual projects on to others his own unrecognised and unaccepted dark impulses. To avoid being divided against his own self, all his potential self-hatred is lavished on third parties: 'Projection is an admirable mechanism for turning the other man into the aggressor, for making hatred appear as a passion for righteousness, for purifying the hate-tormented soul. By this means all war is made into religious war – a crusade for truth and virtue.'[7]

Transformed aggression, displacement and projection have always existed, as mechanisms to resolve what would otherwise be intolerable psychological strain. In the modern period, however, it is the nation-state which has emerged as the main agent of release. That was inevitable, given the state's superior ability to punish private aggression, while its collective nature and size allow it to act with an amorality and lack of conscience which would be intolerable in an individual. So the scene is set for endemic international warfare: 'War is due to nationalism, not because the nation-state is either a peace-making or a war-mongering form of organisation in itself – there are pacific nations and aggressive nations – but because the triumph of aggressive impulses will always manifest itself in a group form and the great group organisation of the age is the nation-state.'[8] But whatever the scale of the agent of our release, it must never be forgotten that the essential unit is the individual human psyche, with all its impulses and frustrations: 'War is due to the expression in and through group life of the transformed aggressiveness of individuals.'[9]

Although Durbin and Bowlby disclaim any great originality, disarmingly describing their work as 'enlightened common sense', their analysis has an appealing cogency. That is due partly, of course, to the depths at which they are operating: in the Stygian darkness of the psyche, a 40-watt bulb seems bright. It is when one applies their concepts – and those of other psychologists – to concrete situations that doubts begin to arise. In particular, there looms the obstinate problem of peace. If only all men at all times in all societies were engaged in war, then the psychological sequence of aggression – frustration – projection would be a sufficient cause. Awkwardly, war is neither permanent nor ubiquitous. In certain societies at certain times it is only intermittent, even exceptional.

The psychologists are well aware of this problem, of course. Durbin and Bowlby concede without further ado that 'Fighting and peaceful cooperation are equally "natural" forms of behaviour, equally fundamental tendencies in human relations. Peaceful cooperation predominates – there is much more peace than war.' All they claim – with a modesty that is now becoming more irritating than disarming – is that 'the willingness to fight is so widely distributed in space and time that it must be regarded as a basic pattern of human behaviour'.[10] But that is to reduce the explanation to the simple, if not banal, formula that: there is war between humans because there are humans. What is needed is an explanation of why peaceful cooperation breaks down and is replaced by war. It is at this point that the limitations of the psychologists' abstract individualism becomes apparent, as their analysis dissolves in a welter of possibilities: 'The nations may fight because of simple acquisitiveness, or simple frustration, or a simple fear of strangers. They may fight because of displaced hatred, or projected hates or fears. There is no single all-embracing cause – no single villain of the piece, no institution nor idea that is wholly to blame.'[11] Psychologists willing to be more precise are more entertaining but no more enlightening, as the following list of 'motives making for war' from another influential work shows: the auto-erotic motive of narcissism (identification with the grandeur of the nation), exhibitionism, the allo-erotic motive of homosexuality (physical contact with a large number of one's own sex in the services), heterosexuality (defence of womenfolk), sadism and the Oedipus complex.[12]

In short, psychologists can explain war (to their own satisfaction, at least) but, by the very nature of their methodology, they cannot explain *wars*. They are aware of this, of course. Durbin and Bowlby announce at the outset that they do not intend to explain the causes of any specific war, only the causes of war *per se*. They conclude later that 'nations *can* fight only because they are able to release the explosive stores of transformed aggression, but they *do* fight for any of a large number of reasons'.[13] Pryns Hopkins is equally blunt: 'Whatever are the *causes* of war – and they may be legion – it is clear that the *fact* of war depends completely upon man's willingness to fight.'[14] But that, surely, is veering perilously close to a tautology. Moreover, if psychology cannot explain *any* specific war, then one must wonder whether it can explain war *per se* – for war *per se* is only the aggregate of all wars, past and present. Just because psychology postulates the universality of human nature, it cannot explain a phenomenon which is intermittent. As Kenneth Waltz has pointed out, human nature may have been the cause of war in 1914, but it was also the cause of peace in 1910 – and whatever else changed in those four years, it was not human nature.[15] It is violence which is universal, not war, which is just one very specialised form of violence. So the formula expressed at the beginning of this paragraph needs to be refined still further: psychologists can explain violence, but they cannot explain wars, or indeed war.[16]

One way round the war–peace dichotomy is to argue that war is a permanent and ubiquitous condition of mankind. That is the solution adopted by Franz Alexander, who has argued that war is the natural and normal way of settling conflicts between groups. Consequently, pacifism is a morbid phenomenon and pacifists (if they are not mentally deficient) are neurotics. What looks like a period of peace is in reality nothing more than a preparation for war: 'A student of European and ancient history can differentiate rightly only between periods of actual and latent war, the latter being misleadingly called periods of peace.'[17] This possesses an attractive simplicity, not to say brutality, but fails on two counts. In the first place, no evidence is presented to show that the periods of war are more 'normal' than the periods of peace (or 'latent war'). It therefore makes just as much – or just as little – sense to say that it is *war* which has never really existed and that what looks like a period of war is in reality nothing more than a preparation for peace. Secondly, it obscures rather than solves the war–peace dichotomy, leaving still unanswered the fundamental question: what determines the incidence of out-and-out war, as opposed to latent war?

If verbal dexterity cannot solve that particular problem, neither can it overcome another defect deriving from psychology's abstract individualism: its populism. Just because psychology can only deal at the level of the individual psyche, it can only explain causation at a mass level. It does not deal with human beings but with *the* human being. So a psychological account of the origin of war is essentially populist, in that it assumes the impulse to come from the people as a whole. For example:

> Those hatreds which in peace-time smoulder in every human soul, varying only in intensity, become licensed then [in war] to vent themselves upon the national enemy. One is allowed – nay ordered – to march against this symbol of the evil father with gun and bayonet, bomb and flame-thrower. The more one tortures, maims, and kills him, the more is one praised. So let there be a holiday from pity. . . .Our native land feeds, clothes and educates us. She therefore becomes to us our *mother*-country whom we love truly as we love our flesh-and-blood mother. When foreign troops threaten our country, we describe their action as one of invading or assaulting her, thus showing who in our unconscious minds we think they are. . . .Unconscious fear of an assault on our mother, therefore, is largely responsible for the clamour that our country shall be 'protected' against potential evil father-figures.[18]

Those murderous impulses, Oedipal and otherwise, which lurk repressed in the subconscious, could only be said to cause wars if it were clear that wars came about as a result of popular pressure. It could then be argued – reasonably – that the patriotic claptrap which precedes wars derives ultimately from the repression of frustrated impulses. To paraphrase Dr Johnson: 'patriotism is the last refuge of the neurotic.' Unfortunately for this line of argument, it is very difficult to find *any* war which was launched as a result of popular pressure. It played a certain part in the War of Jenkins's Ear, the American War of Independence, the French revolutionary war of 1792, the Crimean War, the Franco-Prussian War, perhaps the First World War, but however generous one's category, the list would not be long. Moreover, even in these cases popular pressure was just one of many forces, and not usually the most important. Even in an age of mass democracy, decision-making remains concentrated in the hands of a few.[19] Sometimes the few follow – or are impelled – by the many, but more usually the relationship is reversed. So it is with wars. It is the *outbreak* of a war which creates a great surge of bellicose enthusiasm among the masses, not the other way round. Until perhaps the very eve of war, popular interest in foreign affairs is, at best, tepid. Nor is there any clear correlation between those popular attitudes that do exist and actual conflicts. The collective attitude of the British towards the Germans is one of admiration and respect, that towards the French one of dislike and contempt, but it has not prevented them waging two wars this century against the former in alliance with the latter.[20]

The populist flaw in the psychologists' explanation of the causes of war derives of course from their methodology. They are most confident and convincing when dealing with human nature *per se*, with all human beings, past present and future. One individual human being they can also treat with relative ease – but only if sufficient data are available. Ideally, the subject should be available for first-hand examination, a condition which is rarely, if ever, fulfilled. The psychologists' method really breaks down when it is required to deal, not with one or all human beings, but with *some* human beings. To generalise on man's projection mechanism or to speculate about Hitler's megalomania is one thing, to arrive at a psychological profile of the British Cabinet, the Austrian *Staatskonferenz* or the Soviet Politburo is quite another. It cannot be done. But that is just what has to be done if a valid psychological explanation of wars – and of war – is to be achieved. The insoluble problem was well posed by Emile Durkheim: 'The psychological factor is too general to predetermine the course of social phenomena. Since it does not call for one social form rather than another, it cannot explain any of them.'[21]

It is only when the psychologist is able to identify an exceptional condition that he can be of much assistance to the historian investigating the origins of wars. A good example is William Brown's analysis of national paranoia:

> [It is] the mental tendency of a person who is in a self-assertive mood, rather cut off from others, unable to develop within the group or system, and yet, having to repress his tendencies, feels in repressing them that he is being checked by others and that others wish him ill. Thus he becomes suspicious and obstructive, and may later become somewhat megalomaniac. . . . A paranoid state in any nation makes it a danger to itself and to its neighbours. It may break out into open aggression through the very fact of fear.[22]

That could hardly be bettered as a description of the collective mentality of the decision-makers in revolutionary France on the eve of the war of 1792, (see pp. 99–112), in imperial Germany on the eve of the First World War or in the state of Israel throughout its trouble-torn history. So one is tempted to conclude that only psychopathology, not psychology in general, can be of assistance. That may well be so, but even the more specialised concepts of mental illness leave too great a gap between theory and practice. When reading an abstract diagnosis of the kind offered above by William Brown, its applicability to concrete historical events is often striking: 'Yes, that sounds just like France in 1792.' On the other hand, it is difficult to get much beyond the level of coincidence. The behaviour of the deputies of the National Assembly during the winter of 1791–92 certainly *sounds* like a prime example of group paranoia, but it is hard to be confident, let alone sure. It is clear that the Girondin orators, who persuaded those deputies to vote for war, did appeal to their self-assertiveness, their sense of isolation and persecution and their pre-emptive aggressiveness. It is equally clear that those Girondin orators themselves were also acting for very different reasons, of a purely political kind: to expose the Court, to drive the Revolution left and to seize power. And what was true of a front-line spokesman like Brissot, about whom a great deal is known, may also be true of some silent back-bencher, who is just a name on a list and about whom nothing is known.

If one reverses the exercise and uses the psychopathological categories as a guide, then to seek is to find: but without much consequence. Any group is so rich in psychological diversity, especially at a time of crisis, that almost any hypothesis can be made to fit. That is hardly surprising, since it is the theory itself which governs the selection of the evidence. With unerring accuracy, the psychologist can hit the barn-door time after time after time.[23] What he can also do – as Brown does in the passage quoted above – is to provide the historian with a hypothesis whose terms allow him to describe a prevailing mood with greater precision. But it cannot be anything more than a hypothesis.

Their investigations of the human psyche have not made psychologists optimistic on the subject of war. If the fundamental cause is 'the timeless and ubiquitous urge to fight and kill' (Durbin and Bowlby) and if 'organised societies have always found something to fight about' (Jerome D. Frank), then there seems no reason why it should not continue *ad infinitum*.[24] The daunting nature of the assignment has not deterred some, however, from essaying a cure for war based on a psychological analysis of its causes. In a recent cooperative investigation supervised by Maurice Walsh, those causes were located in the father–mother–son triangle: 'The governing bodies and leaders of the nations of the world are made up predominantly of older males, who recurrently produce mass murder, in recurring 'wars', of younger males of each new generation. . . .This would strongly suggest an intense and murderous, albeit unconscious, hostility of older males for younger males.'[25]

Allied to this is man's fatal propensity for choosing as his leaders at times of crisis 'aggressively perverted and psychiatrically abnormal men', all distinguished by their lack of conscious guilt feelings and by their unconscious homicidal/suicidal tendencies. Alexander the Great, Napoleon, Trujillo, Hitler, Stalin and Mussolini are advanced as illustrations. This diagnosis has suggested to Dr Walsh a course of treatment in five parts: firstly, a world government backed by a world police force; secondly, the removal of the profit motive from the armaments industry; thirdly, 'the creation of a new economic system freed from the unconscious anal influence of wealth and power because of the close association of anality (money is related to faeces in the unconscious), and aggressiveness and destructiveness in present human society'; fourthly, the regular psychiatric examination of world leaders by a team of non-political psychoanalysts; and fifthly, 'massive and continuing multi-disciplinary research projects into such disruptive phenomena as malnutrition, overpopulation, racism and environmental pollution'. As Utopias go, this is on the ambitious side: only the final objective seems capable of realisation in this world. And one may doubt whether the pouring of even unlimited funds into the bottomless pits of the world's social science research councils would be anything more than a placebo.

ETHOLOGY AND THE ORIGINS OF WARS

So for the historian in pursuit of the causes of wars, the psychologists' diagnosis can be of only limited assistance. An alternative kind of explanation has been provided by an even more recent branch of science: ethology, defined by one of its leading practitioners as 'the precise study of innate behaviour patterns in animals'.[26] At first sight the ethological approach shares the psychologists' profundity but adds to it a chronological dimension which they so patently lacked. It is a young science (some would say 'pseudo-science') but already has formulated a set of common premises. Most important is the notion that man is an animal.[27] As such, he is fundamentally a creature of instinct, whose rational faculties occupy a decidedly subordinate status: 'instinct makes use of learning the way a furnace sucks in air.'[28] Indeed, human reason itself is not something unique and peculiar but essentially just another product of evolution: *'Are the qualities that we regard as uniquely human the consequence of being human beings, or have we evolved as human beings because of the earlier evolution of qualities that we regard as uniquely human?'* Robert Ardrey supplies the answer to his own question in one of those pithy aphorisms of which he is so fond: *'Our humanity is not the consequence but the cause of becoming human beings.'*[29]

In both humans and animals, one of the strongest instincts is aggression. That is a natural consequence of evolution, for it has been only through a continuous process of struggle that the fittest have survived. Conflict between species ('inter-specific aggression') and conflict between members of the same species ('intra-specific aggression') have performed a number of important functions. Quite apart from providing basic security against predators, conflict has served to improve the quality of the species by sexual selection and to secure its even distribution over the habitat.[30] So this aggressive instinct is as old as the species itself and a necessary condition of its establishment and survival. Of no species is that more true than of the lord of the earth, of man himself. Only 10,000 years ago did peaceful agriculture begin to provide his livelihood and only 5,000 years ago did it become general. For most of his existence man has been a hunter, relying on killing to stay alive[31]:

From his beginnings in Miocene days through the deprivations of the desperate Pliocene and on into the vagaries, the glaciers, the pluvials of a Pleistocene blowing now hot, now cold, now wet, now dry, the evolution of man has brought him to his present estate: he is the world's most successful predator and the richest of all the world's prey.[32]

Wars occur when this primeval aggressive drive collides with another equally deep-rooted instinct: sense of territory. Like all other higher animals, man is in constant need of identity, stimulation and security. Territory provides all three:

'This place is mine; I am of this place', says the albatross, the patas monkey, the green sunfish, the Spaniard, the great horned owl, the wolf, the Venetian, the prairie dog, the three-spined stickleback, the Scotsman, the Skua, the man from La Crosse, Wisconsin, the Alsatian, the little-ringed plover, the Argentine, the lung-fish, the lion, the Chinook salmon, the Parisian.[33]

So when some other group intrudes, hackles are raised, teeth are bared and claws exposed. Although an apparent truism, it is important to recognise that war is essentially a two-way process, as dependent on the hostile response of the attacked as it is on the aggressive initiative of the attacker. The victim always has a choice between resistance and submission, it always takes two to tango. Almost invariably, he chooses to resist, because in doing so he satisfies his craving for identity, stimulation and security. That is why war has been such a recurrent and ubiquitous phenomenon: 'In all the rich catalogue of human hypocrisy it is difficult to find anything to compare with that dainty of dainties, that sugared delicacy, the belief that people do not like war.'[34]

Although they stress the constructive function of intra-specific aggression and the appeal it makes to basic instincts, the ethologists do not claim that modern human warfare is just the same as territorial disputes among red deer or robins. Konrad Lorenz, in particular, argues that at some point human aggression was 'derailed', losing its beneficial relationship with the environment. That fateful development probably occurred during the early Stone Age, by which time man had acquired weapons, clothing and social organisation. Now that the natural hazards of starvation, exposure and wild animals had been overcome, 'an evil intra-specific selection' began, unconnected with environmental demands. This relatively sudden conquest of nature found man unprepared to control the destructive tools now at the service of his aggressive instincts:

No selection pressure arose in the prehistory of mankind to breed inhibitory mechanisms preventing the killing of conspecifics until, all of a sudden, the invention of artificial weapons upset the equilibrium of

9

killing potential and social inhibitions. When it did, man's position was very nearly that of a dove which, by some unnatural trick of nature, has suddenly acquired the beak of a raven.[35]

To view warfare as the consequence of spontaneous instincts, deriving from an evolutionary process as old as mankind itself, is to be pessimistic about the durability of any peace. However stable the surface crust may seem, just below it there seethes an explosive brew, volatile, unstable, ready to erupt at a moment's notice and at the slightest provocation.[36] Man has become a victim of his own success. His conscious ingenuity has so outstripped his unconscious instincts that he now threatens himself with total extinction: 'An unprejudiced observer from another planet, looking upon man as he is today, in his hand the atom bomb, the product of his intelligence, in his heart the aggression drive inherited from his anthropoid ancestors, which this same intelligence cannot control, would not prophesy long life for the species.'[37]

This analysis of war by the ethologists sidesteps some of the pitfalls into which the psychologists plunge but excavates several others equally deep. It has attracted criticism of a ferocity singularly appropriate to the subject-matter. Red in tooth and claw, academic predators have streamed out of the jungles to savage the herds of grazing ethologists: 'over-simplification . . . errors of reasoning . . . ill-defined terms . . . superficial extrapolations . . . anti-rational . . . uncritical . . . a sort of intellectual pizza pie, with tasty tidbits of information embedded in a mass of partially baked ideas . . . scientific-sounding misinformation . . . noisy and foolish . . . very crude . . . completely false'.[38] One cannot help but suspect that some of this vehemence can be ascribed to the extraordinary commercial success enjoyed by their targets. Through best-selling books, television programmes and articles in the colour supplements of the Sunday newspapers, ethologists like Robert Ardrey, Konrad Lorenz and Desmond Morris have reached a genuinely mass audience. Attempts by the opposition to resort to unorthodox media – including *Playboy* magazine and a satirical review – have only served to emphasise the superior commercial acumen of the ethologists.[39]

Of the substantive criticisms which lurk behind the abusive epithets, some can be dismissed without further ado. Whatever the nature of Konrad Lorenz's relationship with National Socialism, it has no bearing on the validity, or otherwise, of his theories.[40] Equally irrelevant is the objection that offensive inferences may be drawn from the ethologists' examination of aggression and submission/resistance: for example, that if all Negroes were Uncle Toms, there would be no racial violence; that if all states submitted to an invader, there would be no war; that if trade unions accepted what they were offered, there would be no class war; and so on.[41] That kind of criticism reveals an attitude

The origins of great wars

to truth not so very far removed from the double-think of the totalitarian regimes the ethologists' critics are so eager to denounce. Indeed, there is an unappealing political edge to much of their invective, which at times seems more concerned with American policy in Vietnam than with what may or may not have happened in the Pleistocene Age.[42]

Other criticisms are best described as 'not proven'. If it really could be demonstrated that the very notion of instincts is untenable, then of course the ethological case would collapse at once. But as a large number of scholars continue to maintain the opposite, and as the very nature of the phenomenon does not lend itself to conclusive refutation or confirmation, the question must remain open. For the time being, the debate seems to have stuck at the 'Yes there are instincts/No there aren't' stage. So long as one camp asserts 'Instinct exists and we cannot dismiss it from our doorstep just because we do not know where it lives' and the other camp asserts with equal confidence that 'In spite of periodic attempts to revive the idea of the existence of instincts in man, the notion has no scientific validity whatsoever', the non-specialist can only suspend judgement.[43]

On certain specific issues, however, the ethologists' opponents appear to have gained the upper hand. Particularly telling has been their attack on the over-facile comparisons made between animal and human behaviour. An analogy, they point out, is just that: useful in illustrating a logically coherent truth, but no substitute for proof. Even if it could be shown that aggression were innate in animals, it would not follow that it was innate in humans. And even if it could be shown that it was innate in humans, it would not follow that it was innate in states.[44] If it be rejoindered in best ethological style that 'Man is no exception to the animal world' (Herbert Friedmann),[45] then one can only reply that when it comes to the conduct of state policy, human behaviour is demonstrably different in numerous important respects:

> Animal behaviour as compared with that of human beings has at least the benefits of relative simplicity and frankness of exposure, but until I see the counterpart in animal life of government bureaucracies, of customs and traditions by which foreign policy and other objectives are determined and pursued, and the ability to predict easily certain gross consequences from the reciprocal use of such gadgets as nuclear weapons, we are clearly wrong in pressing analogies too far.[46]

This sort of argument raises of course the intractable problem of instinct versus learning. If it is difficult to follow Ashley Montagu and his followers in their almost total rejection of heredity – 'Allowing for whatever idiosyncratic contribution the genes may make, everything a human being does as such he has to learn from other human beings'[47] – it is equally difficult to follow their opponents down the opposite road. If one or other has to be chosen, then for the historian the choice seems

11

clear. Man's ability to communicate symbolically, his consequent development of culture, his awareness of past, present and future, his self-awareness and corresponding capacity for reflection – all these peculiarly human attributes make him a creature apart. As John G. Kennedy, one of the ethologists' most effective critics, has pointed out, only man can hate and seek revenge: 'animals kill but men *murder*'. It is not animals but men who wage war.[48]

For the student of the causes of war, this distinction exemplifies the limitations of the ethological approach. Even if all those ambitious hypotheses and imaginative analogies could be sustained, problems would remain. In particular, the generous time-span, reaching back to the very origins of *Homo sapiens* and even beyond, ensures that ethological explanations are so general as to be little more valuable than the psychological equivalents discussed in the previous section. When Robert Ardrey writes: 'Why did Finland fight [in 1939]? No explanation less than ten million years old can provide a significant answer',[49] one can only reply that such an indiscriminate explanation is not worth having. The jump from prehistoric man hunting to stay alive to a war between two states involving well over a million men (as the Russo-Finnish War did) is just too wide. The ethologist cannot explain why fighting between two men became fighting between groups, or why some groups are more aggressive than others, or why some groups fight differently from others.[50] Nor is he any better able to handle the awkward problem of peace than is the psychologist (see p. 3). All he can do is to argue that peace is inherently unstable because it is unexciting and to advance the lame if not fatuous conclusion that 'the history of war is in large part the story of peoples who will risk all for release from boredom'.[51] As this reveals, he is just as populist as the psychologist, obliged by the very nature of his discipline to address man *per se* and unable to deal with specific groups – most notably, decision-making élites. What he *has* done, however, is to show that war is essentially a two-way process, that 'it takes two to tango': 'the principal cause of modern warfare arises from the failure of an intruding power correctly to estimate the defensive resources of a territorial defender.'[52] As we shall see later, that is an insight of real significance (see below, p. 26).[53]

ANTHROPOLOGY AND THE ORIGINS OF WARS

The case against the ethologists has been put with special force and eloquence by anthropologists. Indeed, Ashley Montagu has led something approaching a crusade against what he regards as dangerous error. It is not hard to appreciate why this should be so, for all of anthropology's most cherished axioms are threatened by ethological subversion. Learning is challenged by instinct, culture by evolution, environment by genes, free will by determinism, perfectibility by incorrigibility – and so on, in an apparently endless contrapuntal sequence.

For the student of the causes of war, most important is the anthropologists' rejection of aggression as a basic impulse. In their view, it is essentially *derived*: either from the interruption of some basic biological function (such as breathing, eating or copulation), or from the frustration of some culturally created objective (such as ownership, ambition or ideology). Consequently, aggressive feelings such as hatred or desire for revenge are culturally, not biologically, determined.[54] The implications for an understanding of war are clear: war is not the ineluctable consequence of an ineradicable instinct, but a human invention 'like any other of the inventions in terms of which we order our lives, such as writing, marriage, cooking our food instead of eating it raw, trial by jury or burial of the dead, and so on'.[55] Human beings do not go to war because they have to; they go to war because they are taught to: 'They fight and organise for fighting because, through tribal tradition, through teaching of a religious system, or of an aggressive patriotism, they have been indoctrinated with certain cultural values which they are prepared to defend, and with certain collective hatreds on which they are ready to assault and kill.'[56] In the context of the twentieth century, that means propaganda. Sheep rather than wolves, servile cannon-fodder rather than aggressive predators, the basically pacific humans are induced to take the field of battle by the manipulations of their masters.[57]

This anthropological analysis has a good deal to recommend it. In particular, it makes a clearer – and more convincing – distinction between the various forms of fighting. Bronislaw Malinowski, for example, identified six, ranging from private anger to full-scale interstate warfare. It had been failure to establish these differences, he argued, which had led to a crude short-circuiting of two essentially separate phenomena: the psychological fact of pugnacity and the cultural fact of fighting. In reality, there was a 'complete dysjunction' between the two.[58] His own more precise definition of war – 'an armed contest between two independent political units, by means of organised military force, in pursuit of a tribal or national power' – allowed him to identify a further flaw in the view that it was biologically (or psychologically) determined. As it can be shown that war is of relatively recent origin and, moreover, that it is not practised by all peoples even today, it must follow that it is an artificial creation.[59]

All of this is helpful. As the anthropologists draw their inductions from material which is both concrete and human, they manage to avoid the snares set by the psychologists' abstract individualism or by the ethologists' speculative animalism. Significantly, however, their services have been mainly of a negative, destructive variety. While proficient at exposing the weaknesses of their opponents, they have been less adept at constructing a more satisfactory alternative. It is in the nature of the beast. Their vast chronological scale demands generalisations of equally accommodating dimensions, with predictably nebulous results when it comes to explaining historical phenomena. With a stupefying lack of precision, Keith Otterbein, for example, has concluded that 'wars are caused by military organisations which go to war in order to obtain certain goals . . . wars are caused by the decisions of men as members of organisations, whether they are military organisations or governing bodies.' Any hope that a discussion of those goals might stiffen this flaccid observation is dashed by the further qualification that they vary from time to time and from war to war. Nor is the multiple categorisation of those goals under the headings of subjugation and tribute, land, plunder, trophies and honours, defence and revenge, any more penetrating.[60] None of his colleagues are any more precise.

Another drawback of the anthropologists' approach to war is their espousal of what can be called the 'puppetmaster' view of the relationship between rulers and ruled. So anxious are they to avoid the populist heresy of the psychologists and ethologists that they fall over backwards into an equally unsatisfactory extreme which veers close to a conspiracy theory of historical causation. Typical is the following assertion by Ashley Montagu: 'Wars are usually made by a few individuals in positions of great power, "great leaders", "thoughtful" and "respected" statesmen, generally advised by "the best and the brightest", almost always with calm and deliberation, and the pretence if not the conviction of complete moral rectitude.'[61] As the shrill insistence and heavy sarcasm of this and many other passages reveals, much anthropological writing about civilised societies is marred by a reductionist lack of nuance. A good example is Montagu's liturgical repetition of the adjective 'artificial' in his description of the role of the state: 'A state is not a natural creation but an artificial entity, and it is as such artificial entities that states wage war, with artificial weapons from artificial motives for artificial purposes, conducted for artificial ends.'[62]

At this point, the suspicion begins to harden that an understandable desire to counteract the fatalism of the ethologists is leading to distortion. To depict international conflict in terms of an artificial squabble between a handful of leaders is so much at odds with what is known about the origins of specific wars as to cast doubt on the whole methodology.[63] Even if this élitist interpretation were acceptable, it would not explain why those leaders behaved as they did and, more specificially, why sometimes they chose to wage war – and why sometimes they chose to keep the peace. Moreover, it carries the arresting implication that to explain the origins of wars what is required is a concentration on high politics. That is a fine paradox, for it may be assumed with some confidence that Ashley Montagu did not set out with the intention of providing an anthropological rationale for the work of Mr Maurice Cowling.

QUANTITATIVE EXPLANATIONS OF WAR

To write of anthropologists, ethologists and psychologists as if they were united armies of course is to distort. That unavoidable penalty, imposed by the need to be concise, afflicts doubly any discussion of sociological approaches to the origins of war. So numerous are the studies, so various the methods, so conflicting the conclusions that the wretched historian can only emerge bemused from even a brief encounter with this multi-faceted discipline. Much of that bewilderment derives from the new and inaccessible language invented by its practitioners to convey their findings to each other. After wrestling with such concepts as 'systemic tightness', 'dummy profit analysis', 'parity–fluidity models', 'lock-in effects', 'Walker–Lev tests' and many many more of the same stamp, one has to agree with Bernard Brodie's exasperated verdict: 'Social science has the great disadvantage that its insights are conveyed by the use of words, sometimes many words, and usually badly written ones.'[64] In actual fact, he was only half-right, for many of those insights are conveyed in mathematical symbols of even more baffling opaqueness. Not at all untypical is the following brief extract from Bruce Bueno de Mesquita's recent article 'Systemic polarisation and the occurrence and duration of war':

$$Y = a + b_1 D_1 + b_2 D_2 + b_3 \triangle T + b_4 (\triangle T)(D_1) + b_5 (\triangle T)(D_2)$$

Where
D_1 = a dummy variable coded one for the years 1900 through 1914 and zero for 1915 through 1965. D_2 = a dummy variable coded zero for 1900 through 1945, and one for 1946 through 1965.[65]

Uncomfortably aware that my own quantitative data input threshold is low – that I am not good at sums – I find it difficult to respond to this kind of explanation with more than a helpless shrug of the shoulders. Even the barely numerate, however, can grasp that this sort of approach has drawbacks other than incomprehensibility. The insistence that all evidence – or 'data' – must be quantifiable, so that it can be handled by the computers, requires a definition of war which is highly arbitrary: for example, 'To qualify for this designation [war], a sustained military conflict has to array at least one sovereign member of the interstate system against another member, or an independent non-member, or a colony, and result in at least 1,000 battle deaths to

15

the system member participant(s)' or 'A war is any military action for a particular country in which the number of its soldiers involved equal or exceed 0.02%. of its population.'[66] It is never explained why 1,000 is more appropriate than 500 or why 0.02 per cent is more appropriate than 0.01 per cent, for the very good reason that no such explanation is possible: the essential quality of any isolated figure is its arbitrariness.

Even when the international conflicts have been identified, their components quantified and the data programmed, the results disgorged on the print-outs are perplexingly and – it has to be said – gratifyingly contradictory. After an investigation of the correlation between domestic and foreign conflict in no fewer than seventy-seven different nations, Rudolph J. Rummel concluded that: 'foreign conflict behaviour is generally completely unrelated to domestic conflict behaviour'.[67] That seems unambiguous enough, but, alas, only five years later Jonathan Wilkenfeld reprocessed the same data and came up with a diametrically opposed conclusion.[68] The road to scientific certainty, it seems, is paved with disappointment. After a lengthy investigation of the sources of international conflict, Michael Haas had to conclude that no general explanation can be made to fit: 'In correlating variables indicating warlike behaviour of states with some 200 societal characteristics, very few of the correlation coefficients have exceeded the level of + 0.40.'[69] His findings are, however, vastly if unintentionally entertaining. It is impossible to resist the temptation to quote the following piece of sublime nonsense:

> In our quest to determine sources of international violence at various levels of analysis, three scenarios emerge. The prototypic dove decision-maker is seen as a middle-aged Jewish negress who has received a college education to attain the status of physician or college professor, who resides outside a big city but not too far from the nation's capital; she is non-authoritarian, nonethnocentric, flexible, achievement-oriented, uncynical, nonalienated, optimistic, and an intellectual with much tolerance of ambiguity; her political views are neither conservative nor nationalist; she participates politically, does not anticipate war, does not expect her country to survive or be victorious in war, and takes few risks. Her decisions are peaceful when the information inputs are neither perceptually complex nor cognitively simple and made when mutual trust, friendliness and communications are maintained at high levels (though short of communications overload). Peace is more likely to emerge if the prototypic decision-maker is in possession of accurate information, advisers are in disagreement over alternatives, while stereotypic decoding of inputs and provocative encoding of outputs is absent; there is concern for long-term implications and longer time for making a decision and drawing up contingency plans.[70]

The obsessive concern with abstract categorisation and quantification also affects the kind of evidence employed. It has to be quantifiable, of course, but it also has to be universal (common to all states under consideration) and it has to be eternal (common to all periods under consideration). To reverse Goethe's dictum, 'universum est ineffabile'. A good example of the genre is provided by Alan Ned Sabrosky's study of the origins of the First World War.[71] It consists mainly of graphs (illustrating, for example, 'Military Expenditure Shares (MES)'), diagrams (illustrating, for example, 'Major Power Alliance Configurations') and tables (illustrating, for example, 'Disaggregated Rank-Order Correlations on Nonamicable Perceptual and Behavioural Variables'). Some of this information is both valid and helpful, notably that relating to the military budget. But when one finds such elusive imponderables as the respective desire of the Dual Alliance and the Triple Entente to change the status quo not just quantified but reduced to *three decimal points*, one hardly knows whether to laugh or cry. In spite of all this spurious precision, the net result is very modest and curiously old-fashioned. Professor Sabrosky's only substantive conclusion is that between 1900 and 1914 the position of Germany and Austria-Hungary relative to France, Russia and Great Britain deteriorated.[72] It is rather as if a fully automated, robot-controlled – and extremely expensive – assembly-line had been constructed to turn out a Model 'T' Ford. Although first published as recently as 1975, the article contains no reference to any of the work of Fritz Fischer, Imanuel Geiss, Volker Berghahn, Hans-Ulrich Wehler – or any of their opponents. But of course Sabrosky's main purpose is not to explain the origins of war, but to establish guide-lines for the present, to demonstrate the uncontroversial if unexciting maxim 'that moderation and prudence are more than proverbial virtues'.[73]

This admirable concern to create a world free of war is shared by all social scientists who study the subject. Some of them have invented solutions decidedly more ingenious than Sabrosky's modest recipe. James Miller has argued that the cause of peace would be advanced if a thousand social scientists disguised as Russians could be infiltrated into the Soviet Union to conduct public opinion surveys which would establish just what its citizens were thinking. Less hazardous is Gordon Allport's proposal that the entrances to the United Nations General Assembly, Security Council and Unesco be so arranged that delegates would have to pass through the playground of a nursery school before starting work. The prospect of Mr Gromyko dandling a baby on his knee prior to approaching the negotiating table is certainly arresting. More simple was J. Cohen's suggestion that all men in government be replaced by women – that was made, of course, before the Falklands War.[74] Following Alexander Pope's celebrated advocacy of enlightened self-interest – 'That REASON, PASSION, answer one great aim;/That true SELF-LOVE and SOCIAL are the same' – a group of social scientists mustered by Unesco called for 'the cooperation of social scientists on broad regional and international levels, the creation of an international university and a series of world institutes of the social sciences under international auspices'.[75]

As these solutions to the problems of war indicate, underpinning the social scientists' analysis of its causes is a concern for contemporary relevance, often overtly political in character. This sense of commitment often lends a welcome vigour to their analysis but also has other less satisfactory consequences. So evil is war, especially nuclear war, that the assumption is made that its causes must be evil too. For the Unesco group just quoted, they are social injustice, economic inequality, national pride, propaganda, colonial exploitation and the oppression of ethnic minorities within a country.[76] For Stanislav Andreski, they are poverty and despotism.[77] For Richard J. Barnet, they are the concentration of power in a national security bureaucracy, the nature of the capitalist system and the business creed which sustains it, and the vulnerability of the public to manipulation on national security issues.[78] Not for the first or last time, the problem of peace now intrudes. If any or all of those evils were responsible for war, their opposites would be responsible for peace. Yet most if not all of them are greatly *intensified* by war, so, logically, wars should be infinite in duration. One cannot help but suspect that the social scientists are approaching the problem from the wrong angle, misled by their contemporary polemical purpose. Whether consciously or not, they select certain institutions or phenomena of which they disapprove (racialism, capitalism, the Pentagon, or whatever), hold them responsible for the absolute evil – war – which now threatens the very existence of mankind and then use the relationship to promote a programme of social and/or political change. And it all stems from a reluctance or inability to recognise that unequivocally evil consequences can result from ethically neutral forces.

No more secure are the empirical foundations of this evil causes–evil consequences interpretation. Certainly some of the former can be identified in any pre-war period – and just as certainly in any post-war period too. Some of them are sometimes conspicuously absent: neither of the world wars of this century, for example, was preceded by pauperisation. During the last four decades since the last of them, the USA has fought two major wars, in Korea and Vietnam, while the incontestably poorer and more despotic USSR has confined itself to minor punitive expeditions. Such poverty-stricken dictatorships as Franco's Spain, Peron's Argentina or Duvalier's Haiti were very models of pacifism in their foreign policy. Even Scandinavia, in Andreski's view the only peaceful part of the world on account of its liberty and prosperity,[79] will not fit the theory. For Denmark, Norway and Finland *were* all involved in war between 1939 and 1945. That they were the invaded rather than the invaders is neither here nor there, for what is to be explained is not aggression but war. That Sweden remained at peace during that period had nothing to do with any superiority of its economic and constitutional arrangements.

The social scientists who adopt this position are heirs to a long tradition of naive liberalism. In a speech at Leeds in 1849, Richard Cobden anticipated Stanislav Andreski by more than a hundred years when he blamed war on despotism and predicted that the advance of popular representation would put an end to it. Only eight years later, his own constituents gave the lie to this optimistic forecast by turning him out of his parliamentary seat as a penalty for his opposition to the Crimean War.[80] Cobden moreover had had his own precursor: in the late 1780s Jeremy Bentham had written in his *Plan for an Universal and Perpetual Peace*: 'Europe . . . would have had no wars but for the feudal system, religious antipathy, the rage of conquest and the uncertainties of succession. Of these four causes, the first is happily extinct everywhere, the second and third almost everywhere – at any rate in France and England – and the last might, if not already extinguished, be so with great ease.'[81] Bentham was certainly a clever man, but he was no historian – and consequently had little understanding of the causes of wars. The same – or at least the second part – could be said of many social scientists today.

THE PRIMACY OF DOMESTIC POLICY?

The influence of sociology is not confined, however, to its own discipline. Especially in the last two or three decades it has colonised large tracts of historians' territory as well. No area has been more affected than the study of war and its origins. Since controversy erupted over Fritz Fischer's book on Germany's aims in the First World War,[82] first published in 1961, there has been a broad and constant flow of books and articles on the subject based on models drawn from the social sciences. The leitmotiv of this new approach was summed up with admirable if rare conciseness in the title of a collection of essays by Eckart Kehr: *Der Primat der Innenpolitik* (the primacy of domestic policy).[83] Kehr had died at the age of thirty in 1933, leaving an *œuvre* of necessarily modest dimensions and little immediate impact. It was not until after 1945 that his use of sociological concepts (drawn mainly from Max Weber but with a dash of Karl Marx added), in combination with a radical critique of German politics past and present, began to command a following.[84] Thanks in part to the tireless advocacy of the prolific Hans-Ulrich Wehler, *Der Primat der Innenpolitik* has become established as virtually axiomatic for the younger generations of German historians.

The implications of this principle for the origins of wars hardly need explaining. If foreign policy is determined by domestic forces, the place to look for those origins is at home. The history of international relations ceases to be of any consequence. What is now required is an investigation of economic development, the social structures it produced and the groups which inhabited them. All the old concerns – negotiations, conferences, diplomatic incidents, military expeditions, Mr A. J. P. Taylor's railway timetables – can be abandoned as so much superficial lumber. Into their place move such concepts as social imperialism, negative integration, organised capitalism and *Sammlungspolitik*.[85] The benefits of this new approach have been considerable. To answer the new questions, new material has been unearthed, forgotten forces have been rediscovered, neglected phenomena have been rescued from obscurity. Whatever response to their findings seems appropriate, it has to be agreed that they have changed decisively the perspective of Wilhelmine Germany. Never again will it be possible to write about the origins of the First World War simply in terms of what one statesman said to another.

Whether the *Primat der Innenpolitik* is an adequate analytical tool for the investigation of the origins of wars is a different matter. Its main defect is its Germanocentric perspective. As Golo Mann pointed out, of the 856 pages of Fritz Fischer's seminal work, 855 are devoted to *German* war aims, with those of the other powers dismissed on a single page.[86] Consequently, the conflicts and problems of Wilhelmine Germany are manifestly exaggerated and are assigned a degree of peculiarity which they patently did not possess. This is a defect inherent to the method, for as soon as a comparative element is readmitted, the exercise reverts to being international relations, albeit of a social or economic rather than diplomatic variety. Correspondingly one-sided is the definition of what is thought to be the opposite position. In particular, Leopold von Ranke is credited with a dogmatic attachment to the *Primat der Aussenpolitik* (the primacy of foreign policy) which he did not possess.[87] While he certainly did believe in the predominance of a state's foreign interests, in both a normative and a practical sense, he was also at pains to stress the interaction of foreign and domestic conditions and the importance of the latter: 'Strange how the conditions of society infuse their predominating traits into each separate institution. . . .All states that count in the world and make themselves felt are motivated by special tendencies of their own. . . . There is a living, unique, inherent principle in each of our great states, by which all its foreign affairs and internal developments are shaped.'[88]

If Ranke was too much a creature of his times to conceive that principle in any but metaphysical terms, at least he was aware of the need to examine both intra-state and inter-state relations. It is the remorseless insistence of the *Primat der Innenpolitik* school on the former which makes their method so one-sided. With a candour amounting to self-condemnation, Hans-Ulrich Wehler has defiantly asserted the value of partiality: 'no objection could be raised *a limine* against even a *consciously* monocausal use of the concept [*Primat der Innenpolitik*], for the insertion of a sharp instrument may be made at the cost of a certain one-sidedness which can then be differentiated and relativised in the course of the second incision.'[89] The obvious reponse to that, of course, is that what is sauce for the goose is sauce for the gander: one cannot expect to be taken seriously if one first condemns Ranke for one-sided monocausality and then announces that one is going to employ the same method oneself!

The fiercely polemical tone of Wehler's writing stems from his desire to turn the study of history into a 'vital, political, critical social science'.[90] He is quite frank about the teleological and didactic nature of the exercise, which can be summarised as follows: in the Federal Republic of Germany we need to build a democratic state and society, therefore we must eliminate any residual loyalty to older rival models, especially to the Wilhelmine Empire; therefore we must demonstrate the essential continuity of the period 1871–1945 and destroy the notion that the period before 1914 represented 'the good old days.'[91] This is a method with success built-in, for the criteria select the evidence which justifies the criteria: 'Ask, and it shall be given you; seek and ye shall find; knock and it shall be opened unto you' (Matthew 7: 7). It is not, however, a method which commends itself for the investigation of the origins of wars.

As war is a conflict between two or more countries, the relations between them must be of central concern. Of course their internal conditions – economic, social, political and ideological – need to be examined, and of course the formation and conduct of foreign policy are strongly influenced by those conditions. But to elevate them to sole primacy, without reference to the international dimension, is an act of wilful self-mutilation. If one's concern is to establish what happened and why – rather than to seek support for a contemporary political cause – it is difficult to see why either foreign or domestic policy should be always elevated at the expense of the other.[92] Their relative strength depends not on some internal dynamic but on concrete circumstances. If the state in question is exposed to danger from outside, then foreign policy will be predominant, both in a normative and a formative sense. If the state in question is exposed to danger from within and/or is secure against foreign interference, then domestic policy will be predominant: indeed a wholly autarchic and isolated state will have no foreign policy at all.[93] Always a very rare bird, such a state became extinct at about the same time as the dodo and for similar reasons. For most people in most ages, foreign policy and international relations have been a matter of vital concern. Anyone familiar with – say – the history of Poland since the late Middle Ages will understand why and will agree with Richard Cobb's maxim: 'foreign policy is at all times more important than domestic matters, for it is a matter of life and death.'[94]

That paraphrase of Ranke from the greatest exponent of 'history from below' would be a fitting, if paradoxical conclusion to this section. But something has to be said about what appears to be a near relative of the *Primat der Innenpolitik* school: Marxism-Leninism. While the founding fathers had little to say about the causes of war *per se*, Lenin returned to the subject again and again, usually with the same form of words. Typical is the following passage from 'War and revolution' of May 1917:

> War is a continuation of policy by other means. All wars are inseparable from the political systems that engender them. The policy which a given state, a given class within that state, pursued for a long time before the war is inevitably continued by that same class during the war, the form of action alone being changed. War is a continuation of policy by other means.[95]

The causes of war are therefore fundamentally economic: war is part of politics, politics is part of the superstructure, so war is determined by the socio-economic base:

> The determinant position of the relations of production stems from the fact that they represent the basic component of socio-economic life, that they determine the social class content of all the superstructure components, such as politics, states and law, morals, ideology, war and peace, and that these superstructure components play a role in the service of the base. In the final analysis, the major causes of war are determined by the nature of the economy, although the immediate causes may lie or may appear to lie in another sphere, since economic causes very often enter the picture in a mediated form.[96]

This characteristically reductionist argument is only formally domestic in character. The arena may be the state but the essential unit is the class and the essential motor is class struggle, neither of which knows national frontiers. Moreover, 'domestic and foreign policy are parts of the overall policy pursued by the ruling class of the state' and cannot be understood in isolation from each other. So both normatively and analytically, the Marxist-Leninist view of war has more in common with the primacy of foreign policy than with the primacy of domestic policy. 'Workers of the world unite!' is, it need hardly be said, a call for international action. Marx and Engels positively welcomed war as a means of accelerating the historical process: 'The next world war will not only cause reactionary classes and dynasties to disappear from the face of the earth, but also entire reactionary peoples. And that too is an advance.'[97] So far as analysis is concerned, Marxists are too well trained in dialectics to suppose that essentially international phenomena can be studied nationally. That is why so many Marxist historians – Eric Hobsbawm, V. G. Kiernan and George Rudé spring at once to mind – write such good international history and why the study of international relations flourishes nowhere in greater abundance than in the Soviet Union. Despite certain misleading resemblances, Fritz Fischer's analysis of the origins of the First

World War is about as far removed from Marxism as it is possible to imagine.

The Marxist approach to the causes of war has certain virtues, a clear understanding of the dialectical nature of a state's national interest and international position being the most important. Also illuminating – usually – is the stress laid on the economic motivation of the belligerents. But while this concern with the material forces at work can often supply a fresh perspective or uncover fresh evidence, its essential monocausality leaves part of the picture unpainted and crams the rest into what is often an anachronistic frame. Symptomatic is the need felt to identify each state by means of a social adjective.[98] That sort of exercise works well enough when 'bourgeois' France is pitted against 'feudal' Austria and Prussia, but begins to show signs of strain when the latter bloc is joined by 'bourgeois' Great Britain and the United Provinces.

The teleological nature of the Marxist approach also causes problems. With all history set on its inevitable course, wars can – and should – be categorised in terms of censure and approval. So Lenin, for example, made a distinction between just wars waged by the oppressed (the wars of the revolutionary bourgeoisie of France, for example) and unjust wars (the wars of imperialist exploitation waged by the decrepit bourgeoisie of late-nineteenth-century Europe, for example).[99] Lenin might well have remembered one of his own aphorisms – 'History is more cunning than any of us' – at this point, for too many wars turn out to be too complex for this kind of classification. For example, particular difficulties are caused by the need to attach the label 'just' to Russia's war of 1812 – 'the great liberation war of the fatherland'. As 'war is a continuation of the policies of a class' and 'to change the character of the war, one must change the class in power',[100] it is very difficult to see how that seal of approval can be justified. For whatever else may have changed between 1799 and 1812, it was not the social structure of France and Russia.[101]

THE ORIGINS OF GREAT WARS

This necessarily lightning review of general explanations of war has been depressingly negative. Exposure of flaws in the structures of others is, of course, a far easier exercise than the construction of an alternative. At least, however, it has uncovered some of the more obvious requirements of a satisfactory theory. It must be able to explain peace as well as war. It must be able to explain the decisions of the élites as well as the impulses of the masses. It must not rely on analogies for its justification. It must be able to explain wars and not just fighting. It must be able to explain geographical and chronological variations. It must be explicable in comprehensible prose, not in some private sectarian language, verbal or mathematical. It must not allow distaste for its subject to introduce the fallacy that evil phenomena must have evil causes. It must allow for the interaction of domestic and foreign policy. It must not be reductionist – for example in reducing all causation to economics. Whether those requirements can be met, remains to be seen: it is highly improbable, but it should not disqualify at least an attempt.

It is important to concede at the outset that this is an exercise conducted by a historian for historians. Just as he derives little benefit from psychologists' investigation of the mind, so he can expect little interest from that quarter. The premises, point of departure and ultimate destination are too different. This caveat has been expressed with especial – and characteristic – cogency by Marc Bloch:

> A graduated classification of causes, which is really only an intellectual convenience, cannot safely be elevated to an absolute. Reality offers us a nearly infinite number of lines of force which all converge together upon the same phenomenon. The choice we make among them may well be founded upon characteristics which, in practice, fully merit our attention; but it is always a choice. Notably, there is something extremely arbitrary in the idea of a cause *par excellence,* as opposed to mere 'conditions'. Even Simiand, who was so possessed by the idea of precision, and who had begun with an attempt (a vain one, I believe) for stricter definitions, seems to have ended by recognising the entirely relative character of such distinctions. 'For a doctor', he wrote, 'the cause of an epidemic would be the multiplication of a microbe and its conditions the dirt and ill health occasioned by poverty; for the sociologist and philanthropist, poverty would be the cause, and the biological factors, the condition.' This is in all honesty to acknowledge the subordination of the perspective to the peculiar angle of the inquiry.[102]

This sage warning is also of value because it raises the important question of whether there are two separate levels of causation: 'the given conditions that make war possible, or even quite likely to occur, and the events and the decisions that immediately lead to it'.[103] A particularly graphic image of what this distinction can mean with regard to a specific case was provided by A. J. P. Taylor in *The Origins of the Second World War:*

> Wars are much like road accidents. They have a general cause and particular causes at the same time. Every road accident is caused, in the last resort, by the invention of the internal combustion engine and by men's desire to get from one place to another. In this sense, the 'cure' for road accidents is to forbid motor-cars. But a motorist, charged with dangerous driving, would be ill-advised if he pleaded the existence of motor-cars as his sole defence.

> The police and the courts do not weigh profound causes. They seek a
> specific cause for each accident – error on the part of the driver; excessive
> speed; drunkenness; faulty brakes; bad road surface. So it is with
> wars. . . .Both enquiries make sense on different levels. They are comple-
> mentary; they do not exclude each other. The Second World War, too, had
> profound causes; but it also grew out of specific events, and these events are
> worth detailed examination.[104]

This is a striking metaphor, but its vivacity should not be allowed to
obscure the weakness of the argument. Like the opponents of the
ethologists, we should be on our guard against any explanation of war
which relies on analogy. Vigilance is rewarded when the two-level
theory founders on the old obstacle of peace. What distinguishes the
'given conditions' or 'profound causes' of war from 'the particular
causes' is their permanence. What the internal combustion engine is to
driving, economic circumstances (for example) are to war. If that
permanence be replaced by a temporary quality – if *the* internal combustion engine be replaced by a special kind of combustion engine –
then the cause gains promotion from profound to particular. The
internal combustion engine plus man's desire for mobility are held to
be responsible for road accidents. But they are equally responsible for
the opposite phenomenon: for safely completed journeys. So they
cannot be held responsible for either. Equally, if the fundamental
causes of war are also fundamental causes of peace, they cannot be
causes of either:

> What is the use of dwelling upon nearly universal antecedents? They are
> common to too many phenomena to deserve a special niche in the genea-
> logy of any of them. I am well aware, from the outset, that there would be no
> fire if the air contained no oxygen: what interests me, what demands and
> justifies an attempt at discovery, is to determine how the fire started. The
> laws of trajectories are as valid for defeat as for victory: they explain both;
> therefore, they are useless as a proper explanation for either.[105]

The motoring analogy also breaks down because accidents are often
caused by wholly unpredictable and uncontrollable mechanical
defects. For most of recorded history there is no equivalent in war.
Until very recently, and the invention of weapons systems which might
conceivably be triggered by computer malfunction, no such possibility
of a fortuitous outbreak existed. Of course most wars take a course and
have results different from those intended by the combatants, but no
war has ever begun by accident – yet. Finally and more generally, it
must be doubted whether the two levels of causation can be made
sufficiently autonomous to justify their separation:

> If the profound causes do not explain the occurrence of war without the
> particular ones, or the particular without the profound ones, how can we
> really speak of two different, but compatible levels of explanation? Is not
> what we have really two parts of a single explanation which recognises the

necessity both of certain predisposing conditions and the actions of certain individuals? The conclusion which suggests itself, in fact, is that historians working at the diplomatic and geopolitical levels simply make different selections from a single set of explanatory conditions – perhaps on no more significant criterion than that certain conditions happen to interest them more than others.[106]

With this methodological red herring consigned to the deeps, we can proceed to the central problem. For a definition, the place to go is still Carl von Clausewitz's *On War,* 'not simply the greatest but the only truly great book on war'.[107] Notwithstanding the celebrity of his maxim that war is nothing but the continuation of politics by other means, Clausewitz identified at an even more fundamental level the two essential characteristics of war – reciprocity and force; 'War is nothing but a duel on a larger scale . . . War is thus an act of force to compel our enemy to do our will.'[108] That war is violent is perhaps a truism, that war requires at least two participants is most certainly not so obvious, or at least has not been so obvious to certain historians (see p. 20). But it is certainly important. Once the reciprocal nature of war is grasped, the way is clear to a general explanation of its causes. However brutal it may sound, the fact of the matter is that every victim of a predator has two choices: he can resist or he can submit. If he chooses the latter course, there is no war.[109] The German invasion of Czechoslovakia in 1938 did not result in war; the German invasion of Poland in 1939 did result in war: the difference lay in the different reactions of the victims. In Michael Howard's more concrete formulation of Clausewitz's twin insights, war 'is simply the use of violence by states for the enforcement, the protection or the extension of their political power'.[110]

This concept of political power supplies the organising principle for the specific objectives of states. At first sight, they comprise such a welter of variations that the temptation to relapse into positivist resignation is almost overwhelming. Another admirer of Clausewitz – Lenin – seemed to succumb when he exclaimed in a letter in January 1917: 'Wars are a supremely varied, diverse, complex thing. One cannot approach them with a general pattern.'[111] However he then buckled down to devising a tripartite categorisation: oppressed nations versus oppressors, oppressors versus other oppressors, conflicts between nations possessing equal rights.[112] What he failed to point out was that all three were essentially concerned with power: the ability to determine or influence the behaviour of others. However generously conceived, concentration on specific war aims can only set a trap, for they are so variable. In particular, they are notoriously prone to inflation once a war has commenced. As Geoffrey Blainey, the author of the most penetrating study of the causes of war yet written, has pointed out:

One generalisation about war aims can be offered with confidence. The aims are simply varieties of power. The vanity of nationalism, the will to spread an ideology, the protection of kinsmen in an adjacent land, the desire for more territory or commerce, the avenging of a defeat or insult, the craving for greater national strength or independence, the wish to impress or cement alliances – all these represent power in different wrappings . . . .The explanations that stress aims are theories of rivalry and animosity and not theories of war. They help to explain increasing rivalry between nations but they do not explain why the rivalry led to war.[113]

The assertion of power lies at the very heart of the state: the word itself derives from the Latin *status* in its sense of standing or position.[114] No state, however small its confines or humble its aspirations, can fail to perform that elemental function. It ceases to do so only at the moment of its extinction. Indeed, every identifiable group develops a conception of power – as soon as it comes into contact with another group with similar and therefore competing interests.[115] All that varies is the currency of power, the way in which it is measured. Football teams use goals, nomadic tribes use grazing land and water-holes, states use territory, population, wealth, armed strength or a permutation of the same. Of course, for states war is not a permanent or even necessary mode of expression of power. Political intercourse between most states in most periods is conducted peacefully. When two states are geographically adjacent or when they pursue their perceived interests in the same area, disputes are bound to arise: over territory, over commerce, over the control of other states, and so on. More often than not, such conflicts can be resolved by negotiation. What has to be determined is why certain states at certain times resort to war. If the dual concepts of reciprocity and force are kept in mind, the answer is clear: because the states concerned decide that they have more to gain by going to war than by staying at peace.[116] That conclusion is simple to the point of banality, but it leads to another: the decision to prefer war to peace is taken by the two parties concerned because they have different assessments of their respective power. When they can agree about their power relationship, they can also agree to settle their differences peacefully. When they cannot, they go to war.[117] War is the most direct, the most effective means of testing that relationship, and when it has allowed agreement to be reached, peace will break out. Consequently, decisive wars are followed by long periods of peace and indecisive wars by the reverse. It was not the superior wisdom of the peacemakers of 1945 which has made their efforts so much more durable than those of their predecessors of 1919 but the more decisive quality of the preceding war.

It follows, therefore, that the investigator of the origins of war should concentrate on those considerations which influence decision-makers' assessments of their power-relationship. Blainey has summarised them as follows:

i. Military strength and the ability to apply that strength efficiently in the likely theatre of war;

ii. Predictions of how outside nations will behave if war should occur;
iii. Perceptions of whether there is internal unity or discord in their land or in the land of the enemy;
iv. Knowledge or forgetfulness of the realities and sufferings of war;
v. Nationalism and ideology;
vi. The state of the economy and also its ability to sustain the kind of war envisaged;
vii. The personality and experience of those who shared in the decision.[118]

When a potential enemy's capability is underestimated and when one's own assets are overrated, then war comes near. When that potential enemy has made a similar miscalculation, then war is unavoidable. This kind of reciprocal error is particularly common during periods of ideological upheaval, for accurate intelligence is hard to obtain and the two sides are using different criteria to assess their relative strength. As we shall see, the French revolutionary wars are a case in point (see p. 123). In short, it is the repeated inability of decision-makers to get their sums right which leads to repeated wars: 'This recurring optimism is a vital prelude to war. Anything which increases that optimism is a cause of war. Anything which dampens that optimism is a cause of peace.'[119]

Paradoxically, that positive, optimistic drive to war is often accelerated and intensified by its apparent opposite: the pessimistic fear that the power of one's state is threatened by the growth of a rival. Both Michael Howard and Martin Wight have taken the same simple sentence from Thucydides' *History of the Peloponnesian War* to make the point: 'What made war inevitable was the growth of Athenian power and the fear this caused in Sparta.'[120] There is no contradiction here; short-term optimism and long-term pessimism not only coexist, they combine to encourage the same calculation: 'We can win now, but we shall lose later, so let us go to war at once.' A particularly clear example was provided by General Helmuth von Moltke on the eve of the First World War,[121] but it is a very common phenomenon. Another good illustration is provided by the French revolutionary wars.[122] As most statesmen at most times fear that in the long run the international position of their states will deteriorate, most wars can be called 'defensive' or 'preventive' – by both sides. Truly preventive wars – when one state takes pre-emptive action in the certain knowledge that attack is imminent – are very rare. Frederick the Great's attack on Austria through Saxony in August 1756 is the only case that springs immediately to mind. Frederick had miscalculated – but so had his enemies. That, alas, is the way with war. Instead of the slick precision instrument for the continuation of policy by other means, it turns out to be clumsy, uncontrollable, ruinously expensive and very, very slow. It is less a sniper's rifle than a blunderbuss, with an alarming propensity for blowing up in the firer's face. In modern times, only Bismarck (and perhaps Mrs Thatcher) have had the satisfaction of seeing short, sharp, decisive wars running roughly according to plan. As Clausewitz put it: 'Everything in war is very simple, but the simplest thing is difficult.'[123]

Wars are about power. As Raymond Aron wrote: 'The stakes of war are the existence, the creation or the elimination of states.'[124] Any attempt to subdivide them into different kinds of wars can only set up contrasts which further investigation reveals to be unjustified. So when A. J. P. Taylor writes that 'wars in fact have sprung more from apprehension than from a lust for war or for conquest',[125] he seems to be unaware that the two impulses are not just compatible but two sides of the same coin. Martin Wight's support for Hobbes' trilogy of wars of gain, fear and doctrine is open to the same objection.[126] All wars for gain – Frederick the Great's invasion of Silesia, Hitler's invasion of Poland, for example – are also wars for security. The reverse formulation is usually, if not invariably applicable too. To elevate wars of ideology to a separate category is also unhelpful. Every war that ever was fought has had an ideological quality, in that the belligerents have justified their participation by appealing to general principles. So far as I ám aware, no state has ever announced: 'We are going to war to obtain this objective because we believe we are the stronger and can get away with it.' Even Frederick the Great in 1740 took his stand on treaties, the law of the Empire and even Protestantism. Of course he did not believe all or even much of it, but neither, one suspects, have many others who have trumpeted their ideological justification. As we shall see, even the fervour of the French revolutionaries, who provide Wight's 'classic example' of a war of doctrine[127], was not unalloyed with more material considerations (see pp. 98–104).

It is high time to turn to those revolutionaries and their wars. Even as formidable a theorist as Clausewitz was aware of the need to avoid too much abstraction: 'Just as some plants bear fruit only if they don't shoot up too high, so in the practical arts the leaves and flowers of theory must be pruned and the plant kept close to its proper soil – experience.'[128] It is with a sense of relief that this amateur theorist reaches for his secateurs. Whether the modest growths he has tended in this chapter can be planted out to any purpose in what follows he rather doubts. At least a few obvious weeds have been pulled out and the ground prepared. Before Clausewitz's horticultural metaphor goes to seed, it should be picked. The final chapter will be the place for a harvest festival.

REFERENCES AND NOTES

1. (London 1978) p. 53.
2. Dorothy F. La Barr and J. David Singer, *The Study of International*

Politics (Santa Barbara and Oxford 1976).

3. Heinrich von Treitschke, *Politics,* (London 1916) pp. 395–6, 599.

4. Albert Einstein and Sigmund Freud, 'Why war?', *The Standard Edition of the Complete Psychological Works of Sigmund Freud,* ed. James Strachey, vol. 22 (London 1964) pp. 199–215.

5. E.F.M. Durbin and John Bowlby, *Personal Aggressiveness and War* London 1939).

6. Ibid., p. 21.

7. Ibid., p. 23.

8. Ibid., p. 38.

9. Ibid., p. 41.

10. Ibid., p. 25.

11. Ibid., p. 28.

12. Pryns Hopkins, *The Psychology of Social Movements. A Psycho-Analytic View of Society* (London 1938) p. 117.

13. Durbin and Bowlby, *Personal Aggressiveness and War,* pp. vii, 28.

14. Hopkins, *The Psychology of Social Movements,* p. 117.

15. Kenneth N. Waltz, *Man, the State and War: A Theoretical Analysis* (New York 1959) p. 28.

16. For further discussion of this point, see Morris Ginsberg, 'The causes of war', *The Sociological Review,* **31** (1939) pp. 139–40.

17. Franz Alexander, 'The Psychiatric Aspects of War and Peace', *The American Journal of Sociology,* **46** (1941), pp. 505–6.

18. Hopkins, *The Psychology of Social Movements,* pp. 129–31.

19. Arno J. Mayer, *Dynamics of Counter-Revolution in Europe, 1870–1956. An Analytic Framework* (New York 1971) p. 135.

20. Werner Levi, 'On the Causes of War and the Conditions of Peace', *Towards a Theory of War Prevention,* eds Richard A. Falk and Saul H. Mendlovitz (New York 1966) p. 152.

21. Quoted in Waltz, *Man, the State and War,* p. 28.

22. William Brown, *War and the Psychological Conditions of Peace* (London 1942) pp. 74–5. For another similarly helpful example, see Z. Barbu, 'Nationalism as a source of aggression', *Conflict in Society,* eds Anthony DeReuck and Julie Knight (London 1966).

23. For some perceptive remarks on this point, see Waltz, *Man, the State and War,* p. 28.

24. Durbin and Bowlby, *Personal Aggressiveness and War,* p. vii. Jerome D. Frank, *Sanity and Survival; Psychological Aspects of War and Peace* (London 1968) p. 287.

25. Maurice N. Walsh, 'Summary and conclusions', *War and the Human Race,* ed. Maurice N. Walsh (New York 1971) p. 93.

26. Robert Ardrey, *The Territorial Imperative* (London 1967) p. 33.

27. 'If we are to understand the nature of our aggressive urges, we must see them against the background of our animal origins' – Desmond Morris, *The Naked Ape* (London 1967) p. 146.

28. Ardrey, *The Territorial Imperative,* p. 41.

29. Robert Ardrey, *The Hunting Hypothesis* (London 1977) pp. 27, 69.

30. Konrad Lorenz, *On Aggression* (London 1966) pp. 30–1.

31. Ardrey, *The Hunting Hypothesis,* pp. 26–7.

32. Ardrey, *The Territorial Imperative,* p. 285.

33. Ibid., p. 362.
34. Ibid.
35. Lorenz, *On Aggression*, p. 207.
36. Herbert Friedmann, 'Animal aggression and its implications for human behaviour', Walsh, *War and the Human Race*, p. 37.
37. Lorenz, *On Aggression*, p. 40.
38. This small but representative sample of abusive epithets is drawn from a collection of essays edited by Ashley Montagu and specifically designed to discredit the views of Robert Ardrey and Konrad Lorenz – *Man and Aggression*, 2nd edn (New York 1973).
39. The article and review in question are to be found in the Montagu collection cited in the previous note.
40. The charge is made by Leon Eisenberg in his contribution to the Montagu collection, pp. 57–8. For a frank appraisal of Lorenz's links with the Nazis, see Alec Nisbett, *Konrad Lorenz* (London 1976) ch. 6.
41. John Lewis and Bernard Towers, *Naked Ape or Homo Sapiens?*, 2nd edn (London 1972) p. 25.
42. See, for example, Montagu, *Man and Aggression*, p. 174.
43. Ardrey, *The Territorial Imperative*, p. 41; Montagu, *Man and Aggression*, p. xiv. It is now forty years since Mark A. May claimed victory over believers in instincts, but the latter refuse to concede – *A Social Psychology of War and Peace* (New Haven 1943) p. 3.
44. John Burton, 'The nature of aggression as revealed in the atomic age', *The Natural History of Aggression*, eds J.D. Carthy and F.J. Ebling (London and New York 1964) pp. 146–8.
45. Friedmann, 'Animal aggression', p. 35.
46. Bernard Brodie, 'Theories on the causes of war', Walsh, *War and the Human Race*, p. 19.
47. Montagu *Man and Aggression*, p. xvii.
48. John G. Kennedy, 'Ritual and intergroup murder: comments on war, primitive and modern', Walsh, *War and the Human Race*, pp. 40–1.
49. Ardrey, *The Territorial Imperative*, p. 259.
50. Keith F. Otterbein, 'The anthropology of war', *Handbook of Social and Cultural Anthropology*, ed. John J. Honigmann (Chicago 1973) p. 928.
51. Ardrey, *The Territorial Imperative*, p. 364.
52. Ibid., p. 257.
53. For reasons of space, I have omitted a discussion of another and even more recent branch of science closely akin to ethology: sociobiology, or the systematic study of the biological basis of social behaviour. Convenient recent summaries can be found in David Barash, *Sociobiology: The Whisperings Within* (London 1980) and Edward O. Wilson, *Sociobiology, The New Synthesis* (London 1975). Sociobiologists are concerned less with the results of evolution than with extrapolating the principle on which it has been based – 'the maximisation of fitness' – and applying it to human phenomena. They differ from the ethologists by not seeing aggression as an instinct. In their view, man engages in aggression because he is told that it is cost effective, a message which comes partly from his genes and partly from his environment. So the causes of war – and of most other forms of fighting too – are to be found in 'resource competition'. These views have attracted just as vehement criticism as

those of the ethologists. See, for example, Ashley Montagu (ed.), *Sociobiology examined* (Oxford 1980). For the latest word, see Stephen Jay Gould, 'Sociobiology goodbye', *The New York Review of Books*, **30** (11) (30 June 1983), which is a review of Charles J. Lumsden and Edward O. Wilson's *Promethean Fire: Reflections on the Origin of Mind* (Cambridge, Mass. 1983). Despite the optimistic title of Gould's review, it is almost certainly 'Au revoir', not 'Adieu'.

54. Bronislaw Malinowski, 'An anthropological analysis of war', *American Journal of Sociology*, **46** (1941) pp. 526–7.

55. Margaret Mead, 'Warfare is only an invention – not a biological necessity', *War: Studies from Psychology, Sociology, Anthropology*, eds Leon Bramson and George W. Goethals (New York 1964) p. 270.

56. Malinowski, 'An anthropological analysis', p. 533.

57. Ashley Montagu, *The Nature of Human Aggression* (New York 1976) pp. 271–2.

58. Malinowski, 'An anthropological analysis', pp. 532, 541. See also his 'War – past, present and future', *War as a Social Institution: The Historian's Perspective*, eds J. Clarkson and T. Cochran (New York 1941) p. 24. His criticisms were directed against psychologists such as Durbin and Bowlby, but they could be applied equally well to the ethologists.

59. Ibid., pp. 22–3. See also Mead, 'Warfare is only an invention', pp. 270–1. For an earlier version of this argument, see Goldsworthy Lowes Dickinson, *Causes of International War*, new edn (New York 1972) pp. 15–16. This book was first published in 1920.

60. Otterbein, 'The anthropology of war', p. 936.

61. Montagu, *The Nature of Human Aggression*, p. 271.

62. Ibid., p. 273.

63. For a specific example, see the main section of this book, especially pp. 99–123 and 135–57.

64. Brodie, 'Theories on the causes of war', p. 15. For a further baffling selection of sociological jargon, see Dean G. Pruitt and Richard C. Snyder (eds), *Theory and Research on the Causes of War* (Englewood Cliffs, NJ 1969) pp. 301–2.

65. In J. David Singer and Associates, *Explaining War. Selected Papers from the Correlates of War Project* (Beverly Hills and London 1979) pp. 132–3.

66. Marvin Small and J. David Singer, 'Conflict in the international system, 1816–1977', Singer and Associates, *Explaining War*, p. 62; Rudolph J. Rummel, 'Dimensions of conflict behaviour within and between nations', *General Systems*, **8** (1963) p. 27.

67. Ibid., p. 24.

68. Jonathan Wilkenfeld, 'Domestic and foreign conflict behaviour of nations', *Journal of Peace Research*, **5** (1) (1968) p. 68.

69. Michael Haas, 'Sources of international conflict', *The Analysis of International Politics: Essays in Honour of Harold and Margaret Sprout* (New York 1972) pp. 263–4.

70. Ibid., p. 271.

71. Alan Ned Sabrosky, 'From Bosnia to Sarajevo. A comparative discussion of interstate crises', Singer and Associates, *Explaining War*, pp. 139–57.

72. Ibid., pp. 154–7.

73. Ibid., p. 157.
74. All these proposals are recorded in Waltz, *Man, the State and War*, p. 46.
75. Hadley Cantril (ed.), *Tensions that Cause War* (Urbana 1950) p. 20.
76. Ibid., pp. 18–19.
77. Stanislav Andreski, 'Origins of war', *The Natural History of Aggression*, eds J. D. Carthy and F. J. Ebling (London and New York 1964) p. 132.
78. Richard J. Barnet, *Roots of War. The Men and Institutions behind US Foreign Policy* (Harmondsworth 1973) p. 339.
79. Andreski, 'Origins of war', p. 132.
80. Waltz, *Man, the State and War*, p. 8.
81. Quoted in F. H. Hinsley, *Power and the Pursuit of Peace. Theory and Practice in the History of Relations between States* (Cambridge 1963) p. 83. For a very similar observation from the same period, see Tom Paine, *Rights of Man*, ed. Henry Collins (Harmondsworth 1969) p. 290.
82. *Griff nach der Weltmacht: Die Kriegszielpolitik des kaiserlichen Deutschlands 1914–1918* (Düsseldorf 1961). It was published in an English translation in 1967 with the title *Germany's Aims in the First World War*. For a fuller discussion of the controversy aroused by the 'Fischer thesis', see the volume in this series by James Joll on the origins of the First World War.
83. Eckart Kehr, *Der Primat der Innenpolitik. Gesammelte Aufsätze zur preußisch–deutschen Sozialgeschichte im 19. und 20 Jahrhundert* (Berlin 1965). For an interesting early attack on the *Primat der Aussenpolitik* as a normative principle, see Rudolf Goldscheid, *Das Verhältnis der äusseren Politik zur inneren* (Vienna and Leipzig 1914). In a pathetic preface, dated September 1914, Goldscheid recorded that originally it had been intended as a lecture to the World Peace Congress, which had been scheduled to meet in Vienna in the autumn of 1914.
84. For Fritz Fischer's acknowledgement of the *Primat der Innenpolitik* school's debt to Kehr, see his preface to Helmut Böhme, *Deutschlands Weg zur Großmacht. Studien zum Verhältnis von Wirtschaft und Staat während der Reichsgründungszeit 1848–1881* (Cologne and Berlin 1966) pp. 1–2.
85. A brief but clear and critical discussion of these concepts can be found in the introduction to Richard J. Evans, *Society and Politics in Wilhelmine Germany* (London 1978).
86. Golo Mann, 'Der Griff nach der Weltmacht', *Deutsche Kriegsziele*, ed. Ernst Wilhelm Graf Lynar (Frankfurt am Main and Berlin 1964) p. 187.
87. Contrary to popular belief, Ranke did not coin the phrase 'Primat der Aussenpolitik' – it was the invention of Wilhelm Dilthey – Karl Dietrich Bracher, 'Kritische Betrachtungen über den Primat der Aussenpolitik', *Faktoren der politischen Entscheidung. Festgabe für Ernst Fraenkel zum 65. Geburstag*, eds Gerhard A. Ritter and Gilbert Ziebura (Berlin 1963) p. 115.
88. 'A dialogue on politics', *The Theory and Practice of History*, eds Georg G. Iggers and Konrad von Moltke (Indianapolis and New York 1973) pp. 110, 118, 123.
89. Hans-Ulrich Wehler, 'Moderne Politikgeschichte oder "Große Politik der Kabinette"?', *Geschichte und Gesellschaft*, 1 (1975) p. 354. For a cogent critique of the arguments advanced in this article, see Klaus

Hildebrand, 'Geschichte oder "Gesellschaftsgeschichte"'? Die Notwendigkeit einer politischen Geschichtsschreibung von den internationalen Beziehungen', *Historische Zeitschrift*, **223** (1976) and Georg G. Iggers, *Neue Geschichtswissenschaft. Vom Historismus zur Historischen Sozialwissenschaft* (Munich 1978) pp. 143–4.

90. Hans-Ulrich Wehler, *Krisenherde des Kaiserreichs 1871–1918* (Göttingen 1970) p. 9. In a particularly trenchant rejoinder, Thomas Nipperdey has pointed out that Wehler's polemics and view of the historian as both prosecutor and judge have made him 'Treitschke redivivus' – 'Wehlers "Kaiserreich". Eine kritische Auseinandersetzung', *Geschichte und Gesellschaft*, **1** (1975) p. 542.

91. Wehler, *Krisenherde des Kaiserreichs*, pp. 10–12.

92. Andreas Hillgruber, 'Politische Geschichte in moderner Sicht', *Historische Zeitschrift*, **216** (1973) pp. 533–9.

93. H. Oncken, 'Über die Zusammenhänge zwischen äusserer und innerer Politik', *Vorträge der Gehe-Stiftung*, vol. 9 (Leipzig and Dresden 1919) p. 18. This point is also well made in two more recent works on the subject: Rudolf L. Bindschedler, 'Zum Primat der Aussenpolitik', *Innen- und Aussenpolitik. Primat oder Interdependenz? Festschrift zum 60. Geburtstag von Walther Hofer,* eds Urs Altermatt and Judit Garamvölgyi (Bern 1980) and Wilhelm G. Grewe, *Spiel der Kräfte in der Weltpolitik. Theorie und Praxis der internationalen Beziehungen* (Düsseldorf and Vienna 1970) p. 255.

94. Richard Cobb, 'To Germany with love', *The Sunday Times*, 21 Sept. 1980, p. 43.

95. V. I. Lenin, 'War and revolution. A lecture delivered May 14 (27) 1917', *Collected Works,* vol. 24: *April–June 1917* (Moscow 1964) p. 400.

96. Karel Kára, 'On the Marxist theory of war and peace', *Journal of Peace Research,* **5** (1) (1968) p. 8. See also V. Kubálková and A. A. Cruickshank, *Marxism-Leninism and Theory of International Relations* (London 1980) p. 104.

97. Karl Marx, *The Revolutions of 1848,* ed. David Fernbach (Harmondsworth 1973) p. 109.

98. For example, Joachim Streisand, *Deutschland von 1789 bis 1815,* 2nd edn (Berlin 1961) p. 23.

99. V. I. Lenin, 'The collapse of the Second International' *Collected Works,* vol. 21: *August 1914–December 1915* (Moscow 1964) p. 221.

100. V. I. Lenin, 'Concluding remarks in the debate concerning the report on the present situation, April 14 (27) (1917)', *Collected Works,* vol. 24: *April–June 1917* (Moscow 1964) p. 151.

101. For a recent example of this sort of problem, see L. G. Beskrovny, *Otechestvennaya Voyna 1812 goda* (Moscow 1962) pp. 4–5, 43, 59. For Lenin's own views, see 'The Junius pamphlet', *Collected Works,* vol. 22 (Moscow 1964) pp. 309–10.

102. Marc Bloch, 'Historical causation', *The Historian's Craft* (Manchester 1976) pp. 192–3.

103. A. J. P. Taylor, *The Origins of the Second World War* (London 1961) pp. 102–3.

104. Ibid.

105. Bloch, 'Historical causation', p. 192.

106. W. H. Dray, 'Concepts of causation in A. J. P. Taylor's account of the origins of the Second World War', *History and Theory,* **17** (1978) p. 173.

107. Bernard Brodie, 'The continuing relevance of *On War*', Carl von Clausewitz, *On War,* eds Michael Howard and Peter Paret (Princeton 1976) p. 53.

108. Clausewitz, *On War,* p. 75.

109. 'A war is always an alternative to some other course and is always known to be so', Hinsley, *Power and the Pursuit of Peace,* p. 331.

110. Michael Howard, 'Military power and international order', *Theories of Peace and security,* ed. John Garnett (London 1970) p. 41.

111. V. I. Lenin, *Letters. February 1912–December 1922, Collected Works,* vol. 35 (Moscow 1964) p. 273.

112. Ibid.

113. Geoffrey Blainey, *The Causes of War* (Melbourne 1977) pp. 149–50. Potential readers of this consistently cogent work should not be deterred by the legend emblazoned on the cover: 'One of Australia's most brilliant authors'.

114. Sir Ernest Barker, Introduction to *The Politics of Aristotle* (Oxford 1952) p. lxiii.

115. R. G. Hawtrey, *Economic Aspects of Sovereignty,* 2nd edn (London 1952) p. 72.

116. 'Whatever may be the underlying causes of international conflict, even if we accept the role of atavistic militarism or of military–industrial complexes or of socio-biological drives or of domestic tensions in fuelling it, wars begin with conscious and reasoned decisions based on the calculation, made by both parties, that they can achieve more by going to war than by remaining at peace' – Michael Howard, *The Causes of War* (Oxford 1983) p. 22.

117. Blainey, *The Causes of War,* pp. 241, 270.

118. Ibid., p. 270.

119. Ibid., p. 53.

120. Howard, *The Causes of War,* p. 10. Martin Wight, *Power Politics,* eds Hedley Bull and Carsten Holbraad (Harmondsworth 1979) p. 138.

121. Imanuel Geiss, 'Origins of the First World War', *The Origins of the First World War,* ed. H. W. Koch (London 1972) pp. 70–1.

122. Clausewitz, *On War,* p. 119.

123. Ibid.

124. Raymond Aron, *Peace and War: A Theory of International Relations* (London 1966) p. 7. Also quoted in Howard, *The Causes of War,* p. 14. See also Hans J. Morgenthau, *Politics among Nations,* 2nd edn (New York 1954) p. 491.

125. A. J. P. Taylor, *How Wars Begin* (London 1980) p. 15.

126. Wight, *Power Politics,* p. 138.

127. Ibid., p. 140.

128. Clausewitz, *On War,* p. 61.

Chapter 2

CONFLICT IN EUROPE BEFORE THE REVOLUTION

THE WARS OF THE EIGHTEENTH CENTURY

Dating the outbreak of the French Revolution is less straightforward than it sounds. Against the traditional Bastille Day of 14 July 1789 can be set a number of other strong competitors, dating back as far as 20 August 1786, when the controller-general of the day, Calonne, informed Louis XVI that his state was insolvent. For the history of international relations, the beginning of an upheaval of corresponding dimensions can be located in time and space with some precision. The date was 17 August 1787, the place was Constantinople (about as far away from Paris as it is possible to go without leaving Europe) and the event was the arrest of Count Bulgakov and his incarceration in the Seven Towers of the Topkapi Palace. That ritual declaration of war by Ottoman Turkey on the Russian Empire was to have untold and unforeseen consequences in a dozen different countries. Within the course of the following year, the war spread to the Balkans and the Baltic. It made possible the Prussian invasion of the United Provinces in the autumn of 1787 and the movement for Polish reform which began in the autumn of 1788 and ended in the second and third partitions. It allowed Belgian dissidents to establish – briefly – an independent state and threatened the rest of the Habsburg Monarchy with disintegration. It allowed Great Britain to establish – briefly – a position of world hegemony, giving the law both on the European continent and overseas. Last but not least, it exercised a profound influence on the French Revolution. If the rest of Europe had not been ablaze, from the North Sea to the Black Sea, with wars and rumours of wars, the Revolution would have developed very differently – might even have been stillborn.

Although quite new in some important respects, the 'revolutionary wars' which began on 20 April 1792 can only be understood properly in the context of this earlier sequence of conflicts and – through them – in the context of old regime rivalries. Those who agitated for war throughout the winter of 1791–92 had not sprung ready-armed from the head of revolutionary ideology. Both their long-term assumptions

and short-term calculations were rooted in past experience and pre-
conceptions. Equally, the response of their enemies was not just to the
Revolution but to France as well. And not only to France: to a greater
or lesser extent, every other part of the European states-system influenced their assessment. In the space of one chapter, no complete
history of that interlocking web of cooperation and conflict can be
attempted. All that is possible – and necessary – is an examination of
what the international relations of the previous half-century or so
contributed to the outbreak of the revolutionary wars.[1]

The point of entry is the influence exerted on the decision-makers of
1792 (and of subsequent years) by their perception of the past. What
that seemed to teach them was that territorial expansion was essential
and that war was the best means of achieving it. To be predator or
prey: that was the choice. It was a lesson taught first and foremost by
the extraordinary frequency of war. Between 1700 and 1790 no fewer
than sixteen wars had been fought between the various combinations
of the major powers of Europe. The point is best made by means of a
simple list:

1700–21 The Great Northern War (Sweden against Russia, Poland, Saxony
and Denmark)
1701–14 The War of the Spanish Succession (France and Spain against
Austria, Great Britain and the United Provinces)
1716–18 Austria against Turkey
1717–19 Spain against Austria, the United Provinces, Great Britain and
France
1733–38 The War of the Polish Succession (France and Spain against
Austria and Russia)
1735–39 Russia against Turkey
1737–39 Austria against Turkey
1739–48 Great Britain against Spain
1740–48 The War of the Austrian Succession (France and Prussia against
Austria and Great Britain)
1741–43 Russia against Sweden
1756–63 The Seven Years War (Austria, Russia, France, Sweden and Spain
against Prussia and Great Britain)
1768–74 Russia against Turkey
1778–83 The American War of Independence (Great Britain against
France, Spain and the United Provinces)
1778–79 The War of the Bavarian Succession (Austria against Prussia)
1787–92 Russia and Austria against Turkey
1788–90 Russia against Sweden

As this reveals, only the 1720s were mainly peaceful. The Ottoman
Turks were at war (with a European power) at some point during five
of those nine decades, Prussia during six, Spain and Sweden during
seven, France, Great Britain and Austria during eight and Russia
during all nine. Only the United Provinces, whose great-power status
was (significantly) by now questionable, managed to remain at peace

for most of the period. If ever there were a time when war was the normal means of intercourse between states, then this was surely it.

This depressing roll-call was made possible partly by the changing nature of warfare itself. Gone – for the time being – were the days when vast hordes of undisciplined and uncontrollable soldiers surged up and down central Europe, laying waste everything that stood in their path. Although no angels of mercy, the armies of the eighteenth century were smaller, more professional and less destructive: 'It might be suggested that it was not the least achievement of European civilisation to have reduced the wolf packs which had preyed on the defenceless peoples of Europe for so many centuries to the condition of trained and obedient gun-dogs – almost, in some cases, performing poodles.'[2] Consequently, they could be used with greater precision – and more often. This more limited character of the actual fighting, which expressed itself in many sieges, much manœuvring, but few battles, also produced inconclusive results. The objective was to secure a favourable negotiating position, not to destroy the enemy and to dictate terms. Over the century as a whole, empires rose and empires fell, but each stage was marked by a truce rather than a peace. There could be no better illustration of Geoffrey Blainey's maxim that the durability of a peace depends on the decisiveness of the preceding war.[3]

The efficiency of war as an instrument of policy was also advertised by its results. In the course of the century, two empires (the Ottoman and the French) were seriously eroded, another (the Swedish) was decimated, while a third (the Polish–Lithuanian) was expunged from the map altogether. From their debris, three new great powers – Great Britain, Prussia and Russia – were constructed and a fourth – the Habsburg monarchy – was given a new lease of life. It was war which made this transfer of power possible. Even the apparently peaceful partitions of Poland were the indirect result of Russo-Turkish conflicts. The days when national interests would be thought best served by a 'Pax Britannica' or whatever were far in the future.

In this massive transfer of territory, a major part had been played by the domestic condition of the states concerned. While the victims were enfeebled by factionalism, insolvency and social unrest, the predators maximised their resources and concentrated their power. In Great Britain, the civil wars of the previous century made way for stable oligarchy. In Prussia, the alliance between king and Junkers was consolidated. In Russia, autocracy was refounded by Peter the Great and – although occasionally tempered by peasant revolt or palace revolution – remained the unchallenged system of government. In the Habsburg monarchy, the defeat of the Hungarian separatists between 1705 and 1711 paved the way for three-quarters of a century of relative harmony. Of the five major powers, only France was threatened from within, caught in a vicious circle, with internal decay leading to external failure, which in turn fed domestic opposition.

In the other four members of the pentarchy, both cause and effect of their resolution of conflict at home was their creation of effective administrations. It was their ability to mobilise men and money which allowed them a share of the spoils. Partly that was due to the general economic expansion which began in the second quarter of the century. The sustained increase in population, in agricultural productivity, in commerce and in manufacturing all generated more wealth to be taxed. Of Britain's fabulous prosperity, drawn from all four corners of the earth, nothing more needs to be said. Dwarfed as they were in absolute terms, the three great powers of eastern Europe could still boast impressive relative success. From a virtually land-locked, mainly natural economy, Russia was transformed in the space of just a few generations into a major commercial power. Between 1775 and 1787 the Russian merchant marine increased *eight times*.[4] By the latter date, moreover, Russian ships were plying the Black Sea as well as the Baltic and were even beginning to penetrate the Eastern Mediterranean.[5]

If Prussia and Austria were unable to match that kind of spectacular commercial expansion, they had more to crow about in agriculture and manufacturing. Not even the most vehement Borussophobe denies Frederick the Great's success in promoting new crops, improving livestock and reclaiming waste land. With some justification he claimed to have conquered a new province in peacetime by attracting around 300,000 immigrants to his state.[6] In the Habsburg monarchy there was a comparable if regionally uneven economic expansion. In Bohemia and Moravia the number of weavers employed in the textile industry increased from 39,000 to 66,000 between 1775 and 1788, while in the same period the number of all workers in woollen goods manufacturing almost doubled from 80,000 to 152,000.[7] A proud Joseph II reported to his brother Leopold in 1786: 'Shipping on the Danube heading for the Levant and the Crimea is increasing every day. . . . Industry and manufacturing are prospering. . . .A large number of Nurembergers, Swabians and even Englishmen, who used to make their living by producing in their own countries, have recently settled here to carry on their business.'[8]

Yet expansion of the economic base is not sufficient by itself to explain the pattern of international power. In terms of depth and diversity of resources, France was still by far the richest state in Europe. Moreover, at least until the depression of the 1770s, she shared fully in the general growth of prosperity. Between *c.* 1720 and *c.* 1790 French overseas trade more than quadrupled in volume.[9] That did not prevent a collapse of French power and prestige. It was the progressive failure of administrative institutions and techniques which condemned the old regime to impotence.[10] Whatever else may have changed between the catastrophic 1750s and the triumphant 1790s, it was not the productivity of the French economy. Indeed, in certain sectors – most notably overseas trade – the Revolution was a good deal poorer than the old regime had been. That resources were not every-thing was demonstrated with conclusive finality by Prussia. Working from a material base markedly inferior to that of adjacent Poland, the Hohenzollerns turned their 'sand-box' (Frederick the Great's descrip-tion) into a power capable of resisting (in the Seven Years War) the combined weight of France, Russia, Austria, Sweden and most of the German princes.

However old-fashioned it may sound, it is clear that the fortuitous coincidence of strong-willed personalities greatly intensified, if it did not cause, international rivalries. The clashes between Peter the Great and Charles XII, Maria Theresa and Frederick the Great, Catherine the Great and Gustavus III, George III and Vergennes, Joseph II and just about everyone – all helped to keep the pot on the boil. Given the autocratic structure of most countries, that could hardly be otherwise. But by the late 1780s the sting of this formidable band was being drawn by death, illness and old age. Those who took their place proved notably less effective. As Sir John Fortescue observed, with charac-teristic astringency, 'This amazing abundance of half-witted sovereigns was one of the many fortunate accidents which allowed the French Revolution to gather so much headway.'[11] By that time, however, the notion that war was an efficient and relatively painless method of settling disputes was too deeply ingrained in the old regime's decision-making habits. In the last war fought in central Europe before the Revolution – the War of the Bavarian Succession of 1778–79 – not a single engagement of any consequence was fought. It was the *reductio ad absurdum* of eighteenth-century warfare. So when the 'half-witted sovereigns' were confronted by the problem of revolu-tionary France, it was natural for them to resort to the sort of solution which had served their forebears so well.

THE CONTINUITY OF REVOLUTIONARY FOREIGN POLICY: AUSTROPHOBIA IN OLD REGIME FRANCE

International conflict before the Revolution not only provided the weapon for the resolution of subsequent disputes, it also suggested the direction in which it should be pointed. If valid, that observation is a paradox: the first revolutionary war was fought by France against Austria and Prussia, yet France had been allied to Austria since 1756, while Austria and Prussia had been inveterate enemies since 1740. Certainly the continuity between old and new regimes, old and new diplomacies should not be exaggerated. The Revolution *did* make a

40

difference. Nevertheless, the decision-makers' conceptions of their respective national interests, prospective allies and prospective enemies were at least strongly influenced by what had gone before.

The French alliance with Austria had always been a squally marriage of convenience, with each partner prone to periodic bouts of doubting whether it was even convenient. It had been born out of the aimless drifting which had afflicted French foreign policy in the 1740s and 1750s. In Albert Sorel's crushing verdict: 'Having risked the loss of Canada in order to conquer Silesia for the King of Prussia, France was to lose it finally in the next war for the pleasure of attempting to restore that province to the Queen of Hungary. France, having played the game of Prussia in the War of the Austrian Succession, was to play that of Austria in the Seven Years War.'[12] Many, if not most contemporary Frenchmen were equally hostile. For two and a half centuries, the guiding principle of French foreign policy had been opposition to the House of Habsburg. This was the tradition of Francis I, Henry IV, Richelieu, Mazarin and Louis XIV and it had brought France security, territory and prestige. If the instinctive opposition aroused by its reversal were to be overcome, the new Austrian alliance of 1756 would have to yield some prompt and impressive returns. If the war which immediately followed had gone according to plan, France would have gained control of Belgium and all might have been well. In the event, it was an unmitigated disaster.

By seeking to wage war simultaneously at sea, in the colonies and on the Continent, France was defeated in all three theatres. And not just defeated – humiliated. Defeats in the Caribbean, Quebec or Bengal might have been stomached, for the French colonial empire was of relatively recent origin. Defeats close to home were a different matter. As so often in the past, a French army had marched east, to chastise another troublesome German prince. On 5 November 1757 it was routed at Rossbach by Frederick the Great and a Prussian army only half its size. Among the numerous possible points of no return in the history of old regime France, that day has a strong claim. Representative of the angry frustration which now infected the French élites, was the reaction of the Comte de Saint-Germain, who commanded the rearguard in the battle. In a letter to a friend in Paris, he wrote:

> No doubt you, like me, were able to predict the Rossbach disaster five months ago. Never has there been such a defective army, and the first cannon-shot determined our rout and humiliation. I am leading a gang of robbers, of murderers fit only for the gallows, who run away at the sound of the first gunshot and who are always ready to mutiny. The King has the worst infantry under the sun, and the worst-disciplined – there is just nothing to be done with troops like these.[13]

With the benefit of hindsight, Rossbach (and Minden, Lagos, Quiberon Bay, Louisbourg, Quebec, Plassey and the rest) derived from a multitude of problems which had eroded French power. Contemporaries preferred an easier answer and fastened on the Austrian alliance as a scapegoat:

> Thus soon after [the Austrian alliance of 1756] the government no longer possessed any dignity, the finances any order and the conduct of policy any consistency. France lost its influence in Europe; England ruled the seas effortlessly and conquered the Indies unopposed. The powers of the North partitioned Poland. The balance of power established by the Peace of Westphalia was broken. The French monarchy ceased to be a first-rank power.[14]

After the war had ended in defeat and disgrace in 1763, France's suffering was not yet over. In the following year, the collapse of her once dominant influence in eastern Europe was revealed by the election of Stanislas Poniatowski as King of Poland. By imposing her own candidate – and superannuated lover to boot – the new Tsarina, Catherine II, demonstrated that Poland was now a Russian satellite. When the last vacancy had occurred, in 1733, France had gone to war to try to impose her candidate. She had failed in that object, but at least had gained Lorraine from the resulting imbroglio. In 1764 she stood helplessly by. There was the same lack of effective response when Poland was partitioned eight years later. What made that episode so offensive in French eyes was the eager participation of Austria, her nominal ally.

Elsewhere in Europe, France's retreat continued apace, with the Austrian alliance apparently only accelerating matters. In the north, Sweden declined from effective ally to expensive liability. In the south-east, the third part of traditional 'leap-frog' diplomacy – Turkey – was savaged by Russia in the war of 1768–74 and weakened further by Catherine's outright annexation of the Crimea in 1783. On the latter occasion, Austria's attitude provoked more intense indignation. Far from giving his French allies the support they had every right to expect, Joseph II coolly revealed that he was now allied to Russia as well and would be doing everything in his power to force the Turks to accept the annexation. In Germany too, French diplomats found themselves elbowed aside by Prussians and even Russians. The Austrian raid on Bavaria in 1778 and the election of Joseph's brother, the Archduke Maximilian Franz, as Elector of Cologne and Prince-Bishop of Münster soon afterwards, signalled at least an attempt to reassert Habsburg power in the Holy Roman Empire.[15] That was directed primarily against Prussia, of course, but the implications for France were also alarming.

This collapse on the Continent might just have been thought worthwhile if it had been counterbalanced by a colonial revival of compensating proportions. Certainly it allowed Vergennes to try another fall with the British in the late 1770s, following the American revolt, but the results were disappointing. Although some vicarious pleasure could be derived from American independence and the humbling of the old enemy, the verdict of the Seven Years War was not reversed. Imminent bankruptcy, defeat at the naval battle of the Saints in April 1782, and the failure to take Gibraltar in the summer of the same year obliged the French to settle for much less than they had expected. A share in the Newfoundland fishing, a couple of West Indian islands and a few trading stations in Senegal and India represented meagre return for more than four years of ruinously expensive fighting.[16] The Spanish, on the other hand, whose war effort had been markedly inferior, emerged with two plums: Minorca and Florida. Once again, it seemed to contemporaries, the French had done all the dirty work but had ended up with next to nothing themselves.

As the diplomatic revolution of 1756 had been followed by a sad sequence of disappointments, it was natural – if not entirely fair – that the Austrian alliance should be blamed. At regular intervals, senior French officials raged impotently at the treachery and ingratitude of their 'ally'. In the very first memorandum he prepared for Louis XVI in 1774, Vergennes denounced 'l'amour-propre, l'avidité, le génie romanesque, le caractère ambitieux' of Joseph II.[17] Louis himself had an equally hostile opinion of his brother-in-law, referring to him the following year in terms similar to those used by his foreign minister: 'usurpateur, un caractère ambitieux et despote'.[18] The passage of time only served to confirm that verdict. In 1783 Vergennes told his ambassador in Vienna, the Marquis de Noailles, that nothing was more shaky ('vacillant') than the Austro-French alliance.[19] Nevertheless, it staggered along somehow or other until eventually killed off in summary fashion by the revolutionaries. The secret of its improbable longevity lay less in its own dubious merits (the most obvious being the neutralisation of Belgium and Italy) than in the certain defects of any alternative. Any attempt to abandon Austria in favour of – say – Prussia would have driven Joseph II straight into the welcoming embrace of the British. It was as simple as that. That sort of negative calculation had no appeal outside government circles. At court, in Paris, in the press, opposition to the Austrian alliance was vocal and sustained. Although perhaps he made too much of it, Albert Sorel had a point when he observed that the foreign policy of the French revolutionaries dated back to 1756 and Favier's *Doutes et questions sur le traité de 1756.*[20] For the kind of man, whether noble or commoner, who went to the Estates General in 1789, it was axiomatic that one of the first things needed by a regenerated France would be a new alliance system. By that time, Austrophobia had come to concentrate with pathological ferocity on Joseph II's sister, Queen Marie Antoinette. Comparing her with Anne of Austria, her friends the Polignacs with Mazarin and the Revolution with the Fronde, Jean-Louis Soulavie wrote:

Ever since the Bourbons had ascended the throne of France, hatred of Austria had always been intense. And whenever the French people had to witness an Austrian princess taking control of the government and ruling through favourites, then their impatience with a foreign yoke was always a prelude to violent reaction.[21]

So far as relations between the two nations were concerned, the Austro-French alliance did more harm than good. Conduct that could be expected from an enemy could not be tolerated in an ally. So relations were worse in 1789 than they had been in 1756. Moreover, this was a two-way process: the Austrians were every bit as disenchanted with the conduct of their allies. If they had not suffered the same losses in the Seven Years War, they had failed in their central objective: the reconquest of Silesia from Prussia. That had been the main purpose of the war, the main purpose of the French alliance, and when it became clear that it was unattainable, so did the alliance lose much of its meaning. Moreover, it was arguable at least that the French war effort had been positively counter-productive. By performing so feebly in Germany, by suffering that epoch-making débacle at Rossbach, the French had raised Frederick the Great to heroic status and had consolidated Austro-Prussian dualism.

That disservice to Austria had been inadvertent. Not even a Habsburg could suppose that battles could be lost on purpose. In the aftermath of the Seven Years War, however, it did become clear that France would make no contribution to any expansion of Austrian power at the expense of Prussia. On the contrary, she would do everything she could to prevent it. As Vergennes put it in 1777, France was obliged to guarantee the integrity of the Habsburg monarchy but was commanded neither by treaty nor by national interest to weaken Prussia.[22] Ten years later, the Austrian *cabinet noir* intercepted and copied a despatch from the Prussian ambassador at Versailles, Count von der Goltz, to his superior in Berlin, in which he recounted a conversation with Vergennes' successor as foreign minister, the Comte de Montmorin.[23] Joseph II and his own foreign minister, Prince Kaunitz, read the intercept with grim satisfaction, for it confirmed all their suspicions about the perfidy of their French ally. Montmorin had told von der Goltz that the Austrian alliance existed in name only, was nothing more than a 'fantôme'. By way of proof, he asked the Prussian what France had done for Austria over the past two decades or more. Without waiting for a reply, he supplied the answer himself – nothing.

He was right. On every occasion that Austria had made a forward move, the French had tried to apply the brakes. In 1772, they had protested noisily if ineffectually about the first partition of Poland. In 1778, they had refused to give any help in the War of the Bavarian Succession. In 1784 they had even threatened to fight against Austria and on the side of the Dutch in the dispute over the Scheldt. In 1785 they had vetoed Joseph II's plan to exchange the Belgian provinces for Bavaria. In the same year they had done nothing to prevent the formation of Frederick the Great's League of Princes. With an ally like that, Austria had no need of enemies.

So the periodic eruptions of wrath from Versailles were more than matched by the almost incessant clamour from Vienna. Time and again the alliance seemed to be – and was stated to be – on the very verge of collapse.[24] Yet however bumpy the ride, it lurched and rattled along throughout the 1770s and 1780s. The reason for its survival was negative but plain: if France were allied to Austria, she could not be allied to Prussia. And if no positive help were forthcoming, at least the Austrians could forget about the Netherlands and Italy and concentrate on Prussia and the Turks.[25] So *raison d'état* kept the two allies together, but could not prevent the festering growth of mutual resentment, at both a governmental and popular level.[26] Indeed, the nominal alliance only made matters worse and helped to ensure that when the Revolution broke out, the two countries were glowering at each other in hatred and incomprehension.

THE CONTINUITY OF REVOLUTIONARY FOREIGN POLICY: ANGLOPHOBIA IN OLD REGIME FRANCE

At first sight, France's relations with her other old enemy – Great Britain – seemed unequivocally and overtly hostile. Since the Nine Years War of 1688–97, they had been locked in 'a second Hundred Years War',[27] interrupted only by peaces that turned out to be truces. The latest inconclusive round had been brought to a close in 1783 by the Treaty of Versailles, leaving a vengeful Great Britain and a disappointed France. Although that combination of restless emotions did not bode well for a stable peace, there were certain forces making for *rapprochement,* or at least coexistence. Both countries had emerged from the American War with a burden of debt which could only encourage future restraint. Both countries were inhibited further by domestic political problems. That Britain would be able to balance her books within three years and that William Pitt would remain prime minister until 1800 was not so obvious at the time. Many contemporaries would have agreed with Leopold of Tuscany, when he observed to his brother, Joseph II, that Britain had 'declined to the status of a second-rate power, comparable to Sweden and Denmark'.[28] France's own – and very real – problems would soon be visible for all to see.

Common anxieties were complemented by common ambitions. In the course of the previous half-century or so, both countries had enjoyed massive commercial expansion. Between 1700 and the outbreak of the American War, the British merchant marine had almost trebled – and then grew at an even faster rate in the 1780s.[29] Even after the French economy as a whole entered a long recession in the 1770s, the commercial sector continued to expand. In 1773, 510 ships with a total tonnage of 122,277 left 11 French ports for Santo Domingo, Martinique, Guadeloupe and Guyana; the corresponding figures for 1788 were 677 and 190,753, a percentage increase of 33 and 56 respectively.[30] In the days of Colbert, mutual expansion might have led to mutual enmity, but by the 1780s more enlightened counsels prevailed. If the physiocrats and Adam Smith had not conquered government opinion in their respective countries, at least the free-trade theories they advocated – powerfully assisted by the logic of international capitalism – had had some effect. Moreover, in the Old World at least, a rough division of zones of interest had been achieved: the French dominated the Levant and the British dominated the Baltic.[31]

That international trade could promote cooperation as well as conflict appeared to be demonstrated by the Anglo-French commercial agreement of 1786, commonly termed 'the Eden Treaty' after the chief British negotiator William Eden. Indeed, there is some evidence that for the French foreign minister, Vergennes, political motives were paramount. By offering the British easier access to French markets, he hoped to gain their support in maintaining the political status quo in Europe. Greatly alarmed by Russian expansion, now aided and abetted by Austria, he realised that France alone, teetering on the brink of bankruptcy, could not cope.[32] The treaty was also designed to deter smuggling, improve customs revenue and stimulate French manufacturing by allowing more competition. Above all, in the view of Calonne, the controller-general of finance, and Rayneval, the chief French negotiator, it was designed to open up British markets for surplus French agricultural produce, especially wine and its derivatives.[33]

If the main motive of the French really was political rather than economic or fiscal, then their initiative was stillborn. When congratulating Eden on the successful conclusion of the negotiations, the British foreign secretary, the Marquis of Carmarthen, added that French compliance on economic matters only made him more suspicious when it came to politics.[34] Although Carmarthen was particularly Francophobe his mistrust was shared by Pitt: 'Though in the commercial business I think there are reasons for believing the French may be sincere, I cannot listen without suspicion to their professions of political friendship.'[35] Those suspicions may have been unfounded, but they were not unreasonable. Since the conclusion of the American War, there had been many smooth professions of friendship issuing from Versailles but without any validating action. On the contrary, such was the gulf between words and deeds that Carmarthen can be forgiven for suspecting a plot to lull the British into a sense of false security.

One major source of alarm was the artificial harbour under construction at Cherbourg. As early as September 1783, with the ink on the Treaty of Versailles barely dry, reports reached London that facilities for no fewer than 100 ships of the line were planned. It was because the new port would be so much closer to British shores than the existing bases at Brest and Toulon that the threat it presented was deemed so serious. Once it was completed, a French force would be able to dash across the Channel, destroy the dockyards at Plymouth and Portsmouth and decide a war before it could properly begin. Most serious of all, it would make a French invasion very much easier: indeed, in August 1784, the Russian ambassador passed on to the British an intelligence report stating that the Cherbourg harbour was being constructed for just that purpose. Confirmation that the French gave the work high priority came with reports that no expense was being spared and that 1,400 labourers and 14 ships were hard at work. When it also became known that the torpid Louis XVI had actually made a personal inspection in the summer of 1786 – one of the very few occasions on which he stirred outside the environs of Paris and Versailles – the warning signals were well and truly posted. No wonder Pitt and Carmarthen found it so difficult to swallow the honeyed words of Vergennes.[36]

Even closer to home – and even more menacing – was the threat from growing French control of the United Provinces. Ever since the personal union achieved by William of Orange, the British had adopted a quasi-proprietary attitude towards their smaller neighbour. Frederick the Great found an appropriately nautical image to express the relationship: 'Holland follows England like a longboat which follows in the wake of the warship to which it is tied', while Edmund Burke – with characteristic overstatement – told the House of Commons on 29 March 1791: 'Holland might justly be considered as necessary a part of this country as Kent.'[37] The majestic insularity of this latter remark was representative of the dominant mood in government and Parliament. Men like the Earl of Shelburne – cosmopolitan, polyglot, as well informed about international affairs as he was free of national prejudice – were very rare. The dominant attitude was well summarised by the Earl of Chesterfield in a letter to his son:

> We are in England ignorant of foreign affairs and of the interests, views, pretensions, and policy of other Courts. That part of knowledge never enters into our thoughts nor makes part of our education . . . and when foreign affairs happen to be debated in Parliament, it is incredible with how much ignorance.[38]

Those words were written in 1748 but were still just as valid in the 1780s. William Pitt made only one brief trip to the Continent, knew little and cared less about its affairs. He took office as prime minister in December 1783, yet it was May the following year before he found time for a conference with his foreign secretary. Carmarthen himself was yet another in a long line of British secretaries of state whose intelligence was not matched by application. Absent from the Foreign Office for weeks at a time, his lethargy was exceptional even in that unhurried age. In January 1788, Sir Robert Keith complained from Vienna: 'This is the fifty third letter I have written to the office, since I have received one word in direct answer to any of them.'[39] Shortly afterwards, the conduct of all British policy with respect to the Habsburg monarchy and the Balkans (now in the throes of a war) was brought to a virtual halt by an acrimonious dispute between Keith and his superior over the ambassador's complaints of neglect.[40]

For relations with other European powers, British politicians' ignorance, deriving from indolence and lack of interest, led to an inability to conceive of any legitimate national interest other than their own. If the Austrians spurned a British offer of an alliance, for example, then they must be knaves or fools, or both. That it might not be in their interest to ally with Britain was not considered.[41] So when Burke laid claim to Holland as part of England, he was expressing a conviction that was as common as it was deep. It was also well founded. Given their geographical location, if the United Provinces ever fell under the control of a hostile power, then British commerce, British prosperity and British security would all be in jeopardy. Once that threat appeared, even the most land-locked booby squire roused himself to take an interest in continental affairs.

That was just the situation in the 1780s. Having failed to support the British during the Seven Years War, the Dutch actually fought against them during the American War. Both symptom and cause of that estrangement was the growing power inside the United Provinces of the political groups opposed to the Stadholder William V, the head of the House of Orange. Given the latter's close relationship with the British, the opposition naturally turned to France for support. After a *de facto* alliance during the last three years of the American War, when they found themselves fighting on the same side, the Dutch and the French concluded a formal alliance in November 1785.[42] With the intermediate Austrian Netherlands (Belgium) ruled by another ally, the French had now acquired, for the first time, control of the entire Channel and North Sea coast. Moreover, they had also acquired the services of the Dutch fleet to help them enforce it.

This was all alarming enough. The British could remember only too well the dreadful summer of 1779, when the French and Spanish fleets cruised unchallenged off the south coast and an invasion seemed imminent. But in the mid and late 1780s the chief threat was thought to be not in the Channel but in India. British sea routes to India were exceedingly vulnerable, there being no base for refuge, supply or refitting after Saint Helena in the South Atlantic. The French, on the other hand, held the key islands Bourbon and Mauritius in the Indian

Ocean, while the Dutch held the even more crucial Cape of Good Hope and Trincomalee on the north-east coast of Ceylon, the only serviceable base in the region during the monsoon.[43] In a despatch sent to Earl Cornwallis, the governor-general of India, in August 1787, William Pitt reviewed the implications of the Franco-Dutch alliance:

> From the maritime strength which it [the United Provinces] might at least be made capable of exerting (when acting under the direction of France, who would naturally turn everything to that object), from its local position, and particularly from that of its dependencies in India, I need not point out to your lordship how much this country would have to apprehend from such an event in any war in which we may be hereafter engaged.[44]

With America independent, India was now the central pillar of the British imperial structure. If the French could repeat their demolition exercise there too, all would come crashing down.[45] This was no illusory nightmare, conjured up by paranoid Francophobia, for there was plenty of evidence that the French were indeed looking east. In the last two years of the American War, a major expedition under the Comte de Bussy had been sent to India to begin the eviction.[46] It had failed, but its objective did not die with it. During the peace negotiations, Vergennes tried everything he knew to regain a significant French presence in India.[47] That failed too, but disappointment did not bring resignation – the promising opportunities presented by the new Dutch connection were sufficient to prevent that. In a memorandum written in the autumn of 1785, the French navy minister, the Maréchal de Castries, argued that Asia was now the main source of British power, so that was where the French – in cooperation with their new Dutch allies – should concentrate their attention.[48] For the time being, France was too exhausted and the United Provinces were too unstable, but there were a few straws in the wind to indicate what was literally the reorientation of French strategy. Between 1784 and 1789 no fewer than ten French naval expeditions were sent to the eastern seas. In 1785 a new *Compagnie des Indes* was founded, ostensibly for commercial purposes only but with clear political overtones. A series of maritime clashes in Indian waters in 1785, which the British believed had been provoked deliberately, soured relations further. In 1786 a French agent was sent to Tippoo Sahib to offer to pay a share of the expenses incurred in the Mysore War against the British.[49]

The British misread these signs. In the aftermath of the American experience, they were too inclined to underestimate their own strength and to overestimate that of France to be able to assess the situation objectively. In the summer of 1784 Carmarthen believed there already existed a treaty between France and the United Provinces, with the avowed aim of expelling the British from India.[50] So when the French came bearing gifts, in the shape of the commercial treaty, the response was not an agreement to cooperate in eastern Europe – as Vergennes had hoped – but redoubled suspicion. The French had only themselves to blame. They could not hope for *rapprochement* while simultaneously seeking to gain control of the United Provinces. Part of the problem here was the characteristic confusion of direction which afflicted the old regime in its twilight years. While Vergennes urged restraint on the French Party in the United Provinces and sought a negotiated settlement with the Stadholder's group, hawks like de Castries called for full steam ahead.[51]

When Vergennes died, on 13 February 1787, the forward party took undisputed control. If France had not been paralysed by political chaos and financial bankruptcy, then almost certainly she would have gone to war against Prussia and Great Britain to prevent their military intervention in Holland in September of that year. On 28 June the Princess of Orange, wife of the Stadholder and sister of Frederick William II of Prussia, had been arrested by a detachment of Freikorps, the para-military wing of the French-backed 'Patriot Party'. Although she was soon released, the Prussians were encouraged by the British to take advantage of the episode to solve the Dutch problem by force. After much hesitation, they agreed, by now secure in the knowledge that the Austrians would be diverted by the war in the Balkans which had broken out in August. Stubborn to the point of folly, the Patriots had refused the satisfaction demanded, confident that their French sponsors would honour earlier promises of military assistance.[52] As it was, with the new chief minister Loménie de Brienne vetoing any response on financial grounds, the French could only stand by in fuming impotence, as their Dutch allies were imprisoned or forced to flee. Once the Stadholder had been restored to his previous dominant position, the United Provinces were duly steered into a new alliance with Prussia and Great Britain (March and June 1788). For the British, the sense of relief was intense. The Dutch navy was back where it belonged (at the disposal of the Admiralty), the threat of French control of the Channel had dissolved and, above all, sea routes to India were safer than they had ever been. George III spoke for everyone when he told Pitt: 'Perhaps no part of the change in Holland is so material to this country as the gaining of that Republic as an ally in India.'[53]

For Franco-British relations, the Dutch affair of 1787 had serious consequences. The temporary ascendancy achieved by the French in the American War was destroyed. Any faint sense that the Treaty of Versailles of 1783 had avenged the Peace of Paris of 1763 was now swamped by a new sense of national dishonour and humiliation. This had been Louis XVI's last chance to assert the old regime's viability. When he declined to take it, his fate was sealed:

A vigorous and determined policy would probably have thrown our enemies into disarray, have reassured Holland, restrained Prussia, made the Turks see reason, and have exported abroad that agitated spirit of unrest which was currently disturbing the country and which clamoured either to be diverted abroad or to explode inside France. . . .This act of weakness and the triumph of our enemies astounded me; all my illusions vanished and from that moment I saw the abyss yawning, into which feeble government on the one side and unbridled passions on the other were dragging my fatherland and its king.[54]

For contemporary Frenchmen, who looked on in furious disbelief as the Prussians and the British trampled across their backyard with impunity, the fate of the United Provinces took on an importance even greater than its actual value. At some point in the future, national regeneration would demand appropriate revenge (see p. 155). For the British too, the episode had left an impression fraught with disruptive potential. In the first place, the alarums and excursions of the 1780s had intensified the conviction that Holland *was* as much a part of England as the county of Kent and that everything *should* be done to make sure it stayed that way. On the other hand, the relative ease with which the United Provinces had been regained from a bankrupt and faction-ridden France encouraged the notion that the combination of the Royal Navy and the Prussian army was irresistible and that the French could not – and would not – stand in its way. In addition, for Pitt and his colleagues the recapture of the Dutch had been their first major success. It made their position in Parliament impregnable and released them from the guiding strings of the King.[55] So they lavished on their prize all the possessive love due to a first-born. Last but not least, Britain had been brought back out of isolation and into an active role in continental affairs.

FRANCE, PRUSSIA AND THE EASTERN QUESTION

So when the Revolution began, France and Great Britain were at daggers drawn. Only French weakness had prevented the outbreak of yet another violent episode in the new Hundred Years War. When France recovered, resumption was very likely, if not inevitable, especially in view of the mutual resentments stoked up – but not released – by the events of 1787. On the face of it, the same sort of remarks should apply to Prussia, except more so, for it had been a Hohenzollern princess who had provided the occasion for the Dutch intervention and it had been a Prussian army which had done all the dirty work. Yet in Franco-Prussian relations the Dutch episode was no more than that – an episode of limited, almost fortuitous character. While for the British fundamental issues were involved, it was very difficult to see why the Prussians got involved at all. Of course the Princess of Orange was the King of Prussia's sister and certainly the Dutch Freikorps had behaved boorishly – to the point of allowing her no privacy even when she relieved herself – but to launch an invasion with an army of 20,000 men smacks of over-reaction. For what did Prussia have at stake in the United Provinces? The answer is surely: nothing at all – nothing political, nothing strategic, nothing economic. It should have been a matter of the utmost indifference to Prussia whether the country was ruled by the pro-French Patriots or the pro-British Orangists.

That had been the conclusion of Frederick the Great, who had declined all requests for assistance from the British with the argument that it would only provoke France into giving the Austrians some real assistance for a change.[56] In his view, Britain neither could nor would give Prussia any material help. Events were to prove him right. Frederick also appreciated that France and Prussia were bound together by common hostility to Austria – even if no formal alliance existed. It was a view shared by the French Foreign Office (see p. 44). So during the last years of his reign, Frederick had preferred isolation to any British connection, relying on his League of German Princes (*Fürstenbund*) to maintain Prussia's position in the Holy Roman Empire.[57] Although he did not enjoy being confronted by an Austria allied to both France and Russia, he could appreciate that all three were deeply divided against each other and that he had nothing to fear so long as he remained passive. Aptly, he likened a possible alliance between Britain and Prussia to two drowning men clutching on to each other – and going down all the faster.[58]

That all changed with Frederick's death on 17 August 1786 and the succession of his nephew, Frederick William II. Now a new ambition and restlessness, not to say incoherence, entered Prussian policy. Of the several competing royal advisers, it was Count Ewald von Hertzberg who gradually achieved predominance. It was his view that the time had come for a new expansionist drive, capitalising on Prussia's favourable position as the holder of the balance between the competing continental powers.[59] He advocated escape from isolation by means of a 'Northern System', which would link Prussia and the League of Princes to Great Britain, the United Provinces, Denmark and Russia.[60] It was in pursuit of this combination that Hertzberg argued and won the case for intervention in the United Provinces. Well aware that no vital Prussian interests were at stake, he was prepared to pay the price for what he hoped would be British support for his scheme in eastern Europe.

This was the famous 'Hertzberg Plan', a multiple exchange of territory designed to bring Prussia significant gains without the effort and expense of war. In all the twists and turns and somersaults of Prussian diplomacy over the next few years, one consistent objective was the acquisition of the towns of Danzig and Thorn, plus their surrounding territories, and thus the rounding-off of the first partition of Poland. In

Sir John Clapham's sonorous metaphor: 'The Prussian diplomatists piped many different airs at this time; but, whatever the air, the drone growled on continuously, "Thorn and Danzig, Danzig and Thorn".'[61] Hertzberg had first mooted this scheme back in 1779,[62] but it was not until the outbreak of the Russo-Turkish War in August 1787 that it became a realistic possibility. All depended on the Turks being defeated by the Russians and the Austrians and thus becoming receptive to any rescue plan, however expensive. Prussia would then intervene, if necessary with an armed demonstration, to propose and enforce the following interlocking exchange: in return for a general guarantee of their remaining territories, the Turks would cede Wallachia and Moldavia to Austria; Austria would cede Galicia to Poland; Poland would cede Danzig, Thorn, the Palatinate of Posen and Kalisch to Prussia. Over the years, several variations were played, notably a scherzo of 1788 which involved Sweden and Russia too, but this remained the basic theme.

With more justification than he is often credited, Hertzberg believed that this scheme would be no more difficult to implement than the first partition of Poland had been. Unfortunately for him, however, the other actors in his carefully plotted drama failed to learn their lines or follow the elaborate stage directions. Instead of exiting right in the first scene, as required, the Turks stood their ground at stage centre, proving much more formidable than anyone had expected. They were greatly assisted by a diversionary exercise launched by a power which had not even featured on Hertzberg's cast-list: Sweden. In July 1788 Gustavus III attacked Russia through Finland with such initial success that Swedish guns could be heard in St Petersburg. So Catherine the Great was obliged to divert her main effort to the north, leaving her hapless ally, Joseph II, to bear the brunt of the Turkish offensive alone. With Austria refusing the cession of Galicia and a resurgent Poland proudly asserting its territorial inviolability, the gabble of improvised voices was such that the curtain had to be rung down on the Hertzberg plan.

By this time – 1789 – Frederick William II had raised his sights well above Hertzberg's programme. He was encouraged to do so by the acute domestic problems of Joseph II. The successful revolt in the Austrian Netherlands, the likelihood that Hungary would follow suit, the discontent which seethed in every other province, all seemed to signal the impending dissolution of the Habsburg monarchy. In August Frederick William decided to launch a full-scale invasion in the spring of the following year, to accelerate the process and to pick up the pieces.[63] Among other things, he proposed to create an independent Belgium and an independent Hungary, the latter to be ruled by a Prussian client, the Duke of Saxony-Weimar. Alliances were negotiated with Poland and Turkey and an army of 160,000 was massed in Silesia.[64] The period of uncertainty which followed the death of Joseph II on 20 February 1790 only seemed to make the moment more propitious.

It was at this point that Prussia's alliance with Great Britain began to fall apart. It had always been inherently unstable because the two participants were fundamentally opposed in their aims. While the British sought to maintain the status quo on the Continent, the Prussians sought to alter it – radically. Sticking to the letter of the 1788 treaty, Pitt and the Duke of Leeds (as Carmarthen had now become) repeatedly stressed that the alliance was defensive. They would do nothing to assist the Hertzberg plan or anything else which involved the rearrangement of eastern Europe.[65] That should have come as no surprise to Frederick William II. As early as February 1789, his man in London, Count von Alvensleben, had warned that their ally could not be relied on and that they would have to go it alone.[66] The disappointment and anger aroused by Albion's perfidy was none the less intense. A particular bone of contention was the fate of the Austrian Netherlands. The Prussians wanted to detach the province from the Habsburgs permanently and so advocated recognition of the 'United States of Belgium'. Hypersensitive about either part of the Low Countries, the British took the (very reasonable) view that an independent Belgium would fall straight under the sway of France.

Prussian hostility deepened still further when Britain moved from being merely inactive to being positively obstructive. That occurred during the spring of 1790, just as the Prussian army was being mobilised for war. Encouraged by the pacific assurances of the new Habsburg ruler – Leopold, Joseph's brother – the British launched an initiative to bring both actual and imminent hostilities in Europe to a peaceful resolution. Its exceedingly complex history need not be recounted yet again here.[67] Suffice it to say that on 27 July 1790 the Convention of Reichenbach gave them all they wanted. The Prussians agreed to demobilise; the Austrians agreed to make peace on the basis of the status quo ante bellum. Of the numerous specific provisions, the most important was that which ordered the return of Belgium to Habsburg rule.

In summary, as the French Revolution began gradually to impinge on international relations, Prussia's position was both very promising and very unsatisfactory. With Austria enfeebled by domestic unrest and an enervating war, with Russia still fully engaged by Sweden and the Turks, with France preoccupied by revolution, Prussia should have been able to give the law to Europe. Time and again the Prussian ministers congratulated themselves on their uniquely favourable position.[68] Yet it had all come to nothing. Despite the enormous expense involved, the Dutch expedition of 1787 and the Silesian mobilisation of 1790 yielded not one scrap of territory. It was the British who had reaped all the benefits. So, not surprisingly, voices were heard in Berlin calling for a change in direction. If territory were not to be won in alliance with the Poles and the Turks against Austria and Russia, because of British opposition, then perhaps a reversal of alliances might be the answer. Early in 1791, Frederick William II's aide-de-camp and confidant, the increasingly influential Johann Rudolf von Bischoffwerder, told the Austrian ambassador that Prussia would welcome a permanent agreement with Austria, to permit liberation from British servitude.[69] Although there was still a long way to go before the formation of the Austro-Prussian alliance against revolutionary France, the first faint signs of *rapprochement* can be seen in the aftermath of Reichenbach. For the time being, however, the Prussians welcomed the Revolution as marking the definitive end of the Austro-French alliance.[70]

FRANCE, RUSSIA AND THE EASTERN QUESTION

So France's relations with Prussia during the closing years of the old regime and early stages of the Revolution had been erratic: informal cooperation under Frederick the Great, then sharp hostility during the Dutch affair of 1787, then mutual indifference as the Prussians turned east. Certainly there was none of the atavistic hostility which had kept France and Austria constantly at odds. There seemed no reason why Prussia and France should not rub along as they had done in the past, although Frederick William II's restless drive for aggrandisement was potentially disruptive if it happened to get pointed in the direction of France. A similar uncertainty marked France's relations with Russia.

For most of the eighteenth century, Russia seemed as natural an enemy of France as did Great Britain. Traditional French control of northern, eastern and south-eastern Europe had been based on 'leap-frog' diplomacy – the use of Sweden, Poland and Turkey to bring pressure on the Habsburgs' rear. The emergence of Russia had put a stop to that. Russia had destroyed Sweden in the Great Northern War (1700–21), had turned Poland into a satellite and had rolled the Turks back to the Black Sea and beyond. By the 1780s even the most sanguine French statesman had to recognise that Sweden and Poland had gone beyond recall. But the Turkish Empire still stood, and the French were very anxious that it should continue to stand. In 1777 Vergennes described the possible destruction of Turkey by Russia as one of the greatest calamities imaginable.[71] The reasons for that concern were mainly economic in character. In 1535, 1604, 1673 and especially in 1740, the Turks had given French merchants significant commercial concessions.[72] In the eighteenth century, this most-favoured status had helped to turn the Levant trade into a virtual French monopoly. On its continued prosperity depended the livelihood of an astonishingly numerous section of Languedoc. Or so it was believed: in 1780 an official memorandum estimated that it sustained between 500,000 and 600,000 people.[73]

All that seemed to be threatened by Russia's inexorable *Drang nach Süden*. Every attempt to arrest it failed:

> If there is one point on which history repeats itself, it is this: that at certain fixed intervals the Russian Empire feels a need of expansion; that that necessity is usually gratified at the expense of the Turk; that the other Powers, or some of them, take alarm, and attempt measures for curtailing the operation, with much the same result that the process of pruning produces on a healthy young tree.[74]

That was just how French contemporaries saw it too. And with good reason, for Catherine the Great made no secret of her ultimate objective. Indeed she flaunted it. Her younger grandson, born on 27 April 1779, was given the provocative name of Constantine and was reared by a Greek nanny. At the festivities organised by Prince Potemkin, Catherine's most influential adviser, to mark the occasion, Greek verses were recited. A commemorative medal was struck, with Santa Sophia depicted on one side and the Black Sea surmounted by a star on the other. The infant prince was taught the Greek language and was given Greek children to play with.[75] This was no mere charade. In September 1782 Catherine proposed to Joseph II that the Turkish Empire should be attacked and its European possessions partitioned. Moldavia, Wallachia and Bessarabia would be combined to form the new kingdom of Dacia, to be ruled by an orthodox Christian (Potemkin, no doubt). All the rest – less whatever Austria wanted – would form a new Byzantine Empire, to be ruled by her grandson Constantine.[76] That scheme may have been visionary, but the drive to the south certainly was not. Only six months later Catherine announced her annexation of the Crimea. No one supposed for a moment that that was the limit of her ambitions. Four years later, in May 1787, Catherine and Joseph paid a visit to her new acquisition: as they entered the new – and thriving – port of Kherson, they passed through a triumphal arch emblazoned with the legend 'The Way to Byzantium'.[77] As Joseph reported to Kaunitz, the Tsarina was 'dying with desire' to attack the Turks again.[78]

In the event, it was the Turks who attacked her, just three months after this provocative exercise. Caught off balance, inadequately prepared, hampered by drought and harvest failure, diverted by the Swedish attack of 1788, it was not until 1789 that the Russian war effort began to get into its stride. By the end of the following year, the Danubian principalities had been overrun and Ismail, the key Turkish fortress at the mouth of the Danube, had been captured. When the war was brought to an end by the Peace of Jassy in January 1792 (following peace preliminaries at Galatz in August of the previous year), the

Russian frontier was rolled forwards another 100 miles or so, up to the river Dniester.

With their vital stake in the survival of the Turkish Empire, the French could not help but be alarmed by this remorseless expansion. Their unease was intensified by the simultaneous expansion of Russian influence in Germany. By mediating in the War of the Bavarian Succession and by guaranteeing the Treaty of Teschen of May 1779 which brought it to a close, Catherine became a guarantor of the status quo in the Holy Roman Empire, as she was already in Poland.[79] Perhaps because she was a German princess herself (of Anhalt-Zerbst), Catherine took a close interest in the development of her new role.[80] A special department was created in the Ministry of Foreign Affairs and diplomatic representation in the Holy Roman Empire was increased. Evidence that her interest was reciprocated was soon forth-coming, as German princes beat a path to her door in search of support in their various disputes.[81] In 1657 Louis XIV had addressed a letter to Tsar Michael, who had been dead for twelve years.[82] By the 1780s Russian diplomatic influence had crossed the Rhine: in January 1785, when the Austrians tried to secure the consent of the Duke of Zweibrücken to the exchange of the Austrian Netherlands for Bavaria (to which he was heir), it was a Russian diplomat – Count Romanzow – who was sent to plead the case.

All this would seem to point to a degree of hostility between France and Russia every bit as natural and intense as that between France and Austria or France and Great Britain. But there were other forces pushing in the opposite direction. Most simply, there was the question of proximity. Russia was so distant geographically and so remote culturally that there was none of that familiarity which bred contempt for nearer neighbours. More specifically, a growing number of French policy-makers began to have increasing doubts about the viability of the Turkish Empire. Vergennes himself had been French ambassador at Constantinople from 1755 until 1768 and so was well aware of its fatal inability to adapt. The current incumbent, Saint-Priest, was even more pessimistic; in February 1783 he reported that both the land and sea forces of the Turks amounted to 'nothing'.[83] So the view gained ground in Paris that there might be more to be gained from the role of predator than that of protector. Attention began to centre on the soft target of Egypt, with Crete to be added as a naval base and entrepôt for the Levant trade. In the course of the 1780s, French diplomatic missions were sent all over the eastern Mediterranean to explore possibilities.[84] For the time being, the temptation to share in a general partition was resisted, but the idea, once sown, never withered. It was to reach maturity in 1798 with Bonaparte's invasion and conquest of Egypt (see p. 179).[85]

This uncertainty over Turkey's fate was strengthened by commercial considerations. For the Russian development of the Black Sea was as

The origins of the French Revolutionary Wars

much an opportunity as a threat. After gaining rights to navigation at
Kutchuk Kainardji in 1774 and to passage through the straits to the
Mediterranean at Ainali Kawak in 1779, the Russians began to expand
this branch of their commerce at impressive speed.[86] The opportunities
for opening up a new and potentially vast market for French goods
were obvious. A French trading company was duly established at
Kherson in 1785 and flourished.[87] There was also an inviting strategic
advantage to be exploited. With the mouth of the Dnieper now under
Russian control, the inexhaustible timber resources of Poland and
western Russia could be diverted away from the Baltic – and the
British – to the south. In 1781, a Marseille merchant resident at
Constantinople, Anthoine, launched an ambitious scheme to supply
France with Polish masts and other naval stores. He was given the
immediate backing of an alert French government, which established a
credit of 100,000 livres for him at an Amsterdam bank. Indeed, in
April 1783 Vergennes urged his navy minister, de Castries, to accelerate the project, to pre-empt any counter-action by the British. By
the time the war of 1787 imposed a halt, several consignments of masts,
spars and hemp had been shipped to Toulon through Kherson.[88]

This reciprocal interest in developing the Black Sea was given
formal expression by the Franco-Russian commercial treaty of
January 1787. By contemporaries it was seen as a sure sign that the
French were about to abandon the Turks to their fate.[89] That fear – or
hope – was premature. What it did show was the deterioration of
Russia's relations with her traditional trading partner: Great Britain.
It was this, more than anything, which encouraged Franco-Russian
rapprochement. In part, that deterioration had been caused simply by
the spectacular growth of Russia's economy over the century. As she
acquired her own merchant marine, own merchant class and own
ancillary services, so she had less need of the British and so she came to
resent what was thought to be British condescension.[90] A major step
towards full economic independence was taken by Catherine the Great
in 1780 when she organised the 'Armed Neutrality'. Despite the im-
partiality implied by its title, this association of most of the European
powers not engaged in the American War was aimed squarely at
Britain's high-handed treatment of neutral shipping.[91] The mutual
ill-will created by this episode had barely begun to fade when a
personal initiative by George III soured relations further. By joining
and helping to recruit for Frederick the Great's League of Princes, he
did irretrievable harm to Catherine's much-cherished but short-lived
influence in Germany. All her plans to create a balance there between
Austria and Prussia, which would have left Russia holding the balance,
were ruined overnight.[92] It was this disappointment which made her
receptive to French proposals for a commercial agreement.[93] But that
was as far as she was prepared to go. When the French came looking
for an alliance in the aftermath of the Dutch débâcle, she declined

politely but firmly: by this stage France was in no condition to ally with anyone.

Anglo-Russian relations never recovered from the League of Princes imbroglio. Catherine had conceived the greatest contempt for George III, the 'marchand drapier' she dubbed 'Ge'. It was matched only by her contempt for Frederick William II, the 'stupid lout' she dubbed 'Gu' (after Frédéric-*Gu*illaume). After their cooperation in the United Provinces in 1787 they were amalgamated to form a single object of derision: 'Gegu'.[94] Behind the malice – on hearing that George III had gone mad, in October 1788, she said she was surprised to learn that he had any wits to lose – lay more substantive grievances. She blamed 'Gegu' for inciting the Turks to declare war in 1787; she blamed 'Ge' for Britain's refusal to give the Russian fleet the facilities it needed to move to the Mediterranean in the spring of 1788; she blamed 'Gegu' for rescuing her enemy Gustavus III from the Danes in the autumn of the same year.[95]

As the war with the Turks progressed and as the Russians began to get the upper hand, so did British hostility grow. With France sliding into chaos, it was Russia which attracted Britain's instinctive anti-hegemonial concern. Once the Austrians had been forced to make peace on the basis of the status quo ante bellum by the Convention of Reichenbach in July 1790 (see p. 54). Pitt and his colleagues sought to repeat the exercise further east. This time they failed. After going to the very brink of war in March 1791, they were obliged to climb down and in effect allow Catherine to make peace with the Turks on any terms she saw fit to accept. There were many reasons for this volte-face: divisions in the Cabinet, opposition in Parliament, the deft manipulation of public opinion by the Russian ambassador Count Vorontsov, the problems involved in bringing military and/or naval pressure to bear on inaccessible Russia, and so on. Essentially, however, Pitt's plan for pacification was ruined by the indomitable will of the Tsarina. While her ministers described Russia's position as 'hopeless' (Bezborodko) and advised compromise, she insisted that not an inch should be given – and had her way.[96]

The repercussions of this episode were far-reaching and bring us close to the origins of the revolutionary wars. Firstly, it delivered the *coup de grâce* to the Anglo-Prussian alliance. Already shaky after the Reichenbach affair of the previous year, it could not survive what seemed to the Prussians to be another act of British treachery. That, in turn, accelerated and cemented the *rapprochement* between Prussia and Austria, to be displayed for all to see in the Declaration of Pillnitz in August the same year (1791). It also prompted the Prussians to put out feelers to Russia about a possible new partition of Poland.[97] It sent the British back into sulky and bruised isolation, determined to have nothing more to do with continental squabbles.

Russia, on the other hand, although left by four years of war in a state of complete exhaustion, 'had triumphed totally'.[98] Moreover, she had done so, not just by her own efforts, but in the teeth of the overt or tacit opposition of most of the rest of Europe. Austria had left her in the lurch by agreeing to a separate armistice in 1790. Great Britain had tried to make her give back her hard-won conquests by a threat of naval war and the destruction of her commerce. Prussia had aided and abetted the British by mobilising her army and by encouraging the Poles in their bid to escape Russian domination. As for the Poles themselves, they had been allowed off the leash only by the Russo-Turkish War. As recently as 3 May 1791 their defiance had reached a climax in the 'revolution' which sought to drag their political and social institutions kicking and screaming into the eighteenth century. Now that her war with the Turks was about to be settled on her terms, the Tsarina could turn her mind to retribution. As we shall see in Chapter 3, the Polish question was to interact with French affairs in a most unfortunate manner.

FRANCE AND SPAIN

With the Eastern Question settled for the time being and with Austria and Prussia about to turn their backs on half a century of conflict, it is almost time to address the immediate origins of the revolutionary wars. Before doing so, a little needs to be said about French relations with Spain, for they exerted an important influence on the development of the Revolution's foreign policy. Moreover, that Spain went to war with France in March 1793, was further evidence that the Revolution *had* made a difference to international relations. Six decades of cooperation, in the course of which the two countries had been allies in three major wars, made way for ferocious if short-lived enmity.

Although the alliances binding the two Bourbon powers were called 'Family Compacts', the ties were more than dynastic. Consanguinity had not prevented the Regent of France from going to war against his cousin, Philip V, just four years after the Treaty of Utrecht (1713), which had recognised the Bourbons as the ruling dynasty of Spain. In the longer term, now that the Spanish had been ejected from Italy and the Netherlands, the old hostility faded. But it was common hostility to the British which provided the main bond.[99] The vast Spanish Empire in the Americas was an irresistible target for the irrepressible British merchants, fuelled by their 'supreme industrial self-confidence'.[100] As the Spanish saw in that same empire the only means for national regeneration and sought to enforce an exclusive trading monopoly for their own subjects, conflict was inevitable. The War of Jenkins's Ear of 1739, launched by the British purely for commercial gain, was the first war fought between two European powers solely for colonial reasons.[101] With the French also colliding with the British in numerous parts of the globe and with increasing impact, the way was open for Franco-Spanish cooperation. It was symptomatic that the third Family Compact, of 1761, should have been motivated by overseas considerations.[102]

Dazzled by the more spectacular rise of Great Britain, Russia and Prussia, both contemporaries and most subsequent historians have underestimated the Spanish achievement of the eighteenth century. In fact they did astonishingly well, not only retaining their existing empire but making huge acquisitions of territory in addition. At the end of the Seven Years War they acquired from the French Louisiana (many times larger than the present-day state of the same name) as compensation for ceding Florida to the British. Twenty years later they regained that too, in the most advantageous peace for Spain for 200 years.[103] Together with the rapid colonisation of north-western America – San Francisco was founded in 1776 – these acquisitions made Spain *the* power in North as well as Central and South America. This success certainly lubricated Franco-Spanish relations but could not prevent all friction. There was a niggling resentment of what was thought to be French arrogance: 'It seems that you look on the King of Spain as a sort of viceroy or provincial governor', was how Count Floridablanca, the foreign minister, voiced the complaint to the French ambassador in 1778.[104] A more specific grievance arose from the failure of the French to lend the expected support in the Falklands crisis of 1770–71, which prompted the Spanish to seek to diversify their foreign alliances.[105] They also felt that the French had not put their best foot forward in the campaign against Gibraltar in 1782.[106]

Nevertheless, the alliance still held when the Revolution turned France inward. The implications for Spain were rubbed in with a vengeance almost immediately. Relations with Great Britain had been deteriorating yet again for some time, following the harassment of British fishing vessels on and off the South American coast, when an incident in May 1789 at Nootka Sound, on the west coast of Vancouver Island, brought the two countries to the verge of war. So remote was the location that it took almost a year for news of the arrest of three British merchantmen by Spanish warships to reach Europe.[107]

The occasion may have been trivial, but the issues it raised were of great importance to both sides. Essentially, it was a collision between the relentless surge of British commercial expansion and the traditional Spanish claim to a monopoly of trade and settlement on the Pacific coast.[108] Both sides armed and both sides blew hot in the negotiations which dragged on acrimoniously throughout the spring and summer of 1790. If Spain had been given the support she requested and had every right to expect from her French ally, war could not have been avoided. Although the appeal provoked a very important debate on foreign policy in the National Assembly in Paris (see p. 79), the revolutionaries were not impressed by such an antiquated relic of the old regime as a 'Family Compact'. The half-hearted offer of token support and the vague talk of a new 'National Compact' sealed Spain's fate. As soon as he learned of the outcome of the May debate in Paris, Floridablanca knew that he would have to capitulate. Resolution of the conflict was delayed until the autumn only by his determination not to give way until court and public opinion had been properly prepared.[109] The moment came on 28 October when a convention was signed at San Lorenzo which gave the British almost everything they had demanded.[110]

Official hostility to the Revolution was so intense in Spain that some ministers had argued that help from such a tainted source was worse than none at all. This ambivalent attitude of the Spanish government was symptomatic of a wider confusion in European affairs during the early stages of the Revolution. If the stark hostility which stamped French relations with Austria and Great Britain was unequivocal enough, there was no indication that it would be expressed in war. Austria was exhausted by war and restrained by domestic unrest. Great Britain was devoting all her energies to avoiding continental conflict. The position of the other great powers was even less clear. Prussia was drifting, pushed this way and that by old rivalries and new ambitions. Russia was preoccupied with the aftermath of the Turkish War and the pressing need to settle with Poland. The range of possible realignments was as complex as the international constellation itself. How the eventual permutation pitched France against the rest of Europe and unleashed the greatest war in the history of both is the subject of the chapters which follow.

REFERENCES AND NOTES

1. Fortunately there is a first-rate and up-to-date general history of international relations in the eighteenth century – Derek McKay and H. M. Scott, *The Rise of the Great Powers 1648–1815* (London 1983). It should be complemented by another outstanding history of Europe in the period – William Doyle, *The Old European Order 1660–1800* (Oxford 1978) – which is more concerned with social, economic and intellectual developments.
2. Michael Howard, *War in European History* (Oxford 1976) p. 73.
3. Geoffrey Blainey, *The Causes of War* (Melbourne 1977) p. 112. See also p. 27.
4. Isabel de Madariaga, *Britain, Russia and the Armed Neutrality of 1780. Sir James Harris's Mission to St Petersburg during the American Revolution* (London 1962) p. 443.

5. A. M. Stanislavskaya, *Russko-angliyskie otnosheniya i problemy sredizemnomor'ya 1898–1807* (Moscow 1962) introduction.
6. Gerd Heinrich, *Geschichte Preußens. Staat und Dynastie* (Frankfurt am Main 1981) p. 237.
7. Hermann Freudenberger, 'Industrialisation in Bohemia and Moravia in the eighteenth century', *Journal of Central European Affairs*, **19** (1960) p. 354; Hermann Freudenberger, 'The woollen-goods industry of the Habsburg Monarchy in the eighteenth century', *Journal of Economic History*, **20** (3) (1960) p. 397.
8. Alfred Ritter von Arneth (ed.), *Joseph II und Leopold von Toscana. Ihr Briefwechsel von 1781 bis 1790*, vol. 2, (Vienna 1872) p. 17.
9. Pierre Goubert, *L'Ancien Régime*, vol. 2 (Paris 1973) p. 198.
10. For a highly original and convincing study of a crucial part of the administration, see J. F. Bosher, *French Finances 1770–1795. From Business to Bureaucracy* (Cambridge 1970).
11. J. W. Fortescue, *British Statesmen of the Great War 1793–1814* (Oxford 1911) p. 82.
12. Albert Sorel, *Europe and the French Revolution*, vol. 1 *The Political Traditions of the Old Regime*, eds Alfred Cobban and J. W. Hunt (London 1969) p. 324.
13. Claude Louis comte de Saint-Germain, *Correspondance particulière du comte de Saint-Germain, ministre d'état, avec M. Paris du Verney* (Paris 1789) p. 157. The letter was written on 11 November 1757.
14. Louis-Philippe comte de Ségur, *Mémoires ou souvenirs et anecdotes*, (Paris 1824–26) pp. 22–3.
15. Karl Otmar Freiherr von Aretin, *Heiliges Römisches Reich*, vol. 1 (Wiesbaden 1967) pp. 131–6. The Archduke did not formally succeed to the electorate and prince-bishopric until the death of the previous incumbent in 1784, but he had been heir apparent since his election as coadjutor in 1780. The territories concerned were large, prosperous and of great strategic importance. The best generally accessible map is in the *Großer Historischer Weltatlas*, vol. 3 (Munich 1957) p. 144.
16. The best account of the peace negotiations and assessment of the final settlement are to be found in V. T. Harlow, *The Founding of the Second British Empire*, vol. 1 (London 1952) ch. 7.
17. A. Tratchevsky, *La France et l'Allemagne sous Louis XVI* (Paris 1880) p. 20.
18. Ibid., p. 30.
19. Albert Sorel (ed.), *Recueil des instructions données aux ambassadeurs et ministres de France depuis les traités de Westphalie jusqu'à la Révolution française*, vol. 1: *Autriche* (Paris 1884) p. 529.
20. Sorel, *Europe and the French Revolution*, vol. 1, pp. 338–42.
21. Jean-Louis Soulavie, *Mémoires historiques et politiques du règne de Louis XVI, depuis son mariage jusqu'à sa mort, ouvrage composé sur des piéces authentiques fournies à l'auteur avant la Révolution, par plusieurs ministres* vol. 1, (Paris 1801) p. 9.
22. Sorel, *Recueil*, p. 513.
23. Alfred Ritter von Arneth and J. Flammermont (eds), *Correspondance secrète du Comte de Mercy-Argenteau avec l'Empereur Joseph II et le Prince de Kaunitz*, vol. 2 (Paris 1891) pp. 134–5.

24. For a (small) sample of complaints by Joseph II and Kaunitz about French treachery, see Alfred Ritter von Arneth (ed.), *Marie Antoinette, Joseph II und Leopold II. Ihr Briefwechsel* (Leipzig, Paris and Vienna 1866) p. 31; Arneth, *Joseph II und Leopold von Toscana*, vol. 1, pp. 232–3; Arneth and Flammermont, *Correspondance secrète*, vol. 1, pp. 166, 195, 206, 209, 236–42 (this is the definitive list of Austrian grievances, compiled by Kaunitz on 8 December 1783), 267–8, 302–6, 375, 381, n. 1.

25. For an elaboration of this argument, see Kaunitz's 'Considérations sur l'alliance de la maison d'Autriche avec la France', of 18 March 1787, reprinted in Arneth and Flammermont, *Correspondance secrète*, vol. 2, p. 87, n. 2.

26. The alliance was just as unpopular in Vienna as it was in Paris – Paul von Mitrofanov, *Joseph II. Seine politische und kulturelle Tätigkeit*, vol. 1 (Vienna and Leipzig 1910) pp. 205–6.

27. McKay and Scott, *The Rise of the Great Powers*, p. 45.

28. Arneth, *Joseph II und Leopold von Toscana*, vol. 1, p. 152.

29. Roy Porter, *English Society in the Eighteenth Century* (Harmondsworth 1982) p. 205.

30. J. Tarrade, *Le commerce colonial de la France à la fin de l'ancien régime: l'évolution du régime de 'l'Exclusif' de 1763 à 1789* (Paris, 1972) vol. 2, pp. 730–1. For other statistics relating to French overseas trade, see A. Foville, 'Le commerce extérieur de la France depuis 1716', *Bulletin de statistique et de législation comparée*, **13**, p. 78 (1883) and Pierre Léon and Charles Carrière, 'La montée des structures capitalistes: l'appel des marchés', *Histoire économique et sociale de la France*, eds Fernand Braudel and Ernest Labrousse, vol. 2: *1660–1789* (Paris 1970) pp. 195–7.

31. Paul Masson, *Histoire du commerce français dans le Levant au XVIIIe siècle* (Paris 1911) p. 373. Dietrich Gerhard, *England und der Aufstieg Russlands* (Munich and Berlin 1933) pp. 4–5.

32. The fullest exposition of this thesis is to be found in Marie Donaghay, *The Anglo-French Negotiations of 1786–1787* (University of Virginia dissertation 1970). See also her articles 'Calonne and the Anglo-French commercial treaty of 1786', *The Journal of Modern History*, On Demand Supplement, **50** (3) (1978) and 'The Maréchal de Castries and the Anglo-French commercial negotiations of 1786–7', *The Historical Journal*, **22** (2) (1979). She develops an argument first advanced by Jonathan R. Dull in *The French Navy and American Independence: A Study of Arms and Diplomacy 1774–1787* (Princeton 1975) pp. 338–43.

33. The primacy of this last motive is made clear in a memorandum composed by the chief French negotiator de Rayneval. It is printed in Felix Salomon, *Wilhelm Pitt der jüngere*, vol. 1, pt 2: *Bis zum Ausgang der Friedensperiode (February 1793)* (Leipzig and Berlin 1906) pp. 225–8.

34. L. G. Wickham Legg (ed.), *British Diplomatic Instructions 1689–1789*, vol. 7: *France*, pt 4: *1745–1789*, Camden 3rd Series, vol. 49 (London 1934) p. 264.

35. William, Lord Auckland, *Journals and Correspondence*, vol. 1 (London 1861) p. 127.

36. This paragraph is based on Paul Webb, *The Navy and British Diplomacy*

1783–1793 (Cambridge dissertation 1971), pp. 231–8. This dissertation is a mine of original insights and information.

37. Sorel, *Europe and the French Revolution*, vol. 1, p. 395. Burke's remark was made in a speech in the House of Commons – *The Parliamentary History of England*, ed. William Cobbett, vol. 29 (London 1817) p. 77.

38. Quoted in C. H. Firth, 'The study of English foreign policy', *Transactions of the Royal Historical Society*, 3rd series, **10** (1916) p. 2.

39. *Memoirs and Correspondence of Sir Robert Murray Keith*, ed. Mrs Gillespie Smyth, vol. 2 (London 1849) p. 219.

40. For further discussion and illustration of the manifold shortcomings of the British foreign service, see Alfred Cobban, *Ambassadors and Secret Agents: The Diplomacy of the First Earl of Malmesbury at the Hague* (London 1954) pp. 14–19.

41. There is a particularly sharp analysis of this endemic British failing in Gerhard, *England und der Aufstieg Russlands*, p. 178.

42. Events in the United Provinces during this period are followed best in Simon Schama, *Patriots and Liberators. Revolution in the Netherlands 1780–1813* (London 1977) ch. 3. The Franco-Dutch alliance had been held up by the dispute between the United Provinces and Joseph II over the latter's attempt to open the Scheldt.

43. Harlow, *The Founding of the Second British Empire*, vol. 1, p. 386.

44. J. Holland Rose, 'The missions of William Grenville to the Hague and Versailles in 1787', *English Historical Review*, **24** (1909) p. 282.

45. E. A. Benians, 'The beginnings of the new empire, 1783–1793', *The Cambridge History of the British Empire*, eds J. Holland Rose, A. P. Newton and E. A. Benians, vol. 2: *The Growth of the New Empire 1783–1870* (Cambridge 1940) p. 12.

46. Harlow, *The Founding of the Second British Empire*, vol. 1, pp. 314–16.

47. Ibid., pp. 319–20.

48. Gerhard, *England und der Aufstieg Russlands*, p. 185.

49. G. C. Bolton and B. E. Kennedy, 'William Eden and the Treaty of Mauritius 1786–7', *The Historical Journal*, **16** (4) (1973) passim. This is a particularly illuminating article on many aspects of Anglo-French relations. See also Frederick L. Nussbaum, 'The formation of the new East India Company of Calonne', *American Historical Review*, **38** (3) (1933) pp. 481–2.

50. Legg, *British Diplomatic Instructions*, p. 249.

51. Louis André and Emile Bourgeois (eds), *Recueil des instructions données aux ambassadeurs et ministres de France depuis les traités de Westphalie jusqu'à la Révolution française*, vol. 23: *Hollande*, pt 3: *1730–1788* (Paris 1924) pp. 357–67.

52. For detailed accounts of events in the United Provinces in 1787, see Cobban, *Ambassadors and Secret Agents*, passim and Schama, *Patriots and Liberators*, ch. 3.

53. Earl Stanhope, *Life of the Right Honourable William Pitt, With Extracts from his MS. Papers*, vol. 1 (London 1961) Appendix, p. xxii.

54. Ségur, *Mémoires*, vol. 3, pp. 263, 307.

55. Their recapture of effective control of British foreign policy antedated George III's first bout of illness, which began in October 1788 – T. C. W. Blanning, ' "That horrid Electorate" or "Ma patrie germanique"?

George III, Hanover and the Fürstenbund of 1785', *The Historical Journal*, **20** (2) (1977) p. 344.

56. Friedrich Karl Wittichen, *Preußen und England in der europäischen Politik 1785–1788* (Heidelberg 1902) p. 31.

57. George III was a member of the League of Princes, but only in his capacity as Elector of Hanover. His decision to join was taken without reference to his British ministers and indeed ran counter to their policy, for at the time they were seeking an Austrian alliance. For a full discussion of this episode, see Blanning, ' "That horrid electorate" or "Ma patrie germanique"?', *passim*.

58. Wittichen, *Preußen und England*, pp. 30–1.

59. The fullest account of Hertzberg's complicated plans is to be found in Andreas Theodor Preuß, *Ewald Friedrich Graf von Hertzberg* (Berlin 1909) especially pp. 138–48.

60. Wittichen, *Preußen und England*, p. 112.

61. J. H. Clapham, *The Causes of the War of 1792* (Cambridge 1899) p. 83.

62. Preuß, *Hertzberg*, p. 64.

63. Friedrich Carl Wittichen, *Preußen und die Revolutionen in Belgien und Lüttich* (Göttingen 1905) pp. 29–30.

64. The alliance with the Turks, concluded in Constantinople on 31 January 1790, was never ratified, since the Prussian negotiator was deemed to have exceeded his brief.

65. See, for example, Pitt's memorandum of 27 August 1789, occasioned by the visit of the Prussian general von Schlieffen, who had been sent to London to discuss military cooperation and to point out the implications of Austria's growing domestic crisis – Salomon, *Pitt*, vol. 2, pp. 453–60.

66. Friedrich Luckwaldt, 'Zur Vorgeschichte der Konvention von Reichenbach: Englischer Einfluß am Hofe Friedrich Wilhelms II', *Delbrück-Festschrift* (Berlin 1908) p. 244.

67. For an English reader, the best account is to be found in R. H. Lord, *The Second Partition of Poland* (Cambridge, Mass. 1915) ch. 7.

68. Albert Sorel, *L'Europe et la Révolution française*, vol. 2 (Paris 1913) p. 25.

69. Leopold von Ranke, *Ursprung und Beginn der Revolutionskriege, 1791 und 1792* (Leipzig 1872) p. 14. As the name of Bischoffwerder will recur frequently in this and subsequent chapters, it is as well that the trivial and tiresome matter of its spelling should be cleared up at the outset. Bischoffwerder himself spelt it like that, while the King and other contemporaries added an 's' to make it Bischoffswerder – Preuß, *Hertzberg*, p. 103. I have preferred his own version.

70. Wilhelm Lüdtke, 'Preußen und Frankreich vom Bastillesturm bis Reichenbach (1789–1790)', *Forschungen zur Brandenburgischen und Preußischen Geschichte*, **42** (1929) pp. 236–8.

71. Sorel, *Recueil*, p. 508.

72. Stanislavskaya, *Russko-angliyskie otnosheniya*, p. 44.

73. M. S. Anderson, 'The Great Powers and the Russian annexation of the Crimea, 1783–4', *Slavonic and East European Review*, **38** (1958) p. 20 n. 9.

74. Lord Rosebery, *Pitt* (London 1892) p. 103. This is only one of many arresting images in this brilliant book, a masterpiece of English prose.

75. Alexander Brückner, *Katharina die Zweite* (Berlin 1883) p. 334.
76. Alfred Ritter von Arneth (ed.), *Joseph II und Katharina von Russland. Ihr Briefwechsel* (Vienna 1869) pp. 143–56.
77. Stanford Jay Shaw, *Between Old and New: The Ottoman Empire under Sultan Selim III, 1789–1807* (Cambridge, Mass. 1971) p. 24.
78. Adolf Beer (ed.), *Joseph II, Leopold II und Kaunitz. Ihr Briefwechsel* (Vienna 1873) p. 261.
79. Aretin, *Heiliges Römisches Reich*, vol. 1, p. 11.
80. Brückner, *Katharina II*, p. 307.
81. S. V. Bakhrushin and S. D. Skazkin, 'Diplomatiya yevropeyskikh gosudarstv v XVIII v.', *Istoriya Diplomatii*, vol. 1, ed. V. P. Potemkin (Moscow 1959) pp. 365–6.
82. M. S. Anderson, *Europe in the Eighteenth Century*, 2nd edn (London 1976) p. 218.
83. Anderson, 'The Great Powers and the Russian annexation of the Crimea', p. 21.
84. Gerhard, *England und der Aufstieg Russlands*, pp. 193, 393. On the growing French interest in Egypt, see Carl Ludwig Lokke, *France and the Colonial Question: A Study of Contemporary French Opinion 1763–1801* (New York 1932) pp. 93–8 and Alfred C. Wood, *A History of the Levant Company* (Oxford 1935) pp. 172–3.
85. The French response to Austrian suggestions about a general partition is best followed in Arneth and Flammermont, *Correspondance secrète* vol. 1, pp. 185–90.
86. Stanislavskaya, *Russko-angliyskie otnosheniya*, pp. 28–30; Norman E. Saul, *Russia and the Mediterranean 1797–1807* (Chicago 1970) pp. 17–18.
87. Gerhard, *England und der Aufstieg Russlands*, p. 119.
88. Paul Walden Bamford, *Forests and French Sea Power 1660–1789* (Toronto 1956) pp. 195–203.
89. J. L. van Regemorter, 'Commerce et politique: préparation et négociation du traité franco-russe de 1787', *Cahiers du monde russe et soviétique,* (3) (1963) p. 251.
90. This is one of the main themes of Gerhard's *England und der Aufstieg Russlands*. See especially pp. 81, 136.
91. Madariaga, *Britain, Russia and the Armed Neutrality*, pp. 166–74.
92. Ernst Herrmann, *Geschichte des russischen Staates*, vol. 6: *Russlands auswärtige Beziehungen in den Jahren 1775 bis 1792* (Gotha 1860) pp. 99–100. Gerhard, *England und der Aufstieg Russlands*, p. 182.
93. Isabel de Madariaga, *Russia in the Age of Catherine the Great* (London 1981) p. 392.
94. Gerhard, *England und der Aufstieg Russlands*, p. 204.
95. There is no space for a discussion of the justice of these complaints; the second and third were certainly accurate, while the first was more doubtful. For authoritative accounts of the three episodes, see Ali Ihsan Bagis, *The Embassy of Sir Robert Ainslie at Istanbul (1776–1794)* (London dissertation 1974) pp. 66–91; Gerhard, *England und der Aufstieg Russlands*, pp. 208–9; R. Nisbet Bain, *Gustavus III and his Contemporaries 1746–1792*, vol. 2 (London 1894) ch. 18.
96. Jerzy Lojek, 'The international crisis of 1791: Poland between the Triple Alliance and Russia', *East Central Europe*, **2** (1) (1975) pp. 41–2. The

literature on this episode – often called the 'Ochakov crisis' after the main sticking point in the negotiations – is vast. For good recent accounts of the British and Russian dimensions respectively, see John Ehrman, *The Younger Pitt*, vol. 2 (London 1983) ch. 1 and Madariaga, *Russia in the Age of Catherine the Great*, ch. 26. The best general account in English remains that in Lord, *The Second Partition of Poland*, ch. 8.

97. Felix Salomon, *Das politische System des jüngeren Pitt und die zweite Teilung Polens* (Berlin 1895) pp. 64–5.

98. Lojek, 'The international crisis', p. 62.

99. Antonio Dominguez Ortiz, *Sociedad y Estad en el siglo XVIII español* (Barcelona 1976) p. 54.

100. Harlow, *The Founding of the Second British Empire*, vol. 2, p. 259.

101. McKay and Scott, *The Rise of the Great Powers*, p. 159. Vicente Palacio Atard, *La España del siglo XVIII. El siglo de las reformas* (Madrid 1978) p. 28.

102. McKay and Scott, *The Rise of the Great Powers*, p. 254.

103. Hermann Baumgarten, *Geschichte Spaniens zur Zeit der französischen Revolution* (Berlin 1861) p. 216.

104. Sorel, *Europe and the French Revolution*, vol. 1, p. 411.

105. Palacio Atard, *La España del siglo XVIII*, pp. 128–9.

106. Baumgarten, *Geschichte Spaniens*, p. 216.

107. The fullest and most satisfactory account of the background to and significance of the affair is to be found in Harlow, *The Founding of the Second British Empire*, vol. 2, ch. 7. Also useful is Christian de Parrel, 'Pitt et l'Espagne,' *Revue d'histoire diplomatique*, **64** (1950), which is based on both British and Spanish sources, although some of the individual judgements – on Pitt's motivation (pp. 66–7), for example – are questionable. The most authoritative account of the British side, predictably, is in Ehrman, *The Younger Pitt*, vol. 1, ch. 17.

108. In a provocative article J. M. Norris argues that Pitt's policy was dictated by the need to be jingoistic in an election year. He has a point but makes far too much of it – 'The policy of the British Cabinet in the Nootka crisis', *English Historical Review*, **70** (1955).

109. Parrel, 'Pitt et l'Espagne', p. 74.

110. Ibid., pp. 96–7. When Palacio Atard records that the Nootka Sound affair was settled 'con un compromiso' – *La España del siglo XVIII*, p. 145 – he is just whistling in the dark.

Chapter 3

THE ORIGINS OF THE WAR OF 1792 (1): from the fall of the Bastille to the Declaration of Pillnitz (27 August 1791)

HISTORIANS AND THE CAUSES OF THE WAR OF 1792

On 20 April 1792, less than three years after the fall of the Bastille, the National Assembly voted to declare war on Austria.[1] The war was expected to be short, decisive and victorious. In the event, it dragged on for more than two decades, punctuated by truces masquerading as peaces, inflicting permanent social, economic and political damage and ending with the destruction of the Revolution. As that primal Austro-French war swelled to embrace almost every other European country, it became incomparably the greatest conflict in the history of the world until that time. If some earlier wars had been longer, none had ranged so widely, required such intense exertion, caused such domestic and international upheaval, or inflicted such casualties. It has been estimated that France alone lost 1.4 million of her inhabitants as a direct result of the war.[2] No wonder then, that this elemental struggle attracted the concern of so many nineteenth-century scholars living in its shadow and generated such fierce controversy. In terms of personal animosity and political axe-grinding, the disputes over the origins of the revolutionary wars were in no way inferior to present-day controversies over the origins of twentieth-century world wars. But once the First World War had set new standards for military carnage, socioeconomic dislocation and political upheaval, interest in that earlier conflict did not so much wane as collapse. With the exception of Karl Otmar Freiherr von Aretin's study of the Holy Roman Empire,[3] no monograph of any substance bearing on the war of 1792 has been published since.[4] So any historiographical review not only has to begin with the literature of the second half of the nineteenth century but has to be largely confined to it.

A central concern has been the role played by ideology. For Ranke and his numerous pupils, the war was a clash not so much between states as between principles: between the monarchical conservatism of the old regime and the republican liberalism of the Revolution. As the master put it in one of his characteristically sonorous passages: 'The question of war and peace became identical with the question of whether the constitution reserving prerogatives for the King should be maintained or not. It was a dual dispute which contained within it the future of the world: monarchy or republic, war or peace with Europe.'[5] So it was argued that through the welter of conflicting aims and considerations ran the essential antagonism between old and new. The precise occasion for and timing of open conflict might remain open to chance, but sooner or later it was inevitable. For that reason, Ludwig Häusser identified 1789 rather than 1792 as the real beginning of the war: 'Compared with this inner necessity of things, all those events outside France, such as Pillnitz and Koblenz, were of subsidiary importance; the Revolution had destroyed not only the old laws of France on 4 August [1789] but also existing international law; it proceeded aggressively – and had to proceed aggressively if it were not to deny its innermost nature'.[6] This view of the war as an inevitable collision of principles (*Prinzipienkrieg*) has had a long life and is still being repeated. A. J. P. Taylor, for example, has described the war of 1792 as 'in some ways the most modern of all wars, a war brought about by rival systems of political outlook'.[7] An even more recent general survey has also concluded that the war had 'primarily ideological causes'.[8]

Significantly, those who have adopted this interpretation have also usually (but not invariably) taken a long-term perspective. Their wide-angle lens has stressed salient features at the expense of detail. However, those historians familiar with the day-to-day conduct of policy, especially with the day-to-day conduct of Austrian policy, were much less impressed by the ideological dimension. One of the most able of them, Heinrich von Sybel, explicitly took his old master, Ranke, to task for demoting individuals to the status of unconscious tools of impersonal ideas.[9] He preferred to stress the paramount role of *raison d'état,* which kept Austria and Prussia out of French affairs for two years after the outbreak of the Revolution and would have kept them at peace in the long term too – if the Girondins had not forced them into war. Without that pernicious Girondin intervention, Sybel argued, revolutionary France could have been absorbed into the European states-system just as easily as the United States of America had been.[10] Albert Sorel chose to dilute the ideological content of revolutionary foreign policy by stressing its continuity with old-regime opposition to the Austrian alliance of 1756 and thus with French traditions which stretched back to Francis I and beyond.[11]

The culpability of Brissot and the Girondins has been stressed repeatedly, by such diverse scholars as Heinrich von Treitschke and

Albert Soboul.[12] The reason for this odd coincidence of opinion between German nationalist and French Marxist is not difficult to fathom: for the former, the Girondins personified French aggression; for the latter they personified bourgeois capitalism. The predominantly neo-Jacobin tone of most French historical writing on the Revolution has cost Brissot and his supporters dear in terms of reputation. Georges Michon, whose detestation of Brissot was matched only by his adulation of Robespierre, delivered the definitive indictment: 'The war', he stated baldly, 'was desired and provoked by the Girondins.'[13] But not even he supposed that they bore the sole responsibility for the war. All of his hero's numerous enemies inside France – with the Feuillants, the Lafayettistes and the court in the van – played their part. It is a fine paradox (albeit one very familiar to students of the First World War) that the most unequivocal statement of French responsibility for the war of 1792 should stem from a Frenchman:

> There was no question of any threat from outside or of any aggression on the part of the foreign powers. War was willed solely to act as a diversion from the social problems which were becoming more serious with every day that passed. For six months several methods had been employed in an attempt to destroy the democratic party and not one had succeeded; so this time the extreme remedy – war – was to be tried, for it would give the government dictatorial powers and would allow it to eliminate its detested enemies. For these groups the war was a grand manœuvre of domestic politics.[14]

Albert Soboul added some economic ingredients to this loathsome stew of social imperialism: in his view, the commercial bourgeoisie also sought war to re-establish the credit of the *assignats* (the Revolution's paper money) and to secure lucrative contracts to supply the army.[15] Yet he – like most other neo-Jacobin historians – has been unable to accept that the war was just the work of one or more political factions. However selfish the intrigues which preceded its outbreak, the war itself was a grand affair of principle: 'simultaneously national and revolutionary, simultaneously a war of the Third Estate against the aristocracy and a war of the nation against the united powers of old regime Europe'.[16]

The role played by those old-regime powers, especially by Austria and Prussia, has also been sharply disputed. At one extreme, Pierre Muret argued that the war was part of a great Prussian-led conspiracy to conquer Alsace and Lorraine – and it comes as no surprise to discover that he was writing while those two provinces were part of the German Empire.[17] But that sort of view has not been confined to French nationalists; A. J. P. Taylor has also asserted that the revolutionaries 'were forced into war by the declared intention of the conservative powers to destroy the French Revolution'.[18] Such a view must be seen as wishful thinking bred by chronic Germanophobia, for the reluctance of the Austrians to go to war is as well documented as anything can be. Indeed, it was von Sybel's main achievement to

71

demonstrate beyond question Leopold II's preoccupation with eastern Europe until 1791 and his aversion to taking any positive action against the Revolution in France.[19] In the course of a long and bitter polemical dispute, he was able to discredit the view of his arch-enemy Ernst Herrmann that Leopold was an arch-reactionary who plotted the destruction of the French Revolution right from the start.[20] Sybel's line has been given authoritative, not to say definitive, confirmation by Leopold's most recent biographer, Adam Wandruszka. Indeed, the central theme of his massive study is the sincerity and consistency of his subject's attachment to constitutionalism. Far from seeking to extirpate the Revolution, Leopold sympathised with and himself sought to realise many of its aims. On the very eve of a war he had neither sought nor relished, he was still seeking to liberalise the constitutional arrangements of his own dominions and was still insisting that there should be no total counter-revolution inside France.[21]

Complementary to this exculpation of the Austrians was the indictment of the Prussians as being far more eager for counter-revolutionary intervention. Once the Prussian and Austrian archives had been opened, the full extent of Frederick William II's restless search for territorial gains became apparent and Ranke's emphasis on Prussian caution had to be modified, if not abandoned. In 1874, for example, Adolf Beer revealed that the Prussians were promoting a scheme for the annexation of French territory as early as September 1790.[22] That was no momentary aberration; at all important stages during the next eighteen months Prussia was consistently the most acquisitive and aggressive of the two German powers. In one of the last and one of the best diplomatic studies of the period, R. H. Lord stressed that the Prussians entered the war not because the French attack on Belgium had activated their defensive alliance with Austria but because they were eager to pick up the rich territorial pickings they erroneously thought would drop into their laps.[23] Such was the weight of evidence that even Prussian historians had to concede the point. In the same year that Lord published his work, Otto Hintze's classic survey of Prussian history – *Die Hohenzollern und ihr Werk* – appeared. In the section dealing with the origins of the war of 1792, Hintze confirmed that Frederick William II had been much more bellicose than his Austrian counterpart.[24]

The dispute about the relative aggressiveness of Austria and Prussia was concerned with intentions rather than consequences. As such, it was rather unreal, for it was the perception of those intentions by the various parties concerned – especially by the French revolutionaries – which did more to determine the course of events. No matter how acquisitive the Prussians may have been, they were in no position to conduct a policy alone. In fact, as was usually the case at the fissiparous court of Frederick William II, more than one policy was being pursued simultaneously (see, for example, p. 82). So the question of Prussian intentions is really neither here nor there. A judicious selection of quotations could be made to allow them the appearance of indifference towards the Revolution as well as of bellicosity. The same applies to Austria. Consequently certain historians have chosen very sensibly to concentrate on the way in which policies were perceived rather than on the policies themselves. That perception was usually misconception. Denied reliable information and working from entirely different premisses, the old-regime powers and revolutionary France held quite erroneous notions of each other's position and intentions. Writing about the period leading up to the outbreak of war, Kurt Heidrich observed: 'They [the French revolutionaries] and their opponents no longer understood each other. They were breathing, as it were, in different political atmospheres.'[25]

This was not a case of myopia, for the image was seen clearly; nor was it a case of distortion, for the image was seen in what were apparently its correct proportions. It can be termed the 'Coppelia effect' (after the magic spectacles which Dr Coppelius gave to the wretched Hoffmann and which for him turned Spalanzani's doll Olympia into a beautiful woman). Frederick William II and Bischoffwerder, Leopold II and Kaunitz, *thought* they knew what was happening in France and acted accordingly. Yet because their image did not correspond to reality, the actions they took had the opposite of the desired effect. The intimidatory exercise launched by Kaunitz with his note of 21 December 1791 was designed to prevent war; thanks to the Coppelian effect, it only served to make it more certain (see p.). Moreover, it afflicted the revolutionaries every bit as much as their enemies. The confident belief that the old regime powers were teetering on the brink of collapse and that one tap on the door would demolish the whole edifice played a major part in sweeping the National Assembly along in the wake of the Girondin warmongers. As will be argued in what follows, it is this approach, concentrating on the miscalculations of the two sides, which has yielded the most cogent analyses of the origins of the war.[26]

THE FORMATION OF REVOLUTIONARY FOREIGN POLICY: NATIONAL SOVEREIGNTY AND SELF-DETERMINATION

When the revolutionaries took control of France in the course of June and July 1789, they also posted several warning signs for the rest of Europe. All of their programmatic statements, and in particular the Declaration of the Rights of Man and Citizen of 26 August, were addressed not only to the French but to all mankind. As Michel Vovelle has observed: 'In this period of "Atlantic" Revolutions there had been other proclamations; no new declaration, however, had ever had such force or such universality.'[27] They found a receptive audience among all the foreign dissident groups who sought change in their own countries. Paris was already the refuge of many thousands of political exiles, notably of Genevans who had fled after the aristocratic counter-coup of 1782 and of Dutch who had fled after the Prussian invasion of 1787 (see p. 50). These were now joined by the oppressed, the radical and the merely curious from all corners of Europe – and beyond. The rich diversity of this international community was dramatised by the appearance at the bar of the National Assembly on 19 June 1790 of a delegation comprising Arabs, Chaldeans, Prussians, Poles, English, Swiss, Germans, Dutch, Swedes, Italians, Spaniards, Americans, Indians, Syrians, Brabanters, Liégeois, Avignonnais, Genevans, Sardinians, Grisons and Sicilians. Their leader, the Prussian Anacharsis Cloots, stressed with some fervour the universal appeal of the Revolution in France: 'the trumpet which sounded the reveille of a great people has reached to the four corners of the globe, and the songs of joy of a choir of 25,000,000 free men have reawakened peoples entombed in a long slavery.'[28] The exiles formed their own clubs, founded their own newspapers and plotted the liberation of their own countries.[29]

Additional warning derived from the reverse process, for if the Revolution attracted sympathisers to France, it also drove opponents out of the country. Just four days after the fall of the Bastille, the King's younger brother, the comte d'Artois, and three other princes of the blood, went into self-imposed exile.[30] The emigration had begun. The 'October Days' three months later, when the royal family was brought back to Paris from Versailles as virtual prisoners, prompted a further wave of departures, as did every other major revolutionary episode over the next few years. On reaching their various places of refuge, the *émigrés* launched an intense and sustained campaign for counter-revolution. Not surprisingly, in the entreaties for help with which they bombarded the crowned heads of Europe, they made great play with the danger of subversion spreading outside France.[31]

On the immediate periphery of France, among the princelings of western Germany, the *émigrés* found enthusiastic supporters. For these were the first casualties of the revolutionary principle of national sovereignty. When the National Assembly voted through the abolition of the 'feudal regime' on 4–5 August, it unwittingly contravened the treaty rights of several princes of the Holy Roman Empire. The Treaty of Westphalia of 1648 had confirmed the cession of Alsace to the French Crown but had reserved in perpetuity for its erstwhile rulers lucrative judicial, seigneurial and ecclesiastical rights.[32] So the question arose: could the sovereignty of the French people, exercised through the National Assembly, be limited by treaties concluded in the past by French kings? The answer took a little time to articulate but was never in doubt. Reporting on behalf of the 'committee on feudalism', Merlin de Douai told the National Assembly on 28 October 1790: 'There is no legitimate title of union binding you and your brothers of Alsace other than the social compact formed between all Frenchmen, ancient and modern, in this self-same assembly last year. . . .Treaties made without the consent of the people of Alsace could not bestow legality on rights to which they had not given their consent. . . .In short, it is not the treaties of princes which regulate the rights of nations.'[33]

Once adopted by the National Assembly, these principles called in question every existing treaty. They also raised the possibility of future disruption of the European states-system by the potentially explosive principle of self-determination. If, as Merlin de Douai put it, 'the Alsatian people are united to the French people because they wished it', what was to prevent some other people seeking annexation to France? Even as he spoke, a test case was in the offing. On 11 June 1790 a rising at Avignon, which was not part of the kingdom of France but was ruled directly by the Pope, had expelled the papal administration. The insurrectionaries had then petitioned the National Assembly for reunion with France. Their example had been followed later in the month by a second papal enclave, the Comtat Venaissin. Once again, the question of the legitimation of power was debated and, once again, radical answers based on self-determination were offered. As Pétion argued: 'The papacy may not retain Avignon against the wishes of the people. Avignon no longer belongs to the Pope because its people no longer wish to have him as their ruler . . . Avignon belongs to France because the Avignonnais wish to be French.'[34] As over Alsace, it took some time for this principle to be fully articulated and generally accepted. After two earlier attempts to win approval for annexation had been defeated by ever-diminishing margins, it was finally voted through on 14 September 1791 'by virtue of the rights of France . . . and in conformity with the wishes freely and solemnly expressed by the majority of communities and citizens'.[35] Count Mercy, the Austrian ambassador to France, observed that by taking this decision the National Assembly had declared war on all other governments.[36]

In addition to these fundamental issues of principle, the old-regime powers had every reason to be alarmed by the new style of diplomacy developed by the Revolution. They were used to conducting their business in conditions of obsessive secrecy. Even in Great Britain the conduct of foreign policy was normally confined to the King and one or two senior ministers, reaching Parliament only at times of acute emergency. From a very early stage, the National Assembly made it plain that no branch of public affairs would escape its well-publicised scrutiny. The alarming implications for the rest of Europe of a policy determined by a revolutionary assembly were revealed by a curious episode at the end of July 1790. It was begun by the news that the Austrian government had asked permission for a detachment of its army to march through French territory *en route* for Belgium.[37] Although in accordance with an existing treaty, this request unleashed a potent combination of fear and hatred in the National Assembly. The revolutionaries' rabid Austrophobia, now fed by a daily diet of rumours about the plots of the court's 'Austrian committee', naturally sought expression. It was intensified by the knowledge that the Austrian troops in question were on their way to destroy the short-lived 'United States of Belgium' and to restore the rebellious provinces to Habsburg rule. But was that their only mission? Was it not possible – likely, even – that this intrusion was the prelude to counter-revolution in *France*? Was it not the case that the French garrisons in the north and the north-east had been reduced in the most suspicious and alarming manner? Was it not also the case that counter-revolutionary troops were massing in Savoy and the Rhineland? Was not Prussia known to be on the verge of *rapprochement* with Austria? And were not the malevolent British using their filthy lucre to finance France's ruin? These assumptions were almost entirely without foundation but they touched such a responsive chord in the revolutionary psyche that they created a surge of Austrophobe paranoia.[38]

Just two months earlier, during the May debates on the control of foreign policy, Mirabeau had made some startlingly prescient comments. In the words of Albert Sorel: 'Mirabeau alone saw clearly; he dispersed the mists, tore aside the veils and for a moment revealed to an incredulous Assembly that strange and fatal future which the Revolution bore within itself and which nothing had predicted. He showed that free peoples were more eager for war and democracies were more slaves to their passions than the most absolute despots.'[39] Among other things, Mirabeau had predicted that if it ever came to a debate on a declaration of war, the deputies would follow the counsels of courage rather than experience, would be carried away by a false sense of invincibility and would fanaticise the masses they should have restrained. Mirabeau died on 2 April 1791, a year before his prophecy was finally fulfilled, but the debate on the Austrian request of July 1790 had shown already that his insights were sound.

Recounted in this manner, the early stages of the Revolution give 1789 the appearance of a watershed in international relations, after which ideology took the place of *raison d'état* as their guiding principle. If sustained, this would lend force to the view of Ranke and others that the war of 1792 was the inevitable result of a clash between two opposing ideologies. Yet behind the rhetorical flourishes of the National Assembly's orators lay a more complex web of interests as well as ideals, traditions as well as principles. The dispute over the rights of the Alsatian princes provides an early and instructive example. This apparently paradigmatic clash between old-regime treaties and revolutionary ideology was not as straightforward as it looked. In the first place, the dispute antedated the Revolution. The administrative and judicial reforms introduced by Calonne and Brienne after 1787 had already trespassed on the rights of the German princes and had already evoked squeals of protest. The decrees of 4–5 August 1789 just made matters worse.[40] Secondly, the attitude of the Holy Roman Empire was decidedly ambivalent. As von Aretin has pointed out, the Alsatian affair was not so much a conflict between historical rights and national sovereignty as a conflict between historical rights and *state* sovereignty. In asserting the latter, the revolutionaries were only following a path long before marked out and followed by the major secular princes of Germany, not only by Prussia and the Habsburg monarchy but also by such lesser states as Bavaria and Saxony. There were many German princes who would dearly have liked to have followed the French example and to have excluded the jurisdiction of outsiders. They were correspondingly unsympathetic when the aggreived parties came looking for support.[41] The Alsatian affair was indeed a conflict between old and new but it was not a conflict which ranged revolutionary France against the Holy Roman Empire in its entirety. Rather it ranged revolutionary France *together with* the major German states against the small fry.

That fundamental division within the German camp was responsible for the halting and confused progress of the dispute. Significantly, it was the ecclesiastical princes who took the lead, for they realised that, if successful, the French example would be followed by their secular colleagues inside the Empire. The secular princes affected would have been happy to have settled for the financial compensation offered by the National Assembly.[42] Indeed, if the Alsatian question had been the only point at issue, then almost certainly it could have been settled by this means. Although determined to stick to the principle that national sovereignty was indivisible, the National Assembly was prepared to pay for its conviction. Indeed, Pierre Muret has argued that Merlin de Douai's resounding statement on self-determination (see p. 75) was designed to make more palatable to the deputies what was an extraordinarily generous offer.[43] Even if the German princes had remained intransigent, there was little they could have done by themselves. However much the Archbishop of Cologne or the Prince-Bishop of Speyer might have railed against the perfidy of the French, they were in no position to take unilateral action. Only if Prussia and Austria were prepared to take supporting action could their angry rhetoric have had any practical effect. There was never any prospect of that. The Prussians assured the French that, while they would be obliged to vote as justice demanded if the matter were brought to the Imperial Diet, they would do nothing to encourage the Alsatian princes.[44] For his part, Leopold dragged his feet. It was not until 14 December 1790 that he finally sent a remonstrance to Louis XVI and then his protest was couched in the most conciliatory terms. When the Imperial Diet called for a new initiative, in August 1791, he waited for four months before responding. By that time, of course, other and far more serious issues were at stake.[45] If they had not intervened, the Alsatian affair would have died of inanition.

A similar qualification has to be made about Avignon. What looks like a clear-cut collision between opposing principles was, at the very least, blurred around the edges. The predatory powers of eastern Europe which had annexed Silesia or partitioned Poland or sought to exchange Belgium for Bavaria were ill-placed to complain about such a minor territorial change as the absorption of two small enclaves. Moreover, the revolutionaries had been careful to fudge the ideological issue by basing their claim on historical precedent as well as the right to self-determination. A team of constitutional lawyers duly unearthed an old *arrêt* of the Aix Parlement maintaining French rights over Avignon.[46] The deputies were also careful to avoid any suggestion that the principle of self-determination should be applied to areas beyond the existing frontiers of France. In any event, it was inconceivable that Protestant Prussia or Josephist Austria would exert themselves unduly to regain territory for the Pope of all people.

It was even more unlikely that they would do anything to help the aristocratic *émigrés*. Joseph II not only refused their request for assistance but also had them ejected from Belgium.[47] The same policy of rejection was adopted by his successor Leopold, who did not even succumb to the blandishments of the beautiful Madame de Cassis, brought from Paris to Vienna by the *émigrés* to exploit the Emperor's fabled 'penchant immodéré pour le sexe'.[48] Throughout 1790 and 1791 the *émigrés* pursued their goal by more orthodox means, but with the same lack of success.[49] They were no more fortunate in their approaches to Frederick William II: as the National Assembly was manifestly anti-Austrian and pro-Prussian, no gesture of support beyond a modest loan was forthcoming.[50] This uncooperative attitude of the German powers was encouraged by the bitter animosity shown towards the *émigrés* by the French royal family. Marie Antoinette, in particular, detested her brothers-in-law with venomous intensity, dismissing them all as cowards and traitors. In her numerous letters to her brother Leopold smuggled out of the Tuileries she was insistent that no assistance be given.[51] Consequently, the *émigrés* were reduced to devising a visionary scheme for counter-revolution with the unstable and ineffective Gustavus III of Sweden. Despite cynical support from Catherine the Great of Russia, who would do anything to promote an imbroglio in the west to allow herself a free hand in Poland, there was no prospect that this adventure would even begin.[52]

Thus the main points at issue during the first two years of the

Revolution – Alsace, Avignon and the *émigrés* – were much less combustible than appeared at first sight. With the advantage of hindsight, we can see that this relative calm was due more to the separate preoccupations of the great powers than to the nature of the issues themselves. The old-regime powers were still enmeshed in the Eastern Question; all the revolutionaries' time and energy were required for the internal reconstruction of France. Moreover, when foreign affairs did impinge on that primary task, they were absorbed into domestic concerns. This consistent 'primacy of domestic policy' was demonstrated by the debate on foreign policy in May 1790. Significantly, it was provoked by outside events: by the dispute between Spain and Great Britain over the Nootka Sound affair (see p. 61). On 14 May 1790 the National Assembly was told that, in response to the major naval armament begun by the British, Louis XVI had ordered the precautionary mobilisation of fourteen ships of the line.[53] As the King was still in full and sole control of foreign policy, this should have been just a matter for report. The deputies were not inclined, however, to let such a golden opportunity to extend their control of the executive go unexploited. As soon as the debate on the King's message began on the following day, Alexandre de Lameth was quick to insist that the principle of who should control foreign policy must be settled first.[54]

From that moment the substantive issue was lost from view and the constitution became the centre of attention. The outcome of the debate was an apparent compromise, which left the King in control of the day-to-day conduct of foreign policy but reserved for the legislature the major decisions of peace and war. In actual fact, as the events of the winter of 1791–92 were to show, that made the National Assembly the master of French Foreign policy. Back in the spring of 1790, that was not so clear; rather it looked as though a mutually constricting balance had been struck which would immobilise France as a European power for the foreseeable future. This impression was strengthened by the celebrated fourth constitutional article voted through on 22 May: 'The National Assembly declares that the French nation renounces the undertaking of any war with a view to making conquests, and that it will never use its power against the liberty of any other people.'[55]

For many contemporaries, the self-imposed impotence of France was then confirmed by the National Assembly's obvious reluctance to help the Spanish over Nootka Sound and by the serious mutinies which wracked the army and navy in the course of the summer. The most majestic expression of the common view that the Revolution had destroyed France as a great power was given by Edmund Burke in a speech to the House of Commons:

> The French have shown themselves the ablest architects of ruin that had hitherto existed in the world. In that very short space of time they have completely pulled down to the ground their Monarchy, their Church, their

79

nobility, their law, their revenue, their army, their navy, their commerce, their arts and their manufactures. They have done their business for us as rivals, in a way which twenty Ramillies or Blenheims could never have done. Were we absolute conquerors and France to lie prostrate at our feet, we should be ashamed to send a Commission to settle their affairs which would impose so hard a law upon the French, and so destructive of all their consequence as a nation, as that they had imposed on themselves.[56]

THE RAPPROCHEMENT BETWEEN AUSTRIA AND PRUSSIA

This account of the early stages of the Revolution's relations with the rest of Europe has sought to argue that there was no linear development towards war. Certainly there were grounds for hostility between France and other countries, but that was no novel phenomenon. Certainly the revolutionary principles of national sovereignty and self-determination were threatening in theory, but the practice had turned out to be much less alarming. Certainly there was some sympathy for the plight of the French royal family and some sense of monarchical solidarity, but those emotions were tempered by rational satisfaction at the collapse of French power. As late as the spring of 1791 the most likely armed conflict in Europe seemed to be that threatening between Great Britain, Prussia and Russia (see p. 59). Yet the obstinate fact remains that just one year later, on 20 April 1792, the National Assembly in Paris voted to declare war on the new ruler of the Habsburg monarchy, Francis, who had succeeded his father Leopold on 1 March.[57]

In trying to explain how that swift transition from peace to war came about, the starting-point must be the vote in the National Assembly. If a majority could not have been found for that motion, the war could not have begun. Of course, if the motion had been lost, the war might still have broken out at some later date, but it is the war which actually happened that is at issue here. In the event, the majority was overwhelming to the point of virtual unanimity: only seven intrepid deputies voted against.[58] So the first question must be: what prompted all those deputies to vote for war? Such an approach does not presuppose that the French revolutionaries were 'to blame' for the war, only that they began it. They may well have taken such a step as a last desperate attempt to pre-empt what was seen as inevitable foreign aggression. Indeed, as we shall see, there is something, but not everything, to be said for this defensive interpretation.

In explaining why such a vote was possible, the first place at which to look is of course the participants' own explanations. In the first instance, that means the text of the motion declaring war and the speech of the foreign minister, Dumouriez, which introduced it. A clear distinction has to be drawn between the reasons advanced for hostility towards Austria and the reasons advanced for declaring war. After all, mutual hostility had been the normal condition of Franco-Austrian relations, yet the two countries had been nominal allies for the past thirty-six years (see pp. 40–5). Indeed, Dumouriez devoted a good part of his speech to upbraiding the Austrians for exploiting the alliance ever since its inception for their own selfish purposes.[59] A more specific and recent grievance was the support allegedly given by Austria to the counter-revolutionary *émigrés* and to those German princes in dispute with the Revolution over their feudal rights in Alsace. But the reason for *war* was given as the alleged imminence of an Austrian invasion. That was held to be proved by the ever-growing concentration of troops on the frontiers of France and by the refusal to dissolve the counter-revolutionary 'concert' of European powers.[60] In short, the Austrians and their various allies were thought certain to attack when the time was ripe, so there was everything to gain and nothing to lose from getting the French blow in first. These were not the only considerations influencing the National Assembly, it need hardly be said. The debate of 20 April 1792 was only the culmination of a process which had begun in the previous October. As will be seen in Chapter 4, all manner of stimulants – ambitions and grievances, hopes and fears – went to make up the final bellicose eruption. For the time being, however, it is the alleged concert of powers which must command our attention.

As an international plan for the forcible repression of the French Revolution, such a concert did not exist, for most of the old-regime powers were not prepared to go beyond verbal reproofs or symbolic gestures. What confronted the revolutionaries in the spring of 1792 was not a European-wide concert but something much simpler: an alliance between Austria and Prussia. In part at least, the history of the origins of the war of 1792 is the history of the *rapprochement* between these two formerly inveterate enemies. It was certainly by no means a sudden affair. Indeed, its slow progress and short duration suggest that ideology was *not* the most powerful determinant of international relations after 1789.

During the months after the fall of the Bastille, without a thought for the cause of monarchical solidarity, Frederick William II directed a determined campaign to subvert Habsburg authority in Belgium, Galicia and Hungary.[61] *Raison d'état* dictated his policy in 1790 too. When the French *émigrés* urged him to put Prussia at the head of a great counter-revolutionary crusade, he declined. With the French National Assembly vehemently anti-Austrian, this was no time to be upsetting potential allies.[62] To establish whether that potential could be realised, an unofficial envoy – the banker Ephraim – was sent to Paris in the summer of 1790.[63] In the event, his negotiations came to nothing, because the revolutionaries demanded too high a price. Nevertheless, that they took place at all shows what little impression the Revolution had made at this stage on traditional patterns of behaviour. Nor did Austria supply the missing ideological *élan*. During the first two years of the Revolution, Leopold II had his hands more than full with domestic unrest and the war in the Balkans. He regarded the French *émigrés* with contempt and does not even appear to have felt much sympathy for his sister, Marie Antoinette, whom he had not seen for twenty-five years. An opponent of the French alliance and liberal constitutionalist, he had greeted the Revolution with sympathy, not to say enthusiasm.[64]

In short, the Austro-Prussian *rapprochement* was not an instinctive reaction to the collapse of the old regime in France. On the first anniversary of the fall of the Bastille, the two German powers appeared more likely to go to war against each other than against the Revolution (see p. 53). But once they had teetered back from that particular brink, other forces developed which replaced enmity with cooperation. From the beginning, it was the Prussians who took the initiative, albeit in a series of confusing staccato jerks. As Frederick the Great had predicted, once his febrile but indecisive nephew took control, the old coherence was lost. At the court of Frederick William II members of the old guard such as Hertzberg, Lucchesini, Finckenstein and the Duke of Brunswick jostled for position with each other and with a host of new men such as Schulenburg, Bischoffwerder, Alvensleben and Haugwitz.[65] With the exception of the last-named, none of them lasted long on the slippery perch of the King's favour, as his indecision spun it this way and that. Through all the oscillations of Prussian policy, however, there ran one constant thread: the search for territorial expansion. Given Hohenzollern traditions, Frederick William II's anxiety to emulate his predecessor and Prussia's advantageous position after 1787, that could hardly be otherwise (see pp. 52–4).

The precise direction of that acquisitive urge was much less clear. Until the summer of 1790 the target was the Habsburg monarchy. Once that option had been closed by the Convention of Reichenbach (see p. 54), Prussian sights swivelled westwards. In September 1790 Lucchesini was sent down to Vienna to canvass support for a joint expedition against France. Austria was to be rewarded with French Flanders, while Prussia would take the long-coveted duchies of Jülich and Berg, whose current ruler – the Elector of the Palatinate and Bavaria – was to be compensated with parts of Alsace.[66] It was characteristic of the multidirectional quality of Prussian policy that this *démarche* should have been launched at a time when another envoy (Ephraim) was exploring the possibility of an *alliance* with France.[67] Lucchesini's plan for monarchical solidarity was given short shrift by Emperor Leopold, who told him crisply that the French Revolution should be regarded as an urgent warning to all sovereigns to treat their subjects with greater consideration.[68]

So, for the time being, France receded as a possible prey and the Prussians redirected their attention to the east. Together with their British and Dutch allies, they intended to impose on the Russians the same sort of settlement they had just forced the Austrians to swallow at Reichenbach. Catherine the Great was to be compelled to restore to the Turks her numerous and extensive conquests and to make peace on the basis of the status quo ante bellum. It was also intended that Russian influence in Poland would be destroyed in perpetuity and hoped that the grateful Poles would cede to Prussia the twin prizes of Danzig and Thorn. If accomplished, this *Pax Borussica* would make Prussia the dominant power in central and eastern Europe. But before it could be accomplished, Austria would have to be enlisted or at least neutralised, for Austria was still allied to Russia and could cause all manner of mischief if it came to war. To attend to this vital task, Bischoffwerder was sent on a secret mission to Vienna at the end of February 1791.[69] The most striking characteristic of his instructions was the total absence of any mention of France: it was Russia that was the target.[70] Predictably, the exercise failed. The Austrians could see no good reason to help their traditional enemy to humiliate their sole remaining ally, and evaded Bischoffwerder's clumsy overtures.

Nothing daunted, the Prussians pressed on with their attempt to coerce Russia. In the spring of 1791, an army was mobilised in east Prussia and Frederick William II's field equipment was despatched to Königsberg.[71] But at almost the last moment Great Britain backed down, for all manner of reasons, not the least of them being uncertainty about Austrian policy in the event of war.[72] That left the Prussians railing impotently against perfidious Albion but forced to return home empty-handed once again. It also left them more anxious than ever before to obtain the Austrian alliance, for that would release them from dependence on the unreliable British. In June 1791 Bischoffwerder was sent on his travels once more, to intercept Leopold on his current tour of his Italian possessions and to renew the attempt to conclude an alliance.

Until now, the Prussians' wooing had been unrequited. They had so little of substance to offer, while their own territorial ambitions were so patent, that the Austrians could see no reason to abandon Russia. Significantly, it was not France but Poland which provided the first impetus for change. Austro-Polish relations were usually cordial. A common religion, a sense of shared traditions and a mutual mistrust of Protestant Prussia and Orthodox Russia created a natural community of interest. Since 1787, however, this harmony had been disturbed by the Polish attempt to escape from Russian tutelage. Seeking support wherever it could be found, the Poles had concluded an alliance with Prussia. Indeed, at one stage they were actually committed to joining the projected Prussian invasion of the Habsburg Monarchy in the spring of 1790. Once that exercise had been aborted by the Convention of Reichenbach, Austro-Polish relations could begin to return to normal.[73] Then the Polish 'revolution' of 3 May 1791 dealt with the most damaging defects of the political system and appeared to offer the inviting prospect of a stable Polish buffer against both Prussian and Russian expansion. Once it had been established that the Poles had been acting on their own account, the Austrians gave the revolution their warmest support and did everything they could to ensure its survival.[74] First and foremost, that meant protecting it against Russia. The Poles had been able to assert their independence only because of the Russo-Turkish War. With that conflict nearing a close in the summer of 1791, it was very likely that Catherine would seek to reassert control over her renegade satellite. For the time being, the Austrians sought only to persuade her that an independent Poland was in Russia's own best interest.[75] But if that singularly unconvincing argument should fail to have the desired effect, Austria would have to seek assistance elsewhere – from Prussia.

By the summer of 1791, however, events in the east were being overshadowed at long last by events in France. That would have happened a great deal earlier, if Leopold had not been so insistent that the immediate concerns of his state had to take priority. Marie Antoinette had issued her first appeal for international assistance against the Revolution as far back as 12 June 1790.[76] Leopold was unmoved. In March of the following year he was still advising his sister not to attempt to escape from France but to play for time, and was still stressing that he could do nothing to help without the agreement and cooperation of all the other European powers.[77] What changed his mind was the sharply deteriorating situation inside France and the news that the flight of the royal family was imminent.[78] Even then he warned that he could take no action until they had reached safety and Louis XVI had issued a formal appeal for help.[79] That he was not quite such a cold fish as this chilly prudence suggests, was shown by his reaction to the (false) news that the great escape had succeeded. In an excited, not to say passionate letter, he praised his sister as the saviour of the King, of the state, of France – of all monarchies indeed – and concluded: 'Everything that I have is yours: money, troops, in fact everything!'[80]

Now that action over France seemed not only unavoidable but desirable, Leopold became an attentive listener to Prussian overtures. His conversion can be dated with some precision: on 10 June 1791 Bischoffwerder arrived in Milan with the latest Prussian invitation, only to find Leopold his usual distant and elusive self. But only two days later news was received from Paris that the great escape was about to be attempted. So Bischoffwerder now found himself overwhelmed with attention and his own earnest desire for a settlement fully reciprocated.[81] Just one stumbling-block remained; Bischoffwerder was under orders to give the proposed alliance an anti-Russian orientation, for when his instructions were composed in May it still seemed likely that Prussia would go to war with Russia. The Austrians, on the other hand, had no intention of offending their Russian ally. On the contrary, it was their intention to take up a median position between Russia and Prussia, allied to both and (so they hoped) controlling both.[82] It was the situation in France that now concerned them most. This difficulty was resolved by Bischoffwerder's inexperience succumbing to Leopold's skill. So pathetically eager was the former to secure the alliance that he made concession after concession. When a preliminary convention was signed at Vienna on 25 July 1791, all the anti-Russian features had been excised.[83] This enraged the Prussian ministers back in Berlin, but they were overruled by their king. Frederick William II was now so anxious for liberation from his treacherous British allies that he was quite prepared to pay the Austrians' price. Moreover, with the Eastern War nearing resolution – leaving the unfortunate Prussians *still* without any territorial gains – he was not averse to taking a closer interest in French affairs.[84]

In short, until the summer of 1791 at the very earliest, there was no international conspiracy to destroy the Revolution and re-establish the old regime. Austria, Prussia and Russia were all far more concerned with events in Poland and the Balkans than with events in France. That did not mean, of course, that they viewed the latter with indifference or equanimity. The universal quality of revolutionary principles and the strident presence in Paris of foreign refugees could not help but alert them to the danger of international contagion. As early as December 1789 the Prussian envoy in France, Count von der Goltz, was reporting that revolutionary missionaries were being despatched to Spain, Italy – and Germany.[85] The Prussian government was unimpressed. With the exception of localised and traditional agrarian disturbances in Silesia, Prussia was largely untroubled by domestic subversion. Even the westernmost provinces adjacent to France were impervious to whatever propaganda may have filtered across the frontier. Although Frederick William II did show occasional signs of anxiety, fear of the Revolution as an ideological threat was not a major determinant of Prussian policy, at this or any other stage.[86]

Habsburg policy-makers of course had much more reason to fear revolutionary contagion. The events of 1789–90, when Belgium had seceded, Hungary and Galicia had threatened to secede and just about every other part of the monarchy had been shaken by unrest, were still painfully fresh in their memories. Moreover, unlike his predecessor, Leopold II was especially anxious to retain his Belgian provinces after restoring Austrian rule there at the end of 1790. Not only did he appreciate their strategic and material significance, he was also aware that if one part of his empire were allowed to secede successfully, all the others would be at risk.[87] With Paris full of Belgian refugees eager for a liberating crusade, Leopold had to be that much more sensitive to the uncomfortably adjacent revolutionary threat than the Prussians. That this concern played some part in determining Austrian policy is beyond question. Both Kaunitz and Leopold himself stated unequivocally that the danger of unrest spreading from France to the rest of Europe, especially the Habsburg possessions in Italy and Belgium, influenced their decision to seek to form an anti-revolutionary bloc.[88] For the time being, however, the threat was muffled if not faint. The revolutionaries were still preoccupied with their domestic concerns. In any case, they had little or no sympathy for most of the Belgian dissidents, who had shown during the course of their short-lived 'revolution' that they were irredeemably clericalist and conservative. In the short and medium term there was no prospect of a French-sponsored insurrection in Belgium, or anywhere else in the Habsburg monarchy. If its eventual possibility was certainly one consideration influencing Austrian policy, it was equally certainly not the most important.

Indeed, it must be doubted whether the Austrians would ever have taken a positive initiative if their hand had not been forced by the abortive escape-plan of the French royal family. It was its imminent attempt which pushed Leopold into the arms of the Prussians and it was news of its failure (the 'Flight to Varennes' of 21 June 1791) which prompted his first public move against the Revolution. This took the form of the 'Padua Circular' of 6 July, an appeal from Leopold to the crowned heads of Europe calling for joint action to restore the French royal family's liberty.[89] The tempo now accelerated rapidly. On 25 July an Austro-Prussian convention was signed at Vienna, giving formal expression to the agreement reached in Italy between Bischoffwerder and Leopold. The war in the east was brought to a close by the preliminary Peace of Galatz between Russia and the Turks on 4 August and by the Treaty of Sistova between Austria and the Turks on the following day.

At the end of the month Frederick William II and Leopold II met at a summit conference in Saxony, concluding their deliberations with the publication of one of the most celebrated, not to say notorious, documents of the revolutionary period: the Declaration of Pillnitz. This stated bluntly that the Holy Roman Emperor and the King of Prussia, having listened to the representations of Louis XVI's brothers, regarded the current situation of the King of France to be a matter of common interest to all the sovereigns of Europe. They appealed to those sovereigns, therefore, to join in a concerted effort to restore their afflicted colleague to a position of complete liberty and to consolidate the bases of monarchical government in France. If this international agreement could be achieved, they were resolved to act promptly and jointly to secure the proposed objectives. In the meantime, the necessary preliminary orders would be issued to their respective armed forces.[90]

As is so often the case with diplomatic documents, there was much more in this than met the eye. Apparently unequivocal in its counter-revolutionary intention, in reality it was anything but that. Almost all of its belligerence was neutralised by that essential condition of international cooperation. After expressing the hope that the European sovereigns would agree to employ 'the most efficient means in proportion to their resources', the Declaration stated 'In that case [*alors et dans ce cas*] their said Majesties, the Emperor and the King of Prussia, are resolved to act promptly and in common accord with the forces necessary to attain the desired common end'.[91] Immediately after the Declaration had been signed, Leopold wrote to Kaunitz that this clause released him from any commitment: '*Alors et dans ce cas* is with me the law and the prophets. If England fails us, the case is non-existent.'[92] As it was exceedingly unlikely that the British would agree to cooperate, the Declaration of Pillnitz was in effect – and in intention – an empty gesture. It was certainly not the prelude to any counter-revolutionary crusade. When the younger of Louis XVI's two brothers, the comte d'Artois, asked Leopold to begin implementing the Declaration by ordering his troops to march westwards, he was told crisply that no action beyond its strict letter was to be taken, either by Austria or by the *émigrés*.[93]

Certainly no member of the diplomatic corps in Vienna was under any illusion as to Austrian intentions. On 5 September 1791 the Sardinian ambassador, the marchese di Breme, reported that Kaunitz had criticised the notion of military intervention in France in the most forthright possible manner. Dismissing the newly drafted French constitution with that searing contempt that came to him so easily, Kaunitz identified just two possible means of restoring stability to France. The first was civil war and, although undeniably unpleasant in the short term, was to be judged the lesser of two evils. For the other was a military expedition by a concert of European powers, an exercise fraught with peril for all concerned. If there were resistance – and Kaunitz was much less convinced than most observers that there would be none – success could be bought only at the price of a blood-bath ('une mer de sang'). Even if the revolutionaries gave up without a fight, an army of occupation would be required for years to come, to guard against a fresh outbreak. Kaunitz even doubted the right of foreign powers to interfere in the domestic affairs of another country. He conceded that Leopold would be justified in reclaiming his sister but could not see what advantage there was to be gained from that. So far as stemming international subversion was concerned, there were better methods available than a war against France. If the new French constitution were viable, it would be an 'act of terrible folly' to destroy it; if it were not, it would collapse of its own accord. Di Breme commented that these views were all the more authoritative in that they were shared by all the chancellor's colleagues and subord-inates.[94]

But were they shared by his sovereign? The answer seems to be: usually. During the course of the summer of 1791 Leopold's policy oscillated between a fraternal instinct to help his sister and a rational assessment of Austrian *raison d'état*. When he was physically removed from the restraining influence of Kaunitz – in Italy in June or in Saxony in August – sentiment threatened to gain the upper hand.[95] It is clear, for example, that the pleading of the comte d'Artois and the *émigrés* did have some influence on the deliberations at Pillnitz.[96] Yet despite these momentary spasms of counter-revolutionary enthusiasm, his natural prudence – and good sense – kept him in the Kaunitz camp. Among other considerations counselling caution, Leopold was only too aware of the fragility of Austrian finances in the aftermath of the Turkish War.[97] So, just before he set out for Pillnitz, he ordered a reduction of the Austrian army to the swingeing tune of 25,000 men.[98] There could hardly be more persuasive evidence than that of Austrian reluctance to embark on a counter-revolutionary crusade.

Not for the first or last time, the Prussians were a good deal more eager for positive action. Allied to an apparently genuine sympathy for the plight of the French royal family was Frederick William II's old restless urge to make a name for himself on the international stage. Ominously, he took only army officers with him to Pillnitz and proved a good deal more susceptible to the pleas of the *émigrés* than did Leopold.[99] In the middle of September 1791, he showed that he, at least, took the terms of the Declaration seriously by sending to Austria a senior general, Prince von Hohenlohe, to concert military action against France. The mission was abortive. Hohenlohe found the Emperor in his best evasive frame of mind, unwilling even to name the commander of the Austrian contingent.[100] Moreover, the Austrians also evaded Prussian pressure to convert the specific convention of 25 July 1791 into a general alliance.[101]

Austrian prudence was then confirmed, and in their eyes justified, by the news from France that Louis XVI had formally accepted the new constitution on 13 September 1791. Although perfectly well aware that this acceptance was utterly insincere and had been granted only under duress, Leopold and Kaunitz heaved a mighty sigh of relief and hastened to signal their pleasure.[102] As Kaunitz observed to his subordinate, Baron von Spielmann, the Austrians had every reason to be grateful to Louis XVI for getting them off the hook.[103] The last danger that Pillnitz might involve them in some sort of action over France now seemed laid to rest.

The degree of pleasure experienced in Vienna can be understood only if it is realised that Austrian policy-makers never did wish to see the restoration of the old regime in France. Whether as ally or enemy, the French absolute monarchy had always been a thorn in Austrian flesh. The fact of the matter was that a strong France and a strong Austria could not coexist amicably, no matter what their formal relationship might be (see pp. 41–5). From the Austrian point of view, the ideal solution to the French problem would be some sort of constitutional monarchy, stable enough not to be a source of revolutionary contagion but too weak to threaten Habsburg interests in the Low Countries, Germany or Italy. In short, France was to become a western version of Poland – but with Austria playing the role of Russia. With Louis XVI's acceptance of the new constitution, that eminently desirable solution appeared to have been achieved.[104]

Much more damaging than this miscalculation, however, was the inability to understand *how* the new constitution had come about. With the Austrian ambassador to France, Count Mercy, residing in The Hague or Brussels since October 1790, Leopold and Kaunitz were denied access to reliable information about what was really happening in France. What they thought they saw was an apparently impeccable sequence of cause and effect: the royal family had tried to escape but had been recaptured and imprisoned; so Leopold had responded with the Padua Circular, the Convention with Prussia and the Declaration of Pillnitz; these warning shots had led in turn to a lurch to the right in France: republican agitation had been halted by the 'massacre of the Champs de Mars', arrests and censorship. The simultaneous split in the Jacobin Club, with most of the deputies of the National Assembly seceding to join the more moderate Feuillants also served to confirm the impression that it was Austrian and Prussian pressure which had made the revolutionaries see reason. The whole process had then been consummated by the modification of the new constitution and its acceptance by the King.[105] This was a natural view to take of the events of the summer of 1791, but it was also almost entirely erroneous. The set-back suffered by the revolutionary left in the aftermath of the Flight to Varennes had had very little if anything to do with the threats issued by the Austrians.[106] On the contrary, their intimidatory tactics helped to lay the foundation for a future surge by the left which would lead to war and the total elimination of the monarchy. For the time being, both Leopold and Kaunitz continued to believe that they had scored a notable victory. As the events of the end of the year were to show, this proved to be a fatal illusion.

REFERENCES AND NOTES

1. *Archives parlementaires de 1787 à 1860: Recueil complet des débats législatifs et politiques des chambres françaises*, 127 vols (Paris 1879–

1913), vol. 42, pp. 217–18. Technically, war was declared on Francis King of Hungary. He did not become the Emperor Francis II until elected Holy Roman Emperor in July 1792.

2. Richard Cobb, *Death in Paris 1795–1801* (Oxford 1978) p. 7, n. 1.

3. Karl Otmar Freiherr von Aretin, *Heiliges Römisches Reich 1776–1806. Reichsverfassung und Staatssouveränität*, 2 vols (Wiesbaden 1967).

4. The wars of 1793 and 1798–99 have fared rather better in this regard: see pp. – . A bulky American dissertation of 1971 has a promising title – *The Girondists and the 'Propaganda War of 1792: a re-evaluation of French Revolutionary Foreign Policy from 1791 to 1793* (Princeton 1971) – but disappointing contents. Its author, Frank L. Kidner, cites nothing in the German language and also appears to be unaware of such important English-language publications as R. H. Lord's *The Second Partition of Poland* (Cambridge, Mass 1915).

5. Leopold von Ranke, *Ursprung und Beginn der Revolutionskriege, 1791 und 1792* (Leipzig 1879) p. 131.

6. Ludwig Häusser, *Deutsche Geschichte vom Tode Friedrichs des Großen bis zur Gründung des deutschen Bundes*, 3rd edn, vol. 1 (Berlin 1861) p. 341. For an almost identical view, see Hans Glagau, *Die französische Legislative und der Ursprung der Revolutionskriege 1791–1792, mit einem Anhang politischer Briefe aus dem Wiener K. und K. Haus-, Hof- und Staatsarchiv*, Historische Studien, vol. 1 (Berlin 1896) p. 271.

7. A. J. P. Taylor, *How Wars Begin* (London 1980) p. 18.

8. Derek McKay and H. M. Scott, *The Rise of the Great Powers 1646–1815* (London 1983) p. 275.

9. Heinrich von Sybel, *Geschichte der Revolutionszeit von 1789 bis 1795*, 4th edn, vol. 1 (Düsseldorf 1877) p. v.

10. Ibid., pp. iv, 325, 340–4, 366.

11. Albert Sorel, *Europe and the French Revolution*, vol. 1: *The political traditions of the old régime*, eds Alfred Cobban and J. W. Hunt (London 1969) pp. 338–42.

12. Heinrich von Treitschke, *Deutsche Geschichte im neunzehnten Jahrhundert*, vol. 1 (Leipzig 1927) p. 119. Albert Soboul, 'La Révolution française 1789–1815', in *Histoire économique et sociale de la France*, eds Fernand Braudel and Ernest Labrousse, vol. 3: *L'avènement de l'ère industrielle (1789–années 1880)*, pt 1 (Paris 1976) pp. 28–9.

13. Georges Michon, *Robespierre et la guerre révolutionnaire* (Paris 1937) p. 9.

14. Georges Michon, *Essai sur l'histoire du parti Feuillant* (Paris 1924) p. 359.

15. Soboul, 'La Révolution francaise,' pp. 28–9. Michel Vovelle, *The Fall of the French Monarchy 1787–1792* (Cambridge 1984) p. 220.

16. Albert Soboul, 'La Révolution francaise. Probléme national et réalités sociales', *Actes du Colloque Patriotisme et Nationalisme en Europe à l'époque de la Révolution française et de Napoléon. XIIIe Congrès international des sciences historiques (Moscou, 19 août 1970)* (Paris 1973) p. 38.

17. Pierre Muret, 'L'affaire des princes possessionnés d'Alsace et les origines du conflit entre la Révolution et l'Empire', *Revue d'histoire moderne et contemporaine*, 1 (1889–1900) pp. 448, 591.

18. Taylor, *How Wars Begin*, p. 14.
19. Sybel, *Geschichte der Revolutionszeit, passim*. It is essential that this fourth edition be used, for it was the first in which von Sybel incorporated the fruits of his researches in the Austrian archives.
20. Herrmann did, however, gain the upper hand over Leopold's participation in the Polish 'revolution' of 3 May 1791, being able to show that Leopold had had no prior knowledge of the affair, let alone had instigated it. Sybel, on the other hand, argued convincingly that Leopold had been much more sympathetic towards the new regime in Poland than Herrmann had allowed. For representative samples of this protracted and tedious dispute, see Ernst Herrmann, 'Die polnische Politik Kaiser Leopold II', *Forschungen zur Deutschen Geschichte*, **4** (1864) and Heinrich von Sybel, 'Noch einmal über Leopold II gegen E. Herrmann', *Historische Zeitschrift*, **12** (1864).
21. Adam Wandruszka, *Leopold II. Erzherzog von Österreich, Großherzog von Toskana, König von Ungarn und Böhmen, Römischer Kaiser*, vol. 2 (Vienna and Munich 1965) pp. 372, 381.
22. Adolf Beer (ed.), *Leopold II, Franz II und Catharina. Ihre Correspondenz. Nebst einer Einleitung: Zur Geschichte der Politik Leopold II* (Leipzig 1874) pp. 36–7. It was proposed that Austria should take part of French Flanders, Prussia should take Jülich and Berg and the Elector of the Palatinate and Bavaria should take part of Alsace.
23. Lord, *The Second Partition of Poland*, pp. 269–70. Unusually, this masterly work delivers much more than its rather narrow title suggests.
24. Otto Hintze, *Die Hohenzollern und ihr Werk*, 8th edn (Berlin 1916) p. 417.
25. Kurt Heidrich, *Preußen im Kampfe gegen die französische Revolution bis zur zweiten Teilung Polens* (Stuttgart and Berlin 1908) p. 45.
26. See, for example, Jacques Droz, *Histoire diplomatique de 1648 à 1919*, 3rd edn (Paris 1972) p. 184.
27. Vovelle, *The Fall of the French Monarchy*, p. 148.
28. *Archives parlementaires*, vol. 16, p. 373.
29. Albert Mathiez, *La Révolution et les étrangers. Cosmopolitisme et défense nationale* (Paris 1918) pp. 31–3.
30. Albert Sorel, *L'Europe et la Révolution française*, vol. 2 (Paris 1913) p. 4.
31. See, for example, the letter from the comte d'Artois to Joseph II dated 12 October 1789: Alfred Ritter von Arneth and J. Flammermont, *Correspondance secrète du Comte de Mercy-Argenteau avec l'Empereur Joseph II et le Prince de Kaunitz*, vol. 2 (Paris 1891) pp. 275–7.
32. The fullest account of this episode is to be found in Theodor Ludwig, *Die deutschen Reichsstände in Elsaß und der Ausbruch der Revolutionskriege* (Strasbourg 1898). Its French equivalent – Muret, 'L'affaire des princes possessionnés' – is marred by an obtrusive anti-German bias and by an exclusive reliance on French sources. This latter defect leads to, among other things, the misspelling of almost every German name mentioned. For a more concise and more recent account, see Aretin, *Heiliges Römisches Reich*, vol. 1, ch. 4, pt 2.
33. *Archives parlementaires*, vol. 20, pp. 75, 83.
34. André Fugier, *La Révolution française et l'Empire napoléonien, Histoire*

des relations internationales, ed. Pierre Renouvin, vol. 4 (Paris 1954) p. 25.

35. *Archives parlementaires*, vol. 30, p. 631.
36. Emile Bourgeois, *Manuel historique de politique étrangère*, vol. 2 (Paris 1897) p. 47.
37. This episode is best followed through the debates in the National Assembly recorded in *Archives parlementaires*, vol. 17, pp. 379–99.
38. Ibid.
39. Sorel, *L'Europe et la Révolution française*, vol. 2, p. 88.
40. Ludwig, *Die deutschen Reichsstände*, pp. 97–101.
41. Aretin, *Heiliges Römisches Reich*, vol. 1, pp. 251–2.
42. Ludwig, *Die deutschen Reichsstände*, pp. 129–31, 154, 158–60, 167.
43. Muret, 'L'affaire des princes possessionnés', p. 456.
44. Häusser, *Deutsche Geschichte*, vol. 1, p. 310.
45. Ludwig, *Die deutschen Reichsstände*, pp. 151, 179.
46. Bourgeois, *Manuel historique*, vol. 2, p. 40.
47. Arneth and Flammermont, *Correspondance secrète*, vol. 2, pp. 275–8; André Guès, 'L'Autriche, la Prusse et la guerre', *Itinéraries: chroniques et documents*, **238** (1979) p. 24.
48. P. Mitrofanov, *Leopold II. Avstriyskiy Vneshnaya Politika*, vol. 1, pt 1 (Petrograd 1916) p. 43.
49. See, for example, Adolf Beer (ed.), *Joseph II, Leopold II und Kaunitz: Ihr Briefwechsel* (Vienna 1873) pp. 370, 410.
50. P. Bailleu, 'Zur Vorgeschichte der Revolutionskriege', *Historische Zeitschrift*, **74** (1895) pp. 259–62.
51. See, for example, Alfred von Arneth, *Marie Antoinette, Joseph II und Leopold II. Ihr Briefwechsel* (Vienna 1866) pp. 143, 166, 204.
52. François de Bourgoing, *Histoire diplomatique de l'Europe pendant la Révolution française*, vol. 1: *Origine de la coalition* (Paris 1865) pp. 356–7; Isabel de Madariaga, *Russia in the Age of Catherine the Great* (London 1981) p. 422.
53. *Archives parlementaires*, vol. 15, p. 510. This episode is best followed through the debates recorded in this volume. There is a good and full account in Sorel, *L'Europe et la Révolution française*, vol. 2, pp. 84–90.
54. *Archives parlementaires*, vol. 15, pp. 516.
55. Ibid., p. 662.
56. Earl Stanhope, *Life of the right Honourable William Pitt, with extracts from his MS. papers*, vol. 2 (London 1861) pp. 47–8.
57. See above, n. 1.
58. *Archives parlementaires*, vol. 42, p. 210. The number of those voting in favour was not recorded; the full strength of the National (Legislative) Assembly was 745 deputies.
59. *Archives parlementaires*, vol. 42, p. 196.
60. Ibid., p. 197.
61. Sybel, *Geschichte der Revolutionszeit*, vol. 1, pp. 161–2.
62. Bailleu, 'Zur Vorgeschichte der Revolutionskriege', pp. 259–62. On Prussian attempts to exacerbate French Austrophobia, see Wilhelm Lüdtke, 'Preußen und Frankreich vom Bastillesturm bis Reichenbach (1789–1790)', *Forschungen zur Brandenburgischen und Preußischen Geschichte*, **42** (1929) pp. 237, 243–4.

63. Kurt Holzapfel, 'Intervention oder Koexistenz: Preußens Stellung zu Frankreich 1789–1792', *Zeitschrift für Geschichtswissenschaft*, **25**, (7) (1977) p. 795.

64. Wandruszka, *Leopold II*, vol. 2, pp. 353, 355.

65. The best account of the factions is to be found in Reinhold Koser, 'Die preußische Politik von 1786 bis 1806', *Zur preußischen und deutschen Geschichte. Aufsätze und Vorträge* (Stuttgart und Berlin 1921) pp. 202–27.

66. Mitrofanov, *Leopold II*, p. 354; Beer, *Leopold II, Franz II und Catharina*, pp. 36–7.

67. Holzapfel, 'Intervention oder Koexistenz', p. 795.

68. Koser, 'Die preußische Politik', p. 214.

69. This expedition is best followed through the copious documentation printed by Alfred Ritter von Vivenot in *Quellen zur Geschichte der deutschen Kaiserpolitik Oesterreichs während der französischen Revolutionskriege, 1790–1801*, vol. 1: *Die Politik des oesterreichischen Staatskanzlers Fürsten Kaunitz-Rietberg bis zur französischen Kriegserklärung, Jänner 1790–April 1792* (Vienna 1873).

70. See especially the proposals submitted to Cobenzl by Bischoffwerder on 21 February 1791 – ibid., pp. 78–9. See also K. T. Heigel, *Deutsche Geschichte vom Tode Friedrichs des Großen bis zur Auflösung des alten Reichs*, vol. 1 (Stuttgart 1899) p. 401.

71. Koser, 'Die preußische Politik', p. 211.

72. J. Holland Rose, *Life of William Pitt*, vol. 1: *William Pitt and National Revival* (London 1912) p. 614. The best account of the British side of the 'Ochakov affair' is to be found in John Ehrman, *The Younger Pitt*, vol. 2: *The Reluctant Transition* (London 1983) ch. 1.

73. The history of Poland's relations with the great powers during this period can be followed in great detail in chs 6–10 of Lord's *The Second Partition of Poland*. A more recent and more concise account can be found in Norman Davies, *God's Playground. A History of Poland*, vol. 1: *The Origins to 1795* (Oxford 1981) ch. 18.

74. Lord, *The Second Partition of Poland*, pp. 204–5.

75. Ibid., p. 206.

76. Sorel, *L'Europe et la Révolution française*, vol. 2, p. 138.

77. Arneth, *Marie Antoinette, Joseph II und Leopold II*, p. 151 – Leopold to Marie Antoinette, 14 March 1791.

78. Heigel, *Deutsche Geschichte*, p. 391.

79. Arneth, *Marie Antoinette, Joseph II und Leopold II*, p. 177 – Leopold to Marie Antoinette, 12 June 1791.

80. Ibid., p. 181 – Leopold to Marie Antoinette, 2 July 1791.

81. Lord, *The Second Partition of Poland*, pp. 210–11. Events in Italy during these weeks can be followed through the documents printed by Vivenot in *Quellen zur Geschichte der deutschen Kaiserpolitik Oesterreichs*, especially in the 'Journal über die Unterhandlung mit Bischoffwerder von seiner Ankunft in Mailand 10. Juni 1791 bis zu seiner Abreise von Mailand 24 Juni 1791'–pp. 176–81.

82. Heinrich von Sybel, 'Polens Untergang und der Revolutionskrieg', *Historische Zeitschrift*, **23** (1870) p. 71.

83. Heigel, *Deutsche Geschichte*, p. 19.

84. Lord, *The Second Partition of Poland*, pp. 214–15. Sybel, *Geschichte der Revolutionszeit*, vol. 1, p. 300.
85. Wilhelm Lüdtke, 'Friedrich Wilhelm II und die revolutionäre Propaganda (1789–1791)', *Forschungen zur Brandenburgischen und Preußischen Geschichte*, **44** (1932) p. 72.
86. Lüdtke – Ibid., p. 81 – argues that fear of subversion did play a part in promoting Prusso-Austrian *rapprochement* but is unable to find any direct evidence. Indeed, he has to concede that the instructions issued to Bischoffwerder on the occasion of his first mission to Vienna did not mention French subversion. Certainly article four of the preliminary treaty of 25 July 1791 provided for joint action against it, but this is best viewed as a ritual gesture, on a par with the pious pledges to defend freedom which adorn modern treaties. Even modern East German historians agree that there was no revolutionary threat inside Prussia at this time – Ingrid Mittenzwei, *Preußen nach dem Siebenjährigen Krieg. Auseinandersetzungen zwischen Bürgertum und Staat um die Wirtschaftspolitik* (Berlin 1979) p. 243.
87. Mitrofanov, *Leopold II*, pp. 13, 221.
88. See, for example, Kaunitz to Ludwig Cobenzl, 8 July 1791 and Leopold to the Elector Max Franz of Cologne (his brother), 5–6 July 1791. Leopold wrote: 'It is high time to save our sister and suppress (*étouffer*) this pernicious French epidemic' – Vivenot, *Quellen zur Geschichte der deutschen Kaiserpolitik Oesterreichs*, vol. 1, pp. 188, 547.
89. Ibid., pp. 185–7.
90. The full text can be found in ibid., p. 234.
91. J. Holland Rose, *Life of William Pitt*, vol. 2: *William Pitt and the Great War* (London 1911) pp. 5–6.
92. Ibid. The full text of this letter, of the Declaration itself and of several supporting documents is to be found in Vivenot, *Quellen zur Geschichte der deutschen Kaiserpolitik Oesterreichs*, vol. 1, pp. 234–43, 554–6.
93. Ibid.
94. Francesco Lemmi, 'Diplomatici sardi del periodo della rivoluzione (1786–1796)', *Miscellanea di Storia italiana*, 3rd series, **19** (1922) pp. 245–6.
95. J. H. Clapham, *The Causes of the War of 1792* (Cambridge 1899) pp. 46–7.
96. Spielmann reported to Kaunitz on 31 August 1791 that, if Artois and his retinue had not been present, no declaration would have been forthcoming – Vivenot, *Quellen zur Geschichte der deutschen Kaiserpolitik Oesterreichs*, p. 236.
97. Beer, *Joseph II, Leopold II und Kaunitz*, p. 414.
98. Wandruszka, *Leopold II*, vol. 2, p. 366.
99. Heidrich, *Preußen im Kampfe gegen die französische Revolution*, p. 23. The Austrian diplomats formed a very low opinion of the Prussian king: Count Philipp Cobenzl reported to Kaunitz that Frederick William was 'an enormous meat-machine' ('eine ungeheuere Fleischmaschine'), inarticulate, ignorant, totally lacking initiative and blindly following the advice of the minister he had spoken to last – Vivenot, *Quellen zur Geschichte der deutschen Kaiserpolitik Oesterreichs*, p. 238.
100. Häusser, *Deutsche Geschichte*, pp. 322–3.

101. Heidrich, *Preußen im Kampfe gegen die französische Revolution*, p. 23.
102. Sorel, *L'Europe et la Révolution française*, vol. 2, p. 277. That Leopold knew that Louis XVI and Marie Antoinette were entirely opposed to the new constitution is shown by his correspondence with the latter – Arneth, *Marie Antoinette, Joseph II und Leopold II*, pp. 193–209.
103. Vivenot, *Quellen zur Geschichte der deutschen Kaiserpolitik Oesterreichs*, p. 259.
104. Bourgoing, *Histoire diplomatique*, p. 427; Sorel, *L'Europe et la Révolution française*, vol. 2, p. 279; Clapham, *The Causes of the War of 1792*, p. 81.
105. Glagau, *Die französische Legislative*, pp. 25–30.
106. See, for example, the most recent account to be published in English: Vovelle, *The Fall of the French Monarchy*, pp. 141–5.

Chapter 4

THE ORIGINS OF THE WAR OF 1792 (II): from the declaration of Pillnitz to the Declaration of war (20 April 1792)

THE LEGISLATIVE ASSEMBLY

After all the excitement caused by the Flight to Varennes and the Austro-Prussian sabre-rattling which followed, the autumn of 1791 saw an apparent return to calm. The Declaration of Pillnitz, although published with an inflammatory and unauthorised commentary by the *émigrés*, did not arouse in Paris the uproar one might have expected. It was not debated by the National Assembly and was ignored by most newspapers.[1] Louis XVI's formal acceptance of the new constitution, on 13 September, seemed to bring the episode to a close and with it perhaps even the Revolution itself. That impression was strengthened when the other European monarchs communicated their pleasure at the constitutional settlement. As Thiers commented: 'Given their replies, none of which was hostile, and given the guaranteed neutrality of England, the uncertainty of Frederick William II and the well-known pacific views of Leopold II, everything pointed to peace.'[2]

As so often in the history of the Revolution, an apparent return to equilibrium was only the prelude to further and more radical dislocation. The vehicle for this next phase of instability, which was to end in war and the final collapse of the monarchy, was the Legislative Assembly established by the new constitution. Its personnel consisted entirely of new faces, for in its dying moments its predecessor had passed a self-denying ordinance.[3] Consequently, the new deputies included many fewer clergymen and nobles and were, on average, appreciably younger. Since most of them had been elected in the tense atmosphere created by the Flight to Varennes, this second generation of revolutionaries was also appreciably more radical.[4] That found early expression in their determination to keep the executive on a much tighter rein. Their twenty-three specialist committees (compared with the Constituent Assembly's seven) subjected the King's ministers to constant surveillance, summoning them at frequent intervals for direct interrogation.[5] Whatever the letter of the new constitution may have said about a constitutional balance of powers, only a short period of practice was needed to show that the legislature was now in the ascendant.[6]

It did not speak, however, with a single voice. From the start, the rifts caused by ideological and factional divisions gave to the executive what should have been ample opportunity to divide and rule. Numerically, the dominant group was the 'Feuillants'. With 264 deputies enrolled at the club which gave them their name, their leaders – the so-called 'triumvirate' of Duport, Barnave and Lameth – were able to exert considerable influence on the choice of ministers. Their most notable coup was to secure the appointment of Delessart as foreign minister when Montmorin resigned on 31 October 1791.[7] Locating the Feuillants on the spectrum of revolutionary politics is made difficult by its mobility: classifiable as left-wing in 1789, by the autumn of 1791 they found themselves in the centre and being propelled rightwards at ever-increasing speed. Broadly speaking, it can be said that they were in favour of a limited monarchy and the stabilisation of the Revolution on the basis of the 1791 constitution. They believed that they had saved the monarchy in the aftermath of Varennes and jumped to the naïve and erroneous conclusion that therefore they enjoyed a special relationship with Louis XVI and Marie Antoinette.[8]

As the next few months were to show, the moderate conciliatory policy of the Feuillants could not be sustained. With both left and right actively seeking polarisation, the centre ground was becoming untenable. Their position was also eroded by internal dissent, as a substantial number of Feuillant deputies preferred to follow the charismatic if more volatile leadership of Lafayette, thus forming another sub-group – the 'Fayettistes'. Hero of the American War of Independence, most prominent of the liberal nobles of the 'pre-revolution', first commander of the National Guard of Paris, orchestrator of the royal family's return to Paris in the 'October Days' of 1789, hammer of the republicans at the massacre of the Champ de Mars in July 1791 – just to mention a few of his more notable exploits – Lafayette had never been out of the revolutionary limelight. Yet he had become increasingly uneasy about the Revolution's inability to achieve political and social stability. That should have made him a natural ally of the triumvirate but, quite apart from the question of conflicting ambitions, he differed from them on certain important points of principle. Well aware that he was loathed implacably by the court, especially by the Queen, Lafayette was much less prepared to cooperate with it. Certainly he wished to see the authority of the King maintained – and if possible strengthened – but he was also determined to organise the operation on his own terms and for his own benefit. Among other things, that meant a rejection of the Austrian alliance personified by the court. Indeed, Lafayette was all in favour of a short, sharp, successful war with Austria, for he supposed it would restore the prestige of the Crown and greatly enhance that of the army's commander (himself). This consideration became more pressing when Lafayette suffered a humiliating defeat in his bid to become mayor of Paris in November.[9]

Belief that a war would serve their domestic political ambitions brought the Fayettistes into tactical alliance with a much more single-minded party – the Brissotins. In fact, although 'party' is a word impossible to avoid, it is something of a misnomer. There were no organised parties in the modern sense of the word, only shifting groups of individuals defined more by a common political colouration than a common political programme. The Brissotins were one such group, taking their name from their unofficial but acknowledged leader, Jacques Pierre Brissot de Warville. They overlapped and increasingly merged with the 'Girondins', a group of deputies from the Gironde department of south-western France.[10] Although these distinctions have to be logged for the sake of accuracy, practical considerations demand that we should regard the Brissotins and Girondins as a single group – just as most contemporaries did. What bound these 130-odd deputies together in the Legislative Assembly was the common conviction that the Revolution was only half-completed and should be driven on to its logical conclusion. That meant the subversion of the constitution which had just been introduced. No one addressed himself to that task with more enthusiastic vigour than Brissot, who had good reason to hate the monarchy. Among other injuries suffered at the hands of the old regime, he had been imprisoned in the Bastille in 1784 and had had to flee to England three years later, pursued by a *lettre de cachet*.[11] He emerged after the outbreak of the Revolution as one of the first declared republicans, advocating (after the Flight to Varennes) the abolition of the monarchy and the prosecution of Louis XVI.[12]

The lurch to the right following the royal family's attempted escape and the introduction of the new constitution appeared to choke these republican ambitions. As it turned out, it was just this new legislature which gave Brissot his chance. For the first time he was able to use a national forum to display his formidable powers of oratory and organisation. Among the Brissotins and Girondins who gathered around him in the Legislative Assembly he found equally effective support. Only a few debates were needed to show that the group included some superb public speakers: Vergniaud, Isnard, Gensonné, Condorcet, just to name a few. With some justification, the historian of the Girondins' foreign policy has observed that it was their oratory which won over the uncommitted centre of the new assembly.[13]

But what made their speeches so appealing was not so much style as substance. Brissot and his followers based their strategy on one obvious but deadly insight: that the royal acceptance of the new constitution was entirely bogus. To demonstrate the fact, they began at once to harry the King over issues on which they knew he could not compromise. They scored an early success over the *émigrés*, when they forced him to veto a decree prescribing the death penalty for all who had not abandoned their counter-revolutionary conspiracy by 1 January.[14] Louis XVI may have been at odds with the *émigrés*, but to threaten his own brothers with execution was too much even for him. His fraternal sentiment only served to confirm what everyone had long suspected – that his attitude towards the new regime in France was decidedly equivocal. So when his veto was communicated to the Legislative Assembly on 12 November 1791, it was greeted by '*murmures prolongés*'.[15]

As one of the most reliable of contemporary memoirs recorded, everyone professed to know that the country's foreign policy was being run by an 'Austrian committee' headed by Marie Antoinette, that all of France's ambassadors at foreign courts were supporters of the old regime, that secret emissaries were being sent from the Tuileries to Koblenz (the headquarters of the *émigrés*) and Vienna to plot counter-revolution and that 'in short, the Court had a constitutional exterior and an anti-constitutional interior'.[16] Although paranoia was one of the most common and potent of revolutionary emotions, these convictions were well founded. The court *was* conspiring against the Revolution and *was* seeking the armed intervention of the European powers.[17] In the radical press, in the Jacobin Club and in the Legislative Assembly itself, the accusation was made repeatedly. As Vergniaud succinctly put it in the debate on the *émigrés* on 25 October, there were men of Koblenz at the Tuileries, and there were men of the Tuileries at Koblenz.[18]

THE BRISSOTIN CAMPAIGN FOR WAR

It was on this general belief in royal treachery and counter-revolutionary conspiracy that the Brissotins played with ever-increasing effect. It was also the premiss on which they built their ultimate solution to all of France's problems: war. The campaign for war was launched by Brissot in his first great speech on foreign affairs on 20 October 1791. In a long but consistently eloquent speech, frequently interrupted by applause, he deftly brought together in one combustible package all of the most emotive grievances of the revolutionaries. The main theme was the existence of a gigantic international conspiracy designed to restore the old regime. After raising the temperature with a vehement attack on what were undeniably counter-revolutionaries – the *émigrés* – he then listed the repeated snubs, slurs and insults inflicted on the Revolution by the other European powers.

The scene was thus set for a series of inflammatory rhetorical questions: why had peace been signed in the east when Russia had been on the point of total victory? Why had the Swedes assembled troops and artillery? Why had there been a congress at Pillnitz and why had the *émigrés* been admitted to it? Why had such implacable enemies as Austria and Prussia sunk their differences? Nimbly changing to an even more speculative gear, Brissot posed a further series of questions prefaced by 'was it true?' – was it true that the Pillnitz congress had agreed to destroy the French constitution? that military action would be taken to support the claims of the Alsatian princes? that a great counter-revolutionary conference of all European states was to be held at Aachen? that Leopold II had sent a large number of troops to western Germany? that Prussia was organising stocks of grain and ammunition on the French frontier? that a cordon of Spanish, Sardinian and Swiss troops was being set up in the south? And so on, and so forth.

This farrago of truths, half-truths and misinformation was brought to a climax by a device that was to prove a persistent feature of Brissotin oratory, an appeal to French honour: 'I tell you that you must avenge your glory, or condemn yourselves to eternal dishonour.'[19] That led naturally to the concrete proposal for a vigorous diplomatic initiative to force the foreign courts to declare their intentions with regard to their armaments and the *émigrés*. In the event of a refusal, 'you will not have to think twice; and you will not have to think just about defending yourselves, you will have to head off the attack, you yourselves will have to attack. (*Applause.*)' To minimise the dangers of such an enterprise, Brissot then stressed the weakness of the Revolution's potential enemies: Great Britain was distracted by problems in Ireland, Scotland and India, Austria by financial weakness and Belgium, Prussia by her essential hostility to Austria, Russia by war exhaustion and serf revolts. In other words, the international conspiracy was just a paper tiger, a war would be easy.[20] Not forgetting his primary purpose, Brissot concluded with a thinly veiled attack on the treachery of the court: 'Ah! If only the heavens could suddenly reveal, unmask before our eyes the mysteries of our equivocal diplomacy, then perhaps we would find there the original threads of all these intrigues which surround us and of all these manoeuvres which threaten us!'[21]

The reception given to this speech showed that Brissot had hit upon a formula of potent appeal. When the tumultuous applause had died down, the Assembly voted almost unanimously to have the speech printed and despatched to the eighty-three departments for distribution. The few intrepid deputies who opposed the motion were rewarded by a storm of jeering and booing from the public galleries.[22] During the weeks which followed, the Brissotin orators replayed this martial theme with mounting stridency. None was more

100

effective than the silver-tongued Isnard, who on 29 November roused the Assembly to a frenzy of excitement with a speech as eloquent as it was extreme. Particularly striking was his repeated appeal to national pride: 'The French have become the foremost people of the universe, so their conduct must correspond to their new destiny. As slaves, they were bold and great; are they to be feeble and timid now that they are free? (*Applause*.)'[23] Emotion was supported by calculation, as several speakers stressed the links between the *émigrés* abroad and the counter-revolutionaries inside the country, especially the refractory priests. While the enemies without were allowed to carry on their wicked work, it was argued, the enemies within would continue to flourish.[24]

Yet the Brissotins were not the only deputies to press for military action to deal with the *émigrés*. The motion to demand from Louis XVI a prompt and vigorous initiative to secure their dispersal came from a Fayettiste – Daverhoult.[25] Voted through 'almost unanimously' on 29 November, this made war at least very likely, since it was expected – with good reason – that Leopold II would be obliged to come to the aid of the German princes if they were attacked.[26] It soon turned out, however, that the bellicose deputies had underestimated the flexibility (or timidity) of their prey. The Electors of Trier and Mainz, the chief patrons of the *émigrés*, positively scrambled to remove all cause of offence.[27] Within a few weeks the Assembly had been given categorical and undeniable assurances that the *émigrés*' 'armies' had been disbanded.[28] The war-party had also been wrongfooted by Louis XVI's response. On 14 December he appeared in person to announce that the Elector of Trier had been told that unless he dispersed the *émigrés* by 15 January 1792, he would be treated as an enemy of France. This surprisingly forthright compliance with the motion of 29 November was accompanied by a pious pledge to uphold the constitution and a ringing appeal for future cooperation to show the foreign powers that the King and the nation were as one.[29]

The Brissotin–Fayettiste initiative had clearly backfired. Not only had they failed to engineer their war, they had allowed the King to score a personal triumph. The official account of the reception accorded to Louis XVI's statement is revealing:

> The applause lasted for several minutes. From several members the shout resounded through the Assembly: Long live the King of the French! This shout was repeated by the galleries and by a large number of citizens who had found their way into the chamber in the wake of the King and had placed themselves at the end of the party on the right. The public galleries at each end of the chamber and the members of the Assembly sitting on the extreme left maintained the most profound silence.[30]

As the triumvirate who had composed the royal statement had foreseen correctly, a sharp warning to the German princes harbouring the *émigrés* did head off war and did cut the ground from under the

Brissotins' feet.[31] It was to be the peace-party's last tactical victory.

It was also short-lived. Even as the left sat sulking on their benches as Louis XVI enjoyed his moment of popularity, new life was being breathed into the cause of war in a most improbable quarter: Vienna. The Austrians had watched the events in Paris during October and November with mounting anxiety. It had become increasingly clear that the apparent stability achieved by the new constitution had been a false dawn. No sooner had it been implemented than the balance had begun to shift decisively towards the legislature, as the beleaguered king was harried from pillar to post. To rub the message home, Marie Antoinette was sending to her brother via Count Mercy increasingly frantic appeals for assistance. Only an armed demonstration by a concert of European powers, she claimed, could save the French monarchy from total ruin at the hands of the republicans.[32] It was also becoming manifestly clear that those same republicans had Austria fixed firmly in their sights. As news of one provocative Brissotin speech after another was carried east, the temptation to respond grew. A more specific advocate of action was the deteriorating situation in Belgium, more restless than ever under restored Habsburg rule and the obvious first target of revolutionary expansion.[33]

At the beginning of December, Leopold II decided that the time had come for action. On 3 December he wrote to Louis XVI to protest against the National Assembly's unilateral abrogation of the rights of the German princes in Alsace. Taking his stand on the sanctity of treaties, he demanded that all innovations introduced since 4 August 1789 be reversed.[34] To show he meant business, one week later he ratified the Imperial Diet's resolution on Alsace of the previous August, taking the opportunity of an accompanying note to accuse the French of fomenting subversion in Germany. This *démarche* was followed by an even more abrasive communication from Kaunitz to the French ambassador in Vienna on 21 December, in response to news of the order issued to the Elector of Trier to disperse the *émigrés*. In tersely provocative language, Kaunitz stated that, while his master was convinced of the pacific intentions of Louis XVI, he was much less confident that moderation would prevail in France as a whole. So orders had been issued to the Austrian commander in Belgium, General Bender, to provide immediate military assistance for the Elector of Trier, should French troops cross the frontier. Just to lend the threat of military retaliation more weight, Kaunitz added that any such invasion would bring down on the French 'inevitable consequences, not only from the head and members of the Holy Roman Empire, but also from the other sovereigns who have united in a concert for the maintenance of public order and for the security and honour of monarchs'.[35]

The Austrians had made a gross and fatal miscalculation. They supposed that if they brandished the whip once again, the same sequence of events which had apparently followed their intimidatory exercise of the previous summer would be repeated: the left would be cowed and the centre–right would reassert control. Once again, 'the Coppelia effect' – their ignorance of what was really happening in France – produced a policy which achieved the reverse of what they had intended. They *thought* that the triumvirate-led Feuillants were still in control and they *thought* that their sabre-rattling would only help.[36] In the event, their clumsy initiative only served to destroy what little chance the Feuillants might have had of regaining influence. It is important to recognise the fluidity of the political scene in Paris before Leopold and Kaunitz blundered in. As the events in the Legislative Assembly on 14 December (see p. 101) had shown, the majority of deputies were still uncommitted. Certainly they were hypersensitive to any threat to the Revolution, especially when roused by the oratory of Isnard or Brissot, but equally certainly they were prepared – eager – to support the King when he seemed to be acting in the national interest.

Although speculative, it is difficult to avoid the conclusion that if the Austrians had minded their own business and if Louis XVI had been prepared to cooperate wholeheartedly with the new constitution, political stability could have been restored and peace maintained. Certainly the Brissotin campaign to persuade the Legislative Assembly that a great counter-revolutionary conspiracy was afoot would have lost much of its cogency. In the event, the Brissotins could listen with grim satisfaction and eager anticipation on 24 and 31 December as the foreign minister Delessart read out the Austrian notes. They could hardly believe their good fortune. Just as it looked as though the *émigrés* issue was slipping through their hands, along came their enemies with a far more emotively promising cause for contention: the revival of the European concert for the purpose of interfering in the domestic affairs of France. On 1 January 1792 the King's two brothers – the comte d'Artois and the comte de Provence – together with four other prominent *émigrés* were indicted by the Assembly for high treason.[37] With these small fry out of the way, the Brissotins could turn to hunt bigger game.

Their chance came with the great debate on the Austrian note of 21 December, beginning on 14 January 1792 and ending ten days later. In a series of truly remarkable speeches, comparable in terms of quality only with the exchanges between Pitt, Burke and Fox in the contemporary House of Commons, the Brissotins brought the Legislative Assembly to the very verge of an outright declaration of war. An episode on the first day conveys the excited, not to say frenzied tone of the proceedings. After Gensonné had reported on behalf of the diplomatic committee in a speech repeatedly interrupted by applause and shouts of approval, Guadet left the presidential chair to fire a broadside against the concert of European powers. What then happened is best expressed by the account recorded in the official minutes:

So, gentlemen, let us tell all these princes [of the Holy Roman Empire] that the French nation is determined to maintain its constitution in its absolute entirety; we shall all die here . . . (*Yes! Yes! Enthusiastic applause.*)

(At these words, all the members of the Assembly, inspired by the same feeling, rise and shout: *Yes, we swear it!* This surge of enthusiasm communicates itself to everyone present, inflames all hearts. The ministers of justice and of foreign affairs [who happened to be present], the ushers, the citizens, male and female, attending the session, join with the representatives of the people, rise, wave their hats, stretch out their arms to the President's desk and take the same oath. The cries of: *We shall live in freedom or we shall die! The Constitution or death!*, are heard and the chamber resounds with applause.[38]

All present were keenly aware that a crucial stage in the history of the Revolution had been reached and passed, that they had burnt their boats. A motion comparing that day's events with the Tennis Court oath and calling for the printing and national distribution of the session's minutes was duly passed.[39] The concrete expression of this great surge of enthusiasm was a decree branding those who cooperated with a foreign concert as 'villains, traitors to the fatherland, guilty of the crime of *lèse nation*'.[40] In effect, that meant that any negotiation with the Austrians on any matter relating to the domestic affairs of France was rendered impossible. As was fully intended, it also put paid to the party which was working for such a compromise: the Feuillants.[41]

In the days which followed, the Brissotins kept the pot on the boil. Aided and abetted by a number of Fayettiste deputies, Brissot himself, Vergniaud, Condorcet and Isnard made one great speech after another to press home their advantage. On 24 January they finally achieved most of what they sought. The decree passed on that day accused the Austrians of breaking the alliance treaty of 1756 and of inciting the other European powers to form a concert for the purpose of interfering in France's domestic affairs. It instructed Louis XVI to seek from Leopold II assurances that he intended to keep the peace and that he renounced any treaty or convention aimed at French sovereignty, independence or security. If complete satisfaction were not given on these points by 1 March, or if the response were evasive or dilatory, a state of war would be deemed to exist. Louis XVI was also instructed to ensure that the French armed forces were ready to take the offensive the moment the order was issued.[42] This was tantamount to a declaration of war. Of course, the Austrians could have submitted, but only at the cost of abject humiliation.

THE CONVERSION OF THE DEPUTIES

The Brissotins and the others who wanted war were still some way from their goal, however. It was one thing to persuade the Legislative Assembly to pass a decree which must lead to war, it was quite another to persuade the executive to cooperate. Showing a rare flash of resolution, Louis XVI informed the Assembly on 28 January that it had exceeded its powers. He reminded the deputies that the constitution reserved to him alone the conduct of foreign policy and that they might discuss a declaration of war only on his initiative. He stated further that he himself had asked the Emperor for the assurances listed in the decree of 24 January more than two weeks previously and would communicate the Austrian reply when it arrived.[43] That single exercise of the royal prerogative was enough to bring the war-party's initiative to an abrupt if temporary halt. Short of a constitutional coup, there was little it could do until the King could be induced to change his mind. Before discussing how and why that vital additional step was taken, it is necessary to pause to examine the nature of the arguments employed by the Brissotins to take the uncommitted deputies down the road to war. This is an essential part of any analysis of the origins of the war of 1792, for Brissot never commanded a party large enough to secure his objectives without other support. He needed the votes of the Fayettistes and, above all, he needed the votes of the unorganised centre.

In the end, by playing on the deputies' hopes and fears, interests and ideals, with truly impressive skill, Brissot achieved virtual unanimity. To isolate the specific arguments employed is somewhat misleading, for they were usually shaken together in one intoxicating cocktail, but the need for analytic clarity allows no other approach. Otherwise the precise, and often eminently practical, reasons for war would be submerged in the ocean of rhetoric on which they were borne. That applies, for example, to the financial considerations which were often to the fore. It was argued that so long as a state of uncertainty prevailed, so long as the *émigrés* were allowed to promote their schemes for counter-revolution, so long would the credit of the Revolution – in both a metaphorical and a literal sense – be artificially depressed. A successful war would demonstrate the permanence of the new regime and give its paper money some much-needed international credibility.[44] As Brissot told the Jacobin Club on 31 December: 'Not to start a war is to seek to destroy the credit of our *assignats*.'[45] The Jacobins were impressed. In their address to affiliated societies of 16 January 1792, they promised that war would restore confidence in France, would re-establish its credit and would return the exchange rate to its proper level. Moreover, in the peace which followed, the *assignats* would flood the rest of Europe and thus give other countries a vested interest in the success of the Revolution.[46] With the value of the *assignats* falling rapidly in the winter of 1791–92,[47] this argument had a topical cogency.

The same could be said of the argument that a war would put an end to the civil strife which was currently plaguing the Revolution. In the Midi, Alsace, Brittany and the Vendeé – just to mention the more troubled areas – violent resistance to revolutionary legislation was well established and growing.[48] To claim that this was the result of outside subversion by the *émigrés*, as Brissot did for example, was bound to be popular, for it allowed evasion of the uncomfortable fact that the Revolution's appeal was less than universal.[49] It also had the merit of being – partly – true. There *were* agents of the *émigrés* roaming France and they *were* fomenting unrest. That they exploited existing dissatisfaction rather than created it was either unknown to, or was ignored by, deputies anxious to believe in a conspiracy theory. The most elaborate version of this argument was given by Isnard, in his major speech of 20 January. He even found a classical precedent to provide extra authority: 'Rome always followed a policy more or less similar. When threatened by some domestic storm, the Senate launched a war far away from Italy, and as a result of this salutary diversion, achieved peace at home and victories abroad.'[50] Although they exaggerated its importance, neo-Jacobin historians such as Georges Michon did have a point when they interpreted the war as *'eine Flucht nach Vorn'* from domestic problems.[51]

These arguments – and those discussed earlier (see pp. 99–101) – were practical and popular, but they were not enough. If the deputies were to be moved to face the uncertainties of war, some deeper impulse had to be tapped, to allow instinct and emotion to join calculation. One obvious route to the collective revolutionary subconscious was Austrophobia, and the Brissotins lost no time in opening it up. In fact, the way was already clear, for hatred of Austria, the Austrian alliance and Marie Antoinette was axiomatic among all revolutionaries, no matter what their precise political colouring. Even before the fall of the Bastille, pamphlets attacking all French foreign policy since the diplomatic revolution of 1756 were circulating (see p. 43). Representative of the widespread feelings of anger and shame at the decline of French power and prestige is the following extract from a pamphlet published in 1789:

> Publicly despised by her allies and insulted with impunity by her enemies, France is today absolutely nothing in the political system of Europe. Chained to the Austrian chariot, what role has France played other than ceaselessly providing the Emperor with money? She gave him money before the Peace of Teschen; she gave him money to end the Scheldt affair; she gave him money to prepare for war against the Turks; she is still giving him money at this very moment! In this fashion, perhaps as much as three hundred million livres have been swallowed up in the Danube.[52]

So the Brissotins were tapping a well-established and powerful source of resentment when they launched their attacks on the Austrian alliance. It was the Treaty of Versailles of 1756 – 'this treaty so fatal to France' (Brissot), 'this deplorable treaty' (Vergniaud) – which had reduced France to being 'an absolute nothing' in European politics.[53] It had led immediately to the loss of most of her overseas possessions in the Seven Years War and to the collapse of her influence within Europe. It had obliged the French to stand idly by as their traditional allies – Sweden, Poland and Turkey – were harassed, partitioned and despoiled. Closer to home, the Austrians had also shown their bad faith by seeking to open the Scheldt and to exchange Belgium for Bavaria.[54] In short, the Brissotin orators concluded, the Austrians had squeezed every last drop of selfish advantage from the alliance, while the French had been left with worse than nothing. As repeated acts of treachery had shown, Austria was an implacable, deadly foe and the sooner that fact was recognised and acted on, the better. That this was the sort of thing the deputies liked to hear was shown by the reception it evoked. Take, for example, the rapture which greeted Vergniaud's denunciation of the 1756 treaty on 18 January 1792: 'We can see that the abrogation of this treaty is a revolution as necessary in foreign affairs, both for Europe and for France, as the destruction of the Bastille has been for our internal regeneration. (*Bravo! Bravo! Enthusiastic applause from the Assembly and from the public galleries.*)'[55]

This Austrophobia was, of course, only the reverse side of a far more positive force: nationalism. Every Brissotin speaker stressed the need for the reassertion of French greatness. In the words of Larivière, the French were 'the most loyal, the most open, the most generous, the most sympathetic and the most human people in the universe' – and it was high time the universe was reminded of the fact.[56] There was much harping on the special virtues, as numerous as they were various, which went to make up 'la grande nation' and no apologies were offered for asserting them: 'If vanity demeans and degrades a private individual, among whole peoples there is a national vanity which makes them great, which elevates them. (*Applause.*)'[57] The best way to express this superior form of vanity, to reassert those special virtues, was to go to war against the power which had been responsible for past humiliations. War against Austria, Gensonné claimed, would raise France 'to the height of her destiny'.[58]

Behind these rather comic claims of French greatness lay a much more important principle: national sovereignty. One speaker after another, and not just the Brissotins, stressed that the affairs of France could only be conducted by Frenchmen. On that fundamental principle there could be no compromise, no negotiation. Hence the decree of 14 January 1792 which established the ultimate crime of *lèse nation* (see p. 104). As Ranke rightly emphasised, the Austrian plan to interfere in the domestic affairs of France touched the Revolution at its most sensitive point.[59] That should have been obvious to anyone able to read the reports of the Assembly's proceedings. Every time a speaker proclaimed his absolute rejection of outside interference, he was rewarded by a storm of vocal approval from all sides of the chamber. To the sound of 'repeated applause', the Fayettiste minister of war, Narbonne, for example, proclaimed on 11 January 1792: 'everything is possible for us, except enduring the shame of a treaty which would allow foreigners to meddle with our political debates.'[60] The Austrians should have been listening, but, if they were, events were to show that they did not understand what they heard.

They should also have paid attention to the extraordinary optimism which suffused the war-party's speeches. Time and again, the same argument was heard: war involved no risk because a quick and easy victory was certain. This confidence was based on what turned out to be an erroneous calculation of the power relationship between France and Austria. Given the revolutionaries' most basic assumptions about political and human behaviour, this miscalculation was understandable, but it was no less fraught with fateful consequences. Chief among them was the rush towards war. With French assets and Austrian weaknesses equally overestimated, the attractions of negotiating a compromise settlement were correspondingly diminished.

First among the Revolution's assets, as viewed by the Legislative Assembly, was numerical superiority. Now that every Frenchman was a citizen, every Frenchman was a potential soldier: 'Louis XIV, with 400,000 slaves, knew how to defy all the powers of Europe; can we, with our millions of free men, fear them?'[61] There was some disagreement as to just how many millions there might be. Rühl's modest estimate of 4 million was raised to 6 million by Brissot and then to every single inhabitant of France by Charlier: 'What is the army? It is the entire population.'[62] It was also believed that this overwhelming quantitative superiority would be made utterly irresistible by a corresponding qualitative advantage. Not without reason, it was assumed that a free man would fight with much more effective dedication than the hired mercenaries of the feudal despots. When making this point with his customary eloquence in the course of his speech of 29 December 1791, Brissot brought the deputies to their feet:

> I do not compare here our military forces with those of our secret and avowed enemies: if we want to remain free, we should ask, as the Spartans did, *where* are our enemies, not how many are there of them (*Applause*); and in any case, if it were necessary to make this comparison, we would see that every advantage is on our side – for now every French citizen is a soldier, and a willing soldier at that! (*Applause*) And where is the power on earth, where is the Genghis Khan, where is the Tamerlaine, even with clouds of slaves in his train, who could hope to master six million free soldiers?[63]

Confidence in the invincibility of the nation-in-arms was enhanced by reassuring reports on the state of the existing regular army. Given the propensity of the rank and file to mutiny and of the officers to emigrate (about 60 per cent had gone by the end of 1791), such reassurance was badly needed.[64] It was duly delivered in authoritative style by the new minister of war, Narbonne, on 11 January 1792. Reporting on his well-publicised tour of the north-eastern frontier, he told the deputies that fortresses, artillery, supplies, ammunition, cavalry and infantry were all in excellent condition. Only 51,000 soldiers were needed to bring the army up to full strength. If the national interest required a war (and he, for one, clearly thought that it did) then the condition of the army was such that it could be waged with success.[65] The finance necessary to make good any defects was not deemed much of a problem, for the Assembly's financial expert, Cambon, preached that the Revolution's resources were inexhaustible. If more money were required, it could be – and was – printed.[66]

Conviction that the revolutionary armies would prove invincible was reinforced by the very low opinion held of the opposition. Well aware of the problems of desertion which plagued old-regime armies, even when fighting each other, they expected the irresistible appeal of revolutionary ideology to provoke mass defections: 'in the face of our brave patriots, the allied armies will fade away like the shades of night in the face of the rays of the sun (*Applause*.)'[67] Units drawn from such oppressed nationalities as the Belgians or the Hungarians were thought, not unreasonably, to be especially susceptible.[68] Not for the first or last time, it was Isnard who found the most striking imagery to convey the argument:

> Let us tell Europe that we shall respect all the constitutions of the various states; but that, if the cabinets of the foreign courts try to raise up against France a war of kings, we shall raise up a war of the peoples against the kings (*Applause*). Let us tell them that conflicts begun between peoples on the orders of despots resemble blows exchanged in the dark by two friends set against each other by some evil intriguer; once day has dawned, they throw away their weapons, embrace and then take revenge on him who deceived them (*Cheers and applause*). In the same way, at the moment that the enemy armies begin to fight with ours, the daylight of philosophy will open their eyes and the peoples will embrace each other in the face of their dethroned tyrants and an approving heaven and earth.[69]

If the military signals were propitious, the international situation was equally promising. The great European concert, it was predicted, would prove impotent, immobilised by internal decay and irreconcilable differences. Of the powers which mattered, Great Britain would be kept neutral by public opinion, ministerial instability, the enormous National Debt and problems in India; Russia was preoccupied by Poland; Spain was bankrupt in every conceivable sense of the word.[70] Most important of all, it was more likely that Prussia would fight on the side of France than against her. This confidence in Prussia was one of the most striking – and misguided – of the war-party's assumptions. It was based in part, of course, on the Austrophobe rejection of the old regime's diplomatic system. To return to a Prussian alliance would be to return to the golden age of French greatness before the fall from grace in 1756. It was also based on a surprisingly but patently sincere admiration of Frederick the Great. The 'immortal glory' of this 'philosopher king' and his stable, just and prosperous state was praised repeatedly.[71] Nor was it only his pacific enlightened virtues which appealed. He was also held up to the Assembly as the model on which the Revolution should base its foreign policy, for when *he* had been confronted by an Austrian-led concert, he had known just what to do: strike first.[72] In short, far from having to fight the rest of Europe, France would only have the feeble Habsburg monarchy to contend with.

In delivering the *coup de grâce* to that moribund hulk, the Brissotins also believed that they could count on the active support of their enemy's own subjects. The belief that the declaration of war would be the signal for a rising against the Habsburg Emperor, and indeed all the princes of the Holy Roman Empire, was repeated constantly during the winter of 1791–92, in the press, in pamphlets, in the Jacobin Club and in the Legislative Assembly. As early as July 1791, Brissot had told the Jacobins that a crusade for the liberation of Europe was both possible and necessary.[73] In the autumn, as pressure for war mounted, so did the predictions of imminent international revolution multiply. Among other things, it was reported that 20,000 Belgian patriots only needed a signal to come to the aid of their French comrades; that all over Germany local insurrections were erupting and could easily be fused into one great revolution; that the Rhenish peasants were buying stocks of tricolour flags and cockades with which to welcome their French liberators; and so on, and so forth.[74]

Belief in these fantastic stories, few of which boasted even a modicum of substance, was encouraged by the foreign refugees with which Paris teemed. Naturally anxious to return home in the wake of a victorious French army, they told the Brissotins just what they wanted to hear, namely that their oppressed fellow countrymen back home groaned under the yoke of the old regime and yearned for liberation.[75] It was one of these exiles, Anacharsis Cloots, who told the Legislative Assembly on 13 December 1791 that within a month of the outbreak of war, the tricolour cockade and the revolutionary song 'Ça ira' would be the proud possessions of *twenty* liberated nations: 'The German and Bohemian peasants will resume their war against their lay and ecclesiastical seigneurs; the Catalans and the Allobrogians will combine to escape from Spanish and Sardinian rule; the Dutch and the Germans, the Italians and the Scandinavians, will shake off and shatter their chains with fury.'[76] The same theme was taken up by the Brissotins in all of their major orations. As Brissot himself told the Jacobin Club:

It will be a crusade for universal liberty. . . . Each soldier will say to his enemy: Brother, I am not going to cut your throat, I am going to free you from the yoke you labour under; I am going to show you the road to happiness. Like you, I was once a slave; I took up arms, and the tyrant vanished; look at me now that I am free; you can be so too; here is my arm in support.[77]

When all these arguments for war were put together, they created in the Legislative Assembly an atmosphere which was always highly charged and which could border on mass hysteria on grand occasions. More than eighteen months before the Terror of Year II actually began, the psychological preconditions were well established.[78] Dangerous as it is to employ psychopathic categories to explain the past, it is difficult to read the accounts of the debates of the autumn and winter of 1791–92 without being struck repeatedly by the symptoms of paranoia evinced by the orators and by the deputies who responded so fervently. The belief in a 'vast conspiracy against the liberty of France and the future liberty of the human race' (Hérault de Séchelles)[79] was repeated with liturgical regularity. Spies and traitors were to be found everywhere – among the courtiers at the Tuileries, among French ambassadors at foreign courts, among the refractory priests, among the *émigrés*' army of agents, among the speculators engaged on economic sabotage, and so on, and so forth. An early and ominous reaction, fuelled by the fear and hatred these denunciations inspired, was the creation of a *comité de surveillance* on 25 November 1791.[80]

Equally ominous were demands for an end to political pluralism and the growing popularity of the concept of political crime. In his passionate intervention on 14 January 1792, which led to the collective oath-swearing ceremony described above, Guadet ended his speech with the demand: 'Let us mark out a place in advance for traitors, and let that place be the scaffold.' (*Bravo! Bravo! Enthusiastic applause.*)[81] That it would be well populated – not least by the Brissotin deputies who were demanding its erection – was ensured by a simultaneous move to see politics strictly in terms of black and white. In the good old days of 1789, Gensonné argued, it had been possible for men of good faith to join all manner of parties; but no longer – now there were only two parties: for the Revolution and against it, right and wrong.[82] As this tendency to view everything in terms of absolutes gathered momentum, so a distinctly nihilist undercurrent rose to the surface. The decision to wage total war, to win absolute victory or suffer absolute annihilation, was taken long before the celebrated *levée en masse* decree of 23 August 1793. The following brief selection of rapturously received appeals for liberty or death conveys some impression of the excited, not to say fanatical tone of the Assembly's debates:

Be ready to fight, to die, even to disappear entirely from the face of the earth rather than put on our chains again . . . Bring back the nobility? Ah! Rather bury ourselves a thousand times under the ruins of the walls which surround us. (Isnard)

Yes, She [the French nation] will disappear from the face of the earth rather than violate her oath. (*Repeated applause.*) (Mailhe)

If there is an attempt to terrorise you into submission to a capitulation unworthy of you, you must implement the oath you have sworn: the Constitution or death! (*Applause.*) (Brissot)[83]

Although difficult to measure, it is at least very likely that this overheating of the Assembly's political temperature was due in part to its physical surroundings. It met in the *Manège*, a former riding school. whose generous dimensions allowed the accommodation of several hundred spectators in the public galleries.[84] In fact, to call them 'spectators' is to underestimate, if not to misinterpret, their role. They were much more like active participants, repeatedly interrupting the debates with cheers for their heroes and boos for their villains. It was a brave man indeed who dared to speak out against the popular current. That current was both bellicose and Brissotin. Through their press, their sectional organisations and the Jacobin Club, the Brissotins proved adept at organising a responsive public gallery. They also used their provincial organisations to assemble and despatch to the Assembly petitions calling for war.[85]

The result was a unique political assembly with a style of doing business all of its own. It was quite unlike other such apparently similar legislatures as the American Congress or the British Parliament. Indeed, it was not really a debating chamber at all, it was much more like an institutionalised political rally, with all the advantages and defects that implies. It was much more exciting, much more open, much more responsive than its Anglo-Saxon equivalents, but it was also much more volatile, emotional and demagogic. As this or that fraternal delegation of Parisian citizens, foreign refugees or volunteer soldiers paraded through the chamber to the rapturous applause of the galleries and (most) deputies, or as this or that debate was brought to a halt by brawling among both deputies and/or spectators, the opportunity for sober, rational debate disappeared.[86] This special environment encouraged a natural temptation to seek simple answers to complex questions, in particular it facilitated the decision to wage war.

Amid the swelling chorus of radical agitation for war, one dissenting voice stood out, for the cogency of its arguments and the eminence of its owner: that of Robespierre. Disqualified from direct participation in the Assembly's proceedings by the self-denying ordinance, Robespierre had to use the Jacobin Club for the expression of his views. There, in the course of the winter, he waged an epic but unavailing struggle against Brissotin war fever. In a series of wonderful speeches, as eloquent as they were prophetic, he countered one Brissotin mis-representation after another. He argued that the famous concert was much less menacing than was claimed, that it was aimed at intimidation, not invasion; that the war would be much more difficult than the Brissotins blithely supposed; that the foreign populations would not rise in support of the revolutionary armies, for 'no one loves armed missionaries'; that the true enemies of the Revolution were located inside not outside France; that the only beneficiaries of a war would be army officers, speculators, the court and noble conspirators.[87] If Robespierre had been able to say all this in the Legislative Assembly, the course of events might have taken a different turn. In the event, even those Jacobins who preferred him to Brissot trimmed their sails when they saw that the war-party was on a flood-tide. Symptomatic of the way it was running was the fact that by the middle of January 1792 not one Parisian newspaper openly opposed the war.[88]

THE RESPONSE OF AUSTRIA AND PRUSSIA

With even Robespierre overwhelmed by the stampede for war, it is time to return to the development of the relationship between France, Austria and Prussia. After Louis XVI's rejection of the decree of 24 January 1792, the war-party was checked (see p. 105). Sooner or later, the Austrians would have to reply to the King's own inquiry about their intentions, but for the time being at least, the Brissotins had lost the initiative. Had they but known it, the revival of their fortunes was already being prepared in the camp of their enemies, in Vienna. Undeterred by the hornet's nest stirred up in Paris by the Kaunitz note of 21 December (see p. 102), the Austrian government continued and extended its campaign of intimidation. On 17 January the Council of State decided that the concert of European powers should be formally reactivated and the following demands put to the French: the armies in the process of being formed on the frontiers of the Holy Roman Empire should be disbanded; all the rights of the German princes in Alsace should be restored; Avignon and the Comtat Venaissin should be returned to the Pope; complete security, liberty and respect should be granted to the French royal family; the monarchical form of government should be upheld in France and everything contrary to it should be abolished; all treaties between France and the other powers should be confirmed.[89]

Once the decision to exert full pressure on the revolutionaries had been taken, the need to cement relations with the Prussians became urgent. Back in the autumn of 1791, Leopold had resisted Prussian moves to have the concert implemented forthwith (see p. 88). Now a personal message was sent to Frederick William II asking for the peripatetic Bischoffwerder to be sent to Vienna, this time to negotiate a formal alliance.[90] There was a ready response from Berlin. All the old acquisitive impulses were just as strong there as in the past (see p. 88). As Frederick William II told his man in Vienna on 14 January 1792, it was high time that the Austrians came up with specific proposals relating to the 'compensation' to be extracted from the French to cover the costs of a military intervention.[91] By early the following month, he was being more specific: Prussia should take the long-coveted prize of Jülich and Berg, while the existing ruler of these two principalities – the Elector of Bavaria and the Palatinate – should be compensated with territory in Alsace and Lorraine, as should the Austrians.[92]

The Austrian search for an alliance with Prussia was also encouraged by the imminence of Russian intervention in Poland. On 9 January 1792 the Peace of Jassy was concluded, finally freeing Catherine the Great's hands by bringing her war with the Turks to an end. At about the same time news reached Vienna that she would soon take military action to destroy the new regime created in Poland by the revolution of 3 May 1791 and to restore Russian control of the country.[93] That was not unexpected, but it was very bad news all the same, for the Austrians had hoped that a stable and independent Poland would become a buffer against both Russian and Prussian expansion (see p. 84). Nor were they under any illusions as to Frederick William II's designs on Poland, knowing full well that he would do almost anything to obtain Danzig and Thorn. Consequently, if the Austrians were not to face total isolation over Poland, some sort of an agreement with Prussia was essential. Of course it was French concerns which were paramount in January–February 1792, but they were intensified by the fact that eastern interests pointed in the same direction.

With the Austrians now anxious to accept the embrace long proffered by Berlin, consummation was swift. On 7 February 1792, just one week after the proposals from Vienna first arrived, the treaty was signed. Although formally a defensive alliance, the clause which envisaged the adhesion of other European powers was clearly intended to lay the basis for a concert to intervene in France.[94] Prussian eagerness to translate the agreement into action was swiftly demonstrated. On 16 February Frederick William II chaired a meeting at Potsdam of his senior military and civilian advisers to draw up a plan of campaign against France. At the end of the month, Bischoffwerder was sent down to Vienna to coordinate allied action.[95] As his instructions made amply clear, the prime aim of Prussian policy was to gain territory; it was to be a war of conquest, thinly disguised as 'compensation' for the costs incurred in restoring order in France.[96] Although Jülich and Berg were still identified as the prime target, an even more monstrous proposal was now being discussed: that Prussia should take its reward in the form of *Polish* territory.[97] In the event, of course, this – the ultimate example of old-regime power politics – was just what happened, in the second partition of Poland of the following year.

In Austria too, acquisitive ambition was beginning to rear its head. In part this was due to the growing assertiveness of a younger generation of ministers. Ever since the accession of Leopold in 1790, the influence of Kaunitz, who was now eighty-one years old, had been on the wane. It was still strong enough to carry the day at real moments of crisis, but was being challenged increasingly by the rival claims of Count Philipp Cobenzl and Baron Anton Spielmann. Trained in the abrasive diplomacy of Joseph II, they put Austria first, and were indifferent to the interests of the Holy Roman Empire.[98] For them, the opportunity to gain territory presented by the French imbroglio seemed too good to miss. In January 1792, Spielmann began to promote the suggestion that Austria should take its compensation in the form of international consent to the exchange of Belgium for Bavaria. This was neither accepted nor rejected by the Council of State, but was pushed to one side by the decision that Prussia should be allowed to make the running over compensations.[99] For the time being, Leopold and Kaunitz kept Austrian policy confined to redressing the constitutional balance in France in favour of the King. It was their intention and conviction that this could be achieved by a modest military demonstration.[100]

Prussian aggression and the less forward but no less confident approach of the Austrians were both encouraged by a gross miscalculation of the will and ability of the French to resist. Recent history seemed to teach that the military effectiveness of revolutionary armies stood in inverse ratio to the bombastic rhetoric of their political leaders. In the autumn of 1787 a small Prussian army had conquered the United Provinces (which two centuries earlier had held the Spanish at bay for eighty years) in less than a month. In the early winter of 1790 a small Austrian army had conquered Belgium in less than a fortnight. France was admittedly much larger and more populous but was also thought to be more enfeebled by internal problems. All reports reaching Berlin or Vienna confirmed what their recipients wanted to believe: that a popular revolution could only lead to anarchy. Civil war in the provinces, factional chaos at the centre, mutinies in the armed forces, financial bankruptcy – this was revolutionary reality. The *émigrés*, Louis XVI and Marie Antoinette, foreign diplomats and secret agents all assured the Austrian and Prussian governments that the revolutionaries were in no condition to begin a war, let alone wage it successfully. Typical of the faulty intelligence coming out of France was the report from the Prussian diplomat von der Goltz on 13 February 1792: 'France is without disciplined armies, without experienced generals, without money, and the highest degree of anarchy reigns in all departments.'[101]

War could be risked, therefore, with a sense of impunity. As the Austrians believed that the revolutionaries would give up without a fight, and as the Prussians believed that France would fall within two months, there was everything to gain and nothing to lose from a policy of intimidation.[102] At the very least, there was an easy diplomatic coup to be scored, while resistance on the part of the French would only increase the spoils of certain victory. The mood of buoyant optimism was expressed well by Bischoffwerder when he told a group of Prussian officers: 'Do not buy too many horses, the comedy will not last long. The army of lawyers will be annihilated in Belgium and we shall be home by the autumn.'[103]

With all three potential combatants believing their side to be invincible and their opponent(s) to be on the verge of collapse, the scene was set for the final lurch into war. It was precipitated by that vital upheaval in the French executive without which the Legislative Assembly's will for war could not be imposed (see p.). The unwitting instrument was the Feuillant foreign minister Delessart, on whom Masson delivered the following crushing verdict: 'discredited with the Assembly's will for war could not be imposed (see p. 105). The unwitting incompetent as a diplomat, knowing nothing of politics, as conceited as Necker, but more stupid'.[104] Inept he certainly was, but poor Delessart was confronted by an almost impossible task. Squeezed between a counter-revolutionary court and a revolutionary legislature and harassed by his ministerial colleagues, especially by the Fayettiste minister of war, Narbonne, *anything* he did was sure to provoke attack. In the event, by trying to steer a middle course, he fell foul of all parties. On 21 January 1792 he sent back to Vienna only a timid response to Kaunitz's minatory note of 21 December. Nothing could have been better calculated to convince the Austrians that their campaign of intimidation was having the desired effect. On 17 February Kaunitz pressed home his advantage with a further note even more provocative than the first.[105]

Once again, the 'Coppelia effect' had prompted the Austrians to commit a gross miscalculation. Instead of strengthening the Feuillants, whom they fondly supposed to be still powerful, their note of 17 February opened the way for the final victory of the war-party. On 1 March the wretched Delessart had to go to the Legislative Assembly and listen while the secretary read both the offending Austrian communication and his own feeble piece of 21 January, to the accompaniment of shouts of anger and derision.[106] This was the opportunity the Brissotins had been waiting for and they seized it with both hands. On the afternoon of the same day they began an assault on the executive, concentrating on Delessart and the even softer target presented by Bertrand de Molleville, the royalist minister of the navy.[107]

116

In their campaign to bring the ministry down, they were given powerful – crucial – support by Lafayette and his supporters. The Fayettistes were important, not so much because of their votes in the Assembly as because one of their number, Narbonne, was already a minister and so able to work from the inside. But not for long: after a series of blistering attacks on Bertrand de Molleville, Narbonne was dismissed by Louis XVI on 9 March. One can understand the King's wish to get rid of such a turbulent minister, but in doing so he sealed his own fate. That night the leaders of the Brissotins and the Fayettistes met to plot their revenge. It was swift and deadly: on the following day, Brissot moved the impeachment of Delessart in one of his longest and most powerful speeches to date. Never had the rally-like atmosphere of the Legislative Assembly been more striking than on this tumultuous occasion. With the public galleries in full cry, only one outcome was possible. 'By a very large majority', Delessart was indicted for the neglect and betrayal of his duties and for having compromised the security and honour of France.[108]

Although Delessart was the immediate target, it was made quite clear that he was just the stalking-horse for more eminent prey. In the course of his speech, Brissot renewed his arguments for war against Austria and also attacked the King and the court more explicitly. Amid a frenzy of excitement, Vergniaud pointed dramatically through the windows at the adjacent Tuileries and summoned the deputies to look at the palace in which civil war and counter-revolution were being plotted.[109] Inside that palace, the royal family viewed this sudden deterioration with alarm bordering on panic. Louis XVI knew enough history not to wish to play Charles I to Delessart's Earl of Strafford. With the benefit of hindsight, the analogy can be seen to have been painfully accurate, but even at the time it looked ominously valid. It was well known that the Brissotins were planning the prosecution of Marie Antoinette for high treason and the suspension of the King. Playing for time in the hope of foreign intervention, the court capitulated. The remaining ministers were dismissed and a more radical government, including some Brissotins, was formed.[110]

As Ranke observed, the fall of the Feuillant ministry represented a decisive breakthrough. Hitherto, the ministers had felt obliged to carry out the wishes of the King – more or less – and had sought to evade the demands for action passed on by the Assembly. The new men regarded the latter's wishes as law.[111] With both legislature and executive now thirsting for war, it could not be long delayed. The dominant figure during the last weeks of peace was the new foreign minister, General Charles François Dumouriez. A veteran of the Seven Years War, the guiding principle of his politics was hatred of Austria.[112] That acted as a natural bond with the Brissotins, with whom he had been in touch for some time through Gensonné, but his ultimate objective was more like that of the Fayettistes. Like the latter, he looked to a short war in Belgium to restore the authority of the Crown – which he would then exercise, of course.[113] For the time being, that did not matter; if the strategy was different, the tactics were the same.

By the time Dumouriez took office on 15 March, matters were also coming to a head at the allied courts. On 1 March Leopold II had died suddenly, after an illness of only three days. It is very doubtful whether that in itself had much influence on what followed, either in Vienna or in Paris. By this time the Austrians had been manœuvred – and had helped to manœuvre themselves – into a position from which they could avoid war only at the cost of humiliation. Leopold's undistinguished successor, his twenty-four-year-old son Francis, had little or no freedom of action. Much more important than the Emperor's death in accelerating the characteristically sluggish tempo of Habsburg policy was the news from the Tuileries. At the end of March, a confidant of Marie Antoinette, Goguelat, arrived in Vienna with the news that war was both certain and imminent and the Queen herself was to be put on trial.[114] On 10 April a further letter arrived via Mercy confirming the earlier warning.[115] Now aware of the change of ministry in France, the Austrian Council of State decided that the Queen's prediction was correct and required immediate action. On 12 April reinforcements of 50,000 were ordered to the frontier and on 21 April a general invitation was issued to the other European powers to form a concert. Finally, on 28 April, two days before news of the French declaration of war arrived, the Council of State decided that an offensive war would have to be waged against France.[116]

Although these decisions were in large measure responses to events in Paris, they were encouraged by growing pressure from Berlin. The Prussians too had received intelligence of an impending French attack on Belgium. It pleased them mightily, for revolutionary aggression would justify generous compensation. So their allies were urged to take positive action. Indeed, Frederick William II now intervened personally, instructing his ministers to send a sharp note to Vienna protesting at what he thought was procrastination. Rightly convinced that the French were about to declare war and afraid lest any further delay might leave them without the Prussian help they needed so urgently, the Austrians decided for war.[117] All the evidence suggests that while they did so with reluctance, the Prussians were thirsting for action. On 24 April Frederick William appointed his retinue for the campaign and army contractors were ordered to make ready.[118]

It is a measure of the complete lack of understanding which governed relations between revolutionary France and the old-regime powers, that Dumouriez should *still* have believed that Prussian neutrality could be negotiated. Although the Prussians had made it abundantly clear that the policy expressed in Kaunitz's notes of 21 December and 17 February was also their policy, such was the power of wishful thinking that they were not really believed. On the very eve of war, Dumouriez was still urging his man in Berlin to argue the naturalness of an *alliance* between France and Prussia, was sending more secret agents to lend support, was offering the Duke of Zweibrücken 1 million livres if he could secure Prussian neutrality, and so on.[119] Certainly there was a party at the Prussian court which opposed the French war, but, for the time being at least, it had no influence on royal policy.[120]

With all parties resolutely set on a course of confrontation, collision could not be long delayed. Dumouriez hurried on the moment of impact by sending an ultimatum to the Austrians: choose between renunciation of the concert and war.[121] In the meantime, he kept the pot on the boil in the Assembly by making periodic visits to read out the latest offensive missive from Vienna.[122] The great day came at last on 20 April. Accompanied by his ministers, Louis XVI arrived in person to conduct the ceremony. First, Dumouriez conducted a review of France's foreign affairs, in the course of which he delivered the definitive attack on the old regime's alliance with Austria:

> Since 1756 Austria has abused an alliance treaty which France has always respected too much. Since its inception, this treaty has drained our blood and our money in the service of wars which were begun by ambition and were ended by treaties dictated by a tortuous and deceitful policy which always left behind the means of inciting new conflict.
> Since that fatal epoch of 1756, France has debased herself to the point of playing a subordinate role in the bloody tragedies of despotism. She has been enslaved to the consistently active and restless ambition of the House of Austria, to whom she has also sacrificed her natural allies.[123]

Dumouriez also rehearsed the Revolution's main grievances against Austria: the support of the *émigrés* and the organisation of the concert to subvert the new constitution. Then, 'with a certain faltering of the voice', as the official record put it, Louis XVI commended this report to the deputies as representative of his own views and those of his government and asked them to declare war.[124] The session which followed sported all the ingredients of war fever: Austrophobia, nationalism, nihilism and, above all, the conviction that victory would be swift and complete: 'victory will be faithful to liberty' was Pastoret's succinct epigram.[125] Roared on by the public galleries, the deputies brushed aside suggestions that the royal proposal should be debated over a period of days. Although held up for a while by a brave and prophetic speech from Louis Becquey, a deputy from the Haute Marne, who predicted that the war would destroy, not save the constitution, would cause financial chaos and would be long and difficult, they had their way. With only seven dissenting votes, war was declared.[126] As Madame de Staël, an eye-witness, observed, it was voted through by acclamation and without the least sense of unease.[127]

AN IDEOLOGICAL WAR?

With the French and the Austrians (soon to be joined by their Prussian allies) at war and about to find all their miscalculations of the other side's strength rudely exposed, it is time to return to the questions posed at the beginning of Chapter 3 (see p. 69). In particular, the role of ideology and the issue of inevitability need to be discussed further. An ideological war, a *Prinzipienkrieg,* can be defined as a conflict in which the two parties adhere to political and social principles so diametrically opposed that each finds the existence of the other to be intolerable and seeks its elimination by force of arms. Put more succinctly: war is made inevitable by the existence of two irreconcilable ideologies. At first sight, the collision between revolutionary France and the old regime appears to provide the classic example: on the one side the principles of liberty, equality, fraternity, national sovereignty and self-determination; on the other the principles of social hierarchy, monarchical authority, prescriptive right and the sanctity of treaties.

Yet, as the last two chapters have endeavoured to show, this macroscopic view is supported only partially by what actually happened in the years between the fall of the Bastille and the outbreak of war. Most obviously, it cannot accommodate relations between France and Prussia. The most bellicose of the revolutionaries – the Brissotins – *admired* Prussia, both for its enlightenment and for its martial exploits, and actively sought a Prussian alliance right up to the very outbreak of war (see pp. 109, 119). They always saw the war with Prussia as a regrettable aberration and as early as September 1792 had begun negotiations for a separate peace.[128] For their part, the Prussians were certainly more inclined to view their relations with the Revolution in terms of hostility based on principle. The excitable Frederick William II was constantly prone to outbursts of rage at French 'anarchy' and to stress the need to promote the cause of Louis XVI as the cause of all kings. Yet it is also abundantly clear that what prompted the Prussians to participate in the war against France was not their hatred of French ideology but their desire for French land (see p. 114). Moreover, there was always a party at the Prussian court which sought to prevent the war, on the very grounds that the natural affinity between Prussia and France outweighed any ideological differences. Not that those differences were held to be great: no less a person than the senior Prussian minister, Count Hertzberg, observed that the principles underlying the French Revolution and the principles underlying the enlightened Prussian state were essentially the same.[129]

Although the antipathy between revolutionary France and Austria was undeniably more intense, the same sort of qualifications need to be made here too. Brissot himself, the arch-Austrophobe, refused to accept that their differences were based on principle. In his last major speech before the outbreak of war, he argued that Leopold II's hostility to the Revolution could only stem from ignorance of the true situation in France, for it had so much in common with his own enlightened principles: 'Are kings doomed never to recognise the truth? How can the Emperor fail to recognise in our Revolution the rule of that philosophy which he himself has promoted?'[130] Hatred of Austria was common to all revolutionaries, indeed it was axiomatic, but it was fuelled not by a sense of irreconcilable principles but by a sense of irreconcilable *interests*. It was because Austria had exploited the 1756 treaty in a fashion so detrimental to French power and prestige, had run French foreign policy through '*l'Autrichienne*' – Marie Antoinette – and was now seeking to keep France weak by interfering in her internal affairs that she was detested so intensely. Certainly there was an issue of principle involved in that last grievance, namely the principle of national sovereignty, but it was as much concerned with the assertion of traditional French interests as with the assertion of revolutionary ideals: hence the allusions to the golden age of Louis XIV with which Brissotin speeches were larded. So attacks on the domestic structure of Austria as the embodiment of the old regime were few and far between. Despotic Russia, with its hordes of oppressed serfs, was a far better candidate for that ignominious title, yet Russia was hardly mentioned in Brissotin diatribes, for the good reason that as yet she barely impinged on French interests. What the Brissotins – and the deputies who were bowled along by their arguments – did believe, however, was that the decayed state of Austria would succumb to the unique power of revolutionary ideology. By helping to inflame revolutionary optimism, that ideology did play an important part in the origins of the war, but that is far removed from an inevitable clash between irreconcilably opposed principles.

The Austrians were undeniably more inclined to view the Revolution in terms of ideology. Complaints about international subversion and declarations of support for the monarchical principle appeared frequently in both public and private communications. That was less because of any special attachment to the old regime than because of the special problems posed by Belgium. For the past thirty years, in the case of Kaunitz, and for the last twenty-five years, in the case of Leopold, the two chief creators of Austrian foreign policy in 1791–92 had sought to implement a programme of domestic reform which had much in common with that of the Revolution in France. Certainly Kaunitz would have no truck with constitutionalism, but Leopold remained its sincere supporter right up until his death.[131] He was equally consistent in his rejection of counter-revolution in France: the settlement he envisaged was designed to serve Austrian interests, no more and no less.[132] Those interests were deemed to require the maintenance of the monarchy to ensure stability, but not to require a return to absolutism, the restoration of the nobility, the abolition of the Civil Constitution of the Clergy or of any of the other major revolutionary achievements.

The timing of the progress towards war also raises doubts as to the primacy of the ideological factor. Until the summer of 1791 there was no real confrontation between the Revolution and the German powers. In the course of 1790 Prussia had even explored the possibility of an alliance with France (see p. 81). The specific causes for contention – Alsace, the *émigrés* and Avignon – were admittedly awkward but were not considered by either side to warrant armed conflict. The revolutionaries themselves had been careful to support the principles of national sovereignty and self-determination with old-regime arguments based on historical claims and treaty rights. Together with Russia, Austria and Prussia were far more concerned with Poland and the Eastern Question than with France and were far more likely to fight each other than to march west. In 1790 the Prussians nearly went to war with Austria and in 1791 they nearly went to war with Russia. Certainly they were looking eagerly for territorial expansion and certainly their eyes lighted on France every now and again, but they were just as likely – more likely indeed – to fasten on Poland as their prey. As the events of the late 1780s had shown, a rounding-off of Prussian territory in the east was the most attractive option (see p. 53). For their part, the Austrians were immobilised by financial problems in the wake of the Turkish War and preoccupied by the need to restore order within their various restless provinces.

What returned France to the centre of the revolutionary stage were developments inside that country. If it can be established that the Revolution was impelled by some inner dynamism which drove it inevitably and irresistibly leftwards, then the notion of an inevitable clash with the old-regime powers can draw fresh validity. This is an issue so complex that it cannot be examined here, let alone resolved. Indeed, the very nature of the issue does not permit definitive resolution. The opinion – and it does not lay claim to any greater status than that – must suffice that the constitutional settlement worked out between 1789 and 1791 was viable and not predestined to collapse. All manner of forces led to its erosion – social, economic and financial problems, popular agitation, political ambitions, religious unrest, just to name a few – but particularly obtrusive was the dogged refusal of the King to cooperate. His backbone stiffened by his formidable queen ('the only man in the family', as Mirabeau called her), the normally invertebrate Louis XVI deliberately wrecked any chance of compromise between old and new. Yet even after his characteristically incompetent flight to Varennes in June 1791, the situation was not beyond repair. The threat of foreign intervention proved short-lived. The constitution established in September was not just acceptable to the Austrians, it was positively welcome. The Prussians were less enthusiastic about suspending the concert, but there was nothing they could or would do without Austrian cooperation.

It was the second move to the left, beginning in the autumn of 1791, which proved decisive. This was due not to the intrusion of any new issue of principle but to the growing influence in the new legislature of a group intent on war, chiefly for the purpose of obtaining political power. When every possible allowance for the Brissotins has been made, it is impossible to avoid the old conclusion that the main drive for war came from them. Yet they could not have succeeded without the assistance of Lafayette and his supporters or without that of the court. As the events of 14 December showed (see p. 101), the volatile Legislative Assembly would still rally to the King – when he appeared to be cooperating wholeheartedly with the new order. By duping his Feuillant ministers and by maintaining a treasonable correspondence with the foreign courts, Louis XVI played straight into the hands of his enemies.

Even so, this deteriorating domestic situation need not have resulted in war if the Austrians and Prussians had not played their role with such counter-productive clumsiness. If they had turned a deaf ear to appeals from the Tuileries, the Brissotins would never have been able to win over the uncommitted deputies in the Legislative Assembly. By seeking to intimidate the revolutionaries, by threatening a new concert to interfere in France's internal affairs, they lent powerful cogency to the war-party's arguments. It was a monumental error of judgement, inspired partly by a sense of fraternal and/or monarchical solidarity, partly by concern at the threat of international subversion, partly by anger at the provocative language of the Brissotin orators – but mainly by a defective appreciation of the events of the summer and autumn of 1791. What they had done, they believed, they could do again. Revolutionary France appeared so weak, so riven by political, social and religious strife, so emasculated by bankruptcy and mutinies, that war could be threatened with complete confidence that a quick and total victory – diplomatic or military – was certain. But their revolutionary opponents were equally convinced of their own invincibility, supremely confident in their own inexhaustible assets, the probable neutrality of Prussia, and the terminal decadence of Austria. In short, it was the mutual miscalculation of the power relationship between the two sides which was essentially responsible for war. The origins of the war of 1792 provide the best possible illustration of the validity of Blainey's insight that: 'Not only is power the issue at stake, but the decision to resolve that issue by peaceful or warlike methods is largely determined by assessments of relative power.'[133]

REFERENCES AND NOTES

1. Georges Michon, *Robespierre et la guerre révolutionnaire* (Paris 1937, pp. 11–12. For a summary of the *émigrés*' additional manifesto, see J. H. Clapham, *The Causes of the War of 1792* (Cambridge 1899, p. 78.

2. M. A Thiers, *Histoire de la Révolution française*, 14th edn, vol. 2 (Paris 1846, p. 17.

3. The nomenclature of the various revolutionary legislatures can easily cause confusion, so an explanatory note may be helpful: on 17 June 1789 the Third Estate of the Estates General declared itself to be the 'National Assembly'. After 7 July, now joined by the other two estates, its full title became 'National Constituent Assembly' (*assemblée nationale constituante*), since its main self-appointed task was the drafting of a new constitution. It is commonly referred to both as the 'National Assembly' and as the 'Constituent Assembly'. When its task was completed with the promulgation of the new constitution and its acceptance by the King in September 1791, it was replaced by the 'National Legislative Assembly' (*assemblée nationale législative*). This new body is commonly referred to both as the 'National Assembly' and as the 'Legislative Assembly'. To avoid confusion, I have referred to it consistently as the 'Legislative Assembly'. It was replaced on 21 September 1792 by the National Convention, following the *journée* of 10 August and the end of the monarchy. The clearest account of these institutional changes is to be found in Georges Lefebvre, *The French Revolution from its Origins to 1793* (London 1962) pp. 109–14, 152–3, 238, 247.

4. Hans Glagau, *Die französische Legislative und der Ursprung der Revolutionskriege 1791–2, mit einem Anhang politischer Briefe aus dem Wiener K.K. Haus-, Hof- und Staatsarchiv*, Historische Studien, vol. 1 (Berlin 1896; p. 41.

5. Ibid., p. 52.

6. Michel Vovelle, *The Fall of the French Monarchy 1787–1792* (Cambridge 1984) p. 154.

7. Lefebvre, *The French Revolution*, p. 213.

8. For the way in which Marie Antoinette, in particular, pulled the wool over the triumvirate's eyes, see the correspondence reprinted in Alfred Ritter von Arneth (ed.), *Marie Antoinette, Joseph II und Leopold II. Ihr Briefwechsel* (Vienna 1866) especially pp. 189–96.

9. The best account of Lafayette's relations with the Feuillants and of the development of his policy during late 1791 is to be found in Georges Michon, *Essai sur l'histoire du parti Feuillant* (Paris 1924) especially pp. 347–52.

10. As if that were not sufficient source of confusion, both groups at this stage adhered to the Jacobin Club and so could also be termed 'Jacobins'. The most satisfactory account of the foreign policy of the Brissotins/Girondins remains H.-A. Goetz-Bernstein, *La Diplomatie de la Gironde. Jacques-Pierre Brissot* (Paris 1912). For his insistence that the two groups did not merge finally until the National Convention in the autumn of 1792, see p. 26. For an even more radical denial that they constituted a party of any description, see M.J. Sydenham, *The Giron-*

dins (London 1961) p. 182. Although Sydenham's book contains much of value on the social background of the Girondins and the like, it is not helpful on the subject of their foreign policy. Indeed, on p. 104 there is a very curious statement which implies a belief that the war began considerably earlier than it actually did.

11. C. Perroud, 'Notice sur la vie de Brissot', *J.-P. Brissot. Correspondance et papiers précédés d'un avertissement et d'une notice sur sa vie*, ed. C. Perroud (Paris 1912) pp. xxxi, xliv–xlv.
12. Ibid., p. lvii; Goetz-Bernstein, *La Diplomatie de la Gironde*, p. 6.
13. Ibid., p. 83.
14. *Archives parlementaires de 1787 à 1860. Recueil complet des débats législatifs et politiques des chambres françaises*, 127 vols. (Paris 1879–1913) vol. 34 pp. 724–5.
15. Ibid., vol. 35, p. 27.
16. Etienne Dumont, *Souvenirs sur Mirabeau et sur les deux premières assemblées législatives*, ed. J. Bénétruy (Paris 1951) p. 201. See also Charles François Dumouriez, *La vie et les mémoires du général Dumouriez*, vol. 2 (Paris 1822) p. 202. For comments on the reliability of Dumont's memoirs, see Bénétruy's introduction, p. 29 and also Goetz-Bernstein, *La Diplomatie de la Gironde*, p. xiii.
17. Max Lenz, 'Marie Antoinette im Kampf mit der Revolution', *Preußische Jahrbücher*, **78** (1894) p. 2.
18. *Archives parlementaires*, vol. 34, p. 402.
19. Ibid., p. 315.
20. Ibid., p. 316.
21. Ibid.
22. Ibid., p. 317. It was, of course, common practice to have particularly popular speeches printed and distributed to the departments.
23. Ibid., vol. 35, p. 441.
24. Ibid., pp. 294, 359–61.
25. Ibid., p. 401.
26. Heinrich von Sybel, *Geschichte der Revolutionszeit von 1789 bis 1795*, 4th edn, vol. 1 (Düsseldorf 1877) p. 330. As Sybel correctly observes, the decree of 29 November was the first step towards war.
27. Joseph Hansen (ed.), *Quellen zur Geschichte des Rheinlandes im Zeitalter der französischen Revolution*, 4 vols (Bonn 1933–38) vol. 1, p. 1071, n. 2; vol. 2, p. 28, n. 3.
28. *Archives parlementaires*, vol. 36, p. 478, vol. 37, pp. 109, 447.
29. Ibid., vol. 36, p. 110.
30. Ibid.
31. Glagau, *Die französische Legislative*, pp. 67–70.
32. Arneth, *Marie Antoinette, Joseph II und Leopold II*, pp. 215–16.
33. Glagau, *Die französische Legislative*, pp. 93, 96–7.
34. On the earlier progress of the Alsatian dispute, see above, p.
35. The full text of all the various communications cited in this paragraph can be found in *Archives parlementaires*, vol. 36, pp. 352–4, 698.
36. Michon, *Essai sur l'histoire du parti Feuillant*, p. 368.
37. *Archives parlementaires*, vol. 36, p. 728.
38. Ibid., p. 413.
39. Ibid., p. 416.
40. Ibid., p. 414.

41. Glagau, *Die französische Legislative*, p. 115.
42. *Archives parlementaires*, vol. 37, pp. 653–6.
43. Ibid., p. 717.
44. For examples of this sort of argument being used in the Legislative Assembly, see the speeches of Brissot and of Condorcet on 29 December 1791 and of Gensonné on 14 January 1792–ibid., vol. 36, pp. 607, 618; vol. 37, p. 412.
45. Michon, *Histoire du parti Feuillant*, p. 365.
46. F.-A. Aulard, *La Société des Jacobins. Recueil de documents pour l'histoire du Club des Jacobins de Paris*, vol. 3 (Paris 1892) p. 325.
47. François Furet and Denis Richet, *The French Revolution* (London 1970) p. 127.
48. Vovelle, *The Fall of the French Monarchy*, pp. 213–15.
49. In his speech of 29 December 1791 Brissot claimed that it was only the machinations of Koblenz which kept the counter-revolutionary intrigues of the aristocrats and 'fanatics' [priests] in being – *Archives parlementaires*, vol. 36, p. 607. For similar observations by Condorcet and Gensonné, see ibid., p. 618 and vol. 37, p. 412.
50. Ibid., vol. 37, p. 547.
51. Michon, *Histoire du parti Feuillant*, p. 359.
52. Jean Louis Carra, *L'Orateur des Etats Généraux pour 1789* (Paris 1789) pp. 28–9. Cf. the self-explanatory title recorded in Alfred Ritter von Arneth and J. Flammermont (eds), *Correspondance secrète du Comte de Mercy-Argenteau avec l'Empereur Joseph II et le Prince de Kaunitz*, 2 vols, (Paris 1889–91) vol, 2 p. 281, n. 1; Charles de Peyssonel, *Situation politique de la France et ses rapports actuels avec toutes les puissances de l'Europe, ouvrage dont l'objet est de démontrer, par les faits historiques et les principes de la saine politique tous les maux qu'a causés à la France l'alliance autrichienne et toutes les fautes que le ministère français a commises depuis l'époque des traités de Versailles de 1756, 1757 et 1758 jusqu'à nos jours* (Neufchâtel and Paris 1789). It was so successful that a new edition was published in the following year. The old regime's classic denunciation of the Austrian alliance – Favier's *Doubts and Questions about the Treaty of Versailles* was reprinted in 1789 with a preface explicitly aimed at the Estates General – Glagau, *Die französische Legislative*, p. 88. The Austrians themselves had to recognise that once the Revolution had taken control, their alliance was over in all but name. As Joseph II observed to Kaunitz on 13 November 1789, France was not only worthless as an ally but had become 'an inveterate enemy' – Adolf Beer, *Joseph II, Leopold II und Kaunitz. Ihr Briefwechsel* (Vienna 1873) p. 349.
53. *Archives parlementaires*, vol. 36, p. 609; vol. 37, p. 492.
54. For a sample of these arguments, see Isnard's speech of 20 January 1792–ibid., vol. 37, p. 546.
55. Ibid., p. 492.
56. Ibid., vol. 39, p. 598.
57. Marie-David Lasource, 1 March 1792–ibid., p. 240.
58. Ibid., vol. 37, p. 412.
59. Leopold von Ranke, *Ursprung und Beginn der Revolutionskriege, 1791 und 1792* (Leipzig 1879) p. 140.

60. *Archives parlementaires*, vol. 37, p. 328.
61. Dubois-Dubais, 22 October 1791–ibid., vol. 34, p. 348.
62. Ibid., vol. 35, p. 398; vol. 36, p. 607; vol. 37, p. 574. Charlier's observation was not as fatuous as it looked: on 23 August 1793 the National Convention did requisition for the war effort every man, woman and child.
63. Ibid., vol. 36, p. 607. See also the address sent by the Jacobin Club to all affiliated societies on 16 January 1792 – Aulard, *La Société des Jacobins*, p. 324.
64. On the condition of the regular army at this time, see Samuel F. Scott, *The Response of the Royal Army to the French Revolution. The Role and Development of the Line Army 1787–1793* (Oxford 1978), especially ch. 3.
65. *Archives parlementaires*, vol. 37, pp. 233–9.
66. Sybel, *Geschichte der Revolutionszeit*, vol. 1, pp. 335–6.
67. Gaston, 20 October 1791–*Archives parlementaires*, vol. 34, p. 319.
68. Ranke, *Ursprung und Beginn der Revolutionskriege*, p. 173.
69. *Archives parlementaires*, vol. 35, p. 442. See also the similar arguments advanced by Vergniaud on 27 December 1791: 'they will try to raise nations against you, but will raise only princes' – ibid., vol. 36, p. 442.
70. For a sample of these comfortable assumptions about the state of the other powers, see the sanguine review of Europe conducted by Brissot in his speech of 29 December 1791: ibid., pp. 601–7.
71. For examples, see ibid., vol. 35, p. 398; vol. 36, p. 614; vol. 37, p. 89.
72. Ibid., vol. 36, p. 607; vol. 37, pp. 412, 493.
73. Michon, *Robespierre*, p. 21.
74. Aulard, *La Société des Jacobins*, p. 258; *Le Patriote français* [A Jacobin publication], nos 785, 866, 870, 877, 894.
75. On the alliance which developed between the Brissotins and the foreign exiles, see Albert Mathiez, *La Révolution et les étrangers. Cosmopolitisme et défense nationale* (Paris 1918) p. 45 and Jacques Godechot, *La Grande Nation. L'expansion révolutionnaire de la France dans le monde 1789–1799*, 2 vols, (Paris 1956), vol. 1 p. 78.
76. *Archives parlementaires*, vol. 36, p. 79.
77. Alphonse Aulard, 'La diplomatie du premier comité de salut public', *Etudes et leçons sur la Révolution française*, 3rd edn, vol. 3 (Paris 1914) p. 53.
78. See the acute observation by Andre Gués in an otherwise unremarkable article: 'The Terror did not derive from the national emergency created by the war, it was the war which was the result of the terrorist design' – Andre Guès, 'La guerre machinée de 1792', *Itinéraires: Chroniques et Documents*, **229** (1979) p. 77.
79. *Archives parlementaires*, vol. 36, p. 613.
80. Ibid., vol. 35, pp. 361–2.
81. Ibid., vol. 37, p. 414. See also above, p. 104. After the fall of the Brissotins, Guadet spent almost a year on the run, but was caught in the end and was executed at Bordeaux on 14 July 1794.
82. Ibid., vol. 36, p. 406.
83. Ibid., vol. 35, pp. 441–2; vol. 37, p. 465; vol. 39, p. 97.
84. For illustrations of the *manège*, see Furet and Richet, *The French*

Revolution, pp. 101, 145.

85. Goetz-Bernstein, *La Diplomatie de la Gironde*, p. 56; Michon, *Robespierre*, p. 79.

86. For examples of participation by the public galleries, see *Archives parlementaires*, vol. 36, pp. 80, 112–13; vol. 37, p. 718. For an account of public participation in the events of 14 January 1792, see p. 104.

87. The best account of Robespierre's campaign against the war is to be found in Michon, *Robespierre*, especially pp. 51–5. See also the debates recorded in Aulard, *La Société des Jacobins*, vol. 3, pp. 278, 292, 309.

88. Michon, *Robespierre*, pp. 31–2.

89. The minutes of the conference are reprinted in full in Alfred Ritter von Vivenot, *Quellen zur Geschichte der deutschen Kaiserpolitik Oesterreichs während der französischen Revolutionskriege, 1790–1801*, vol. I: *Die Politik des oesterreichischen Staatskanzlers Fürsten von Kaunitz-Rietberg bis zur französischen Kriegserklärung, Jänner 1790–April 1792* (Vienna 1873) pp. 327–30.

90. Clapham, *The Causes of the War of 1792*, p. 148.

91. Ernst Herrmann, *Geschichte des russischen Staates. Ergänzungsband: Diplomatische Correspondenzen aus der Revolutionszeit 1791–1797* (Gotha 1866) p. 143.

92. Ibid., pp. 163–4.

93. R. H. Lord, *The Second Partition of Poland* (Cambridge, Mass. 1915) p. 235.

94. Clapham, *The Causes of the War of 1792*, p. 157. The full text can be found, among other places, in Vivenot, *Quellen zur Geschichte der deutschen Kaiserpolitik Oesterreichs*, vol. 1, p. 370.

95. Lord, *The Second Partition of Poland*, pp. 237–40.

96. The full text of Bischoffwerder's instructions can be found in Ranke, *Ursprung und Beginn der Revolutionskriege*, pp. 278–85.

97. Lord, *The Second Partition of Poland*, p. 237.

98. Karl Otmar Freiherr von Aretin, *Heiliges Römisches Reich 1776–1806. Reichsverfassung und Staatssouveränität*, 2 vols, (Wiesbaden 1967), vol. 1 p. 249; P. Mitrofanov, *Leopold II. Avstriyskiy Vneshnaya Politika*, vol. 1, pt 1 (Petrograd 1916) pp. 59–63.

99. Lord, *The Second Partition of Poland*, pp. 261–2; Vivenot, *Quellen zur Geschichte der deutschen Kaiserpolitik Oesterreichs*, vol. 1, p. 340.

100. Kurt Heidrich, *Preußen im Kampfe gegen die französische Revolution bis zur zweiten Teilung Polens* (Stuttgart and Berlin 1908) pp. 38, 48.

101. Ranke *Ursprung und Beginn der Revolutionskriege*, p. 132, n. 2. For other apparently authoritative comments on French weakness, see that made by Marie Antoinette on 16 December 1791 – Arneth, *Marie Antoinette, Joseph II und Leopold II*, p. 234; that made by Montmorin on 16 February 1792 – Glagau, *Die französische Legislative*, p. 92, n. 1; that made by the Comte de la Marck on 23 February 1792 – Herrmann, *Geschichte des russischen Staates*, p. 194; and that made by Goguelat in March 1792 – Ranke, *Ursprung und Beginn der Revolutionskriege*, p. 166.

102. Vivenot, *Quellen zur Geschichte der deutschen Kaiserpolitik Oesterreichs*, vol. 1, p. 338; Louis-Philippe comte de Ségur, *Histoire des principaux événements du règne de F. Guillaume II, roi de Prusse; et tableau*

politique de l'Europe depuis 1786 jusqu'en 1796, ou l'an 4 de la République; contenant un précis des révolutions de Brabant, de Hollande, de Pologne et de France, 3 vols, (Paris 1800), vol. 2 p. 222.

103. Albert Sorel, 'Dumouriez; Un général diplomate au temps de la Révolution', *Revue des Deux Mondes*, **64** (1884) p. 323.

104. F. Masson, *Le Département des affaires étrangères pendant la Révolution 1787–1804* (Paris 1877) p. 124.

105. The full text can be found in Vivenot, *Quellen zur Geschichte der deutschen Kaiserpolitik Oesterreichs*, vol. 1, p. 372 and in *Archives parlementaires*, vol. 39, p. 248.

106. Ibid., pp. 245–9.

107. Ibid., pp. 255–6.

108. Ibid., pp. 530–50. He was committed to prison the same night, languishing there until murdered during the September Massacres later in the year.

109. Ibid., p. 549.

110. Brissot himself and his closest associates were disqualified because they were, or had been, members of the legislature. The most detailed account of this episode is to be found in Glagau, *Die französische Legislative*, chs 7–8. Glagau seeks to show that the final crisis was caused not by the note of 17 February, but by a dispute between the Feuillants and the Fayettistes. One must suspect that this argument derives from his concern to exculpate the Austrians, for it is incompatible with the clear evidence that it was news of the Austrian initiative which allowed the Brissotins to galvanise the Legislative Assembly once more. Although very valuable, Glagau's work has to be treated with caution, since – among other things – he has a dangerous habit of stating as fact what his sources report only as hearsay – for example, that during the dark days after 10 March Louis XVI spent most of his waking hours praying on his *prie-Dieu* and talking of abdication – p. 239.

111. Ranke, *Ursprung und Beginn der Revolutionskriege*, p. 153.

112. Dumont, *Souvenirs*, pp. 218–19. See also Dumouriez's own memoirs – *La vie et les mémoires du général Dumouriez*, vol. 2, pp. 198–202.

113. Lefebvre, *The French Revolution*, p. 225; Richard Munthe Brace, 'General Dumouriez and the Girondins 1792–3', *American Historical Review*, **56** (3) (1951) pp. 493–4.

114. Ranke, *Ursprung und Beginn der Revolutionskriege*, pp. 165–6.

115. Heidrich, *Preußen im Kampfe gegen die französische Revolution*, p. 49.

116. Lord, *The Second Partition of Poland*, p. 267; Clapham, *The Causes of the War of 1792*, p. 206.

117. Heidrich, *Preußen im Kampfe gegen die französische Revolution*, pp. 49–59.

118. Ibid., p. 68.

119. Sorel, 'Dumouriez', pp. 312–13; Jacques Droz, *Histoire diplomatique de 1648 à 1919*, 3rd edn (Paris 1972) p. 184; Arthur Chuquet, *La première invasion prussienne (11 août–2 septembre 1792* (Paris 1886) p. 19. On earlier attempts to secure Prussian support, organised by Narbonne, see Albert Sorel, *L'Europe et la Révolution française*, vol. 2: *La chute de la royauté* (Paris 1913) pp. 334, 350–5. Narbonne had even supposed that the Duke of Brunswick, the Prussian general, might be recruited to serve

as Commander-in-Chief of the French army – Albert Sorel, 'La mission de Custine à Brunswick en 1792', *Revue historique,* **1** (1876), *passim.*
120. Ranke, *Ursprung und Beginn der Revolutionskriege,* pp. 158–62.
121. Glagau, *Die französische Legislative,* pp. 262–3.
122. *Archives parlementaires,* vol. 40, pp. 660–2; vol. 41, pp. 605–8.
123. Ibid., vol. 42, p. 196.
124. Ibid., p. 199.
125. Ibid., p. 203.
126. Ibid., pp. 217–18.
127. G. de Staël, *Considérations sur les principaux événements de la Révolution française,* 3 vols, (Paris 1818), vol. 2 p. 41.
128. Sorel, *L'Europe et la Révolution française,* vol. 3, pp. 53–5.
129. Jacques Droz, *L'Allemagne et la Révolution française* (Paris 1949) p. 80.
130. *Archives parlementaires,* vol. 39, p. 537.
131. Adam Wandruszka, *Leopold II. Erzherzog von Österreich, Großherzog von Toskana, König von Ungarn und Böhmen, Römischer Kaiser,* vol. 2 (Vienna and Munich 1965) p. 372.
132. Ibid., p. 381.
133. Geoffrey Blainey, *The Causes of War* (Melbourne 1977) p. 150.

Chapter 5

THE ORIGINS OF THE WAR OF 1793

BRITISH NEUTRALITY

Less than ten years after the Treaty of Versailles of 3 September 1783 had brought the latest phase of the 'Second Hundred Years War'[1] to an end, France and Great Britain were at each other's throats again. Although both sides believed the war would be short, it lasted for twenty-two years and became a fight to the finish. As this was the sixth time the two countries had been at war within the space of a century, there is a strong temptation to locate its causes in some sort of inevitable continuum of violence. It is a temptation which is strengthened by the discovery that most revolutionaries were as Anglophobe as any old- regime minister. Just two weeks after the fall of the Bastille, the British ambassador, the Duke of Dorset, reported from Paris the general conviction that British money was being spent to encourage French anarchy. He also complained that it was becoming dangerous for him and his fellow-countrymen to appear in public.[2] The not unreasonable belief that British policy was fuelled by an insatiable appetite for new markets and new colonies persuaded most revolutionaries that the interests of the two countries were simply irreconcilable. The most important political figure of the first phase of the Revolution, Mirabeau, wrote in the spring of 1790: 'the enmity of England will be eternal: it will grow each year with the productivity of its industry, and even more than our own.'[3]

An early sign that this prediction would be proved accurate was the Nootka Sound crisis of the same year (see p. 61). This looked all too much like an attempt by the British to take advantage of temporary French impotence to humiliate and despoil France's only reliable ally, Spain. In the debates in the National Assembly on the Spanish request for help, Anglophobia kept breaking in.[4] It was even suggested that the naval armament currently under way in British ports was directed not against Spain, but against France itself.[5]

On the other side of the Channel, this traditional enmity was heartily reciprocated. Given its most celebrated pictorial expression in Hogarth's *O the Roast Beef of Old England, or the Gate of Calais,*

Francophobia was common to all classes. With only slight exaggeration, one French observer recorded: 'Before they learn there is a God to be worshipped, they learn there are Frenchmen to be detested.'[6] It was a prejudice with strong political implications, as William Eden discovered to his anger when the commercial treaty he had negotiated with France in 1786 ran into fierce opposition, despite its manifestly favourable terms. An exasperated Eden wrote to his old friend, Lord Sheffield: 'How can you twist and pervert your own superior understanding so as to affect even to give countenance to all the anti-Gallican nonsense which is encouraged in England?'[7]

That nonsense was not dispelled by the outbreak of the Revolution. Certainly some well-publicised voices hailed a new dawn in Anglo-French relations, but for every poet rhapsodising on the theme of amity, a great mass clung to its traditional aversion. As Edmund Burke put it: 'half-a-dozen grasshoppers under a fern make the field ring with their importunate chink, whilst thousands of great cattle, reposed beneath shadows of the Great British oak, chew the cud and are silent.'[8] The most common British response to news of the Revolution was an unappealing *Schadenfreude,* supported by the complacent assumption that it would eliminate France as an international rival.[9] The foreign secretary; the notoriously Francophobe Duke of Leeds, wrote shortly after the fall of the Bastille: 'I defy the ablest Heads in England to have planned, or its whole Wealth to have purchased, a Situation so fatal to its Rival, as that to which France is now reduced by her own intestine Commotions.' His prime minister, William Pitt, smugly regarded France as 'an object of compassion'.[10]

But mutual antipathy did not necessarily mean conflict. On the contrary, Franco-British relations during the first three years of the Revolution were calmer than they had been for a long time past. In France the revolutionaries were preoccupied with domestic reconstruction. Even when the Nootka Sound affair threatened to disrupt relations, international interests quickly took second place to the overriding concern with the constitution (see p. 79). The British were anxious only that political turmoil should *continue* in France for as long as possible. In the meantime, they busily – and clumsily – set about moving into the vacuum created by the collapse of French power. This initiative certainly demonstrated that Britain could now exert more influence on the Continent than ever before, but it also generated friction with the other old-regime powers. First, the imposition of the Convention of Reichenbach in July 1790, together with the consequential disputes over the restoration of Habsburg authority in Belgium, alienated Austria. Then the Nootka Sound affair alienated Spain. Then the attempt to force Catherine the Great to disgorge her Turkish conquests alienated Russia. Finally, the abandoning of that attempt alienated Prussia. By the summer of 1791 the British had retreated to sulky insularity and inglorious isolation, leaving behind an enhanced reputation for perfidy. (On these incidents, see p. 54–62.)

So far as revolutionary France was concerned, both the opportunity for continental involvement and its dissipation dictated neutrality on the part of the British. It was a policy they observed right from the start and with complete consistency – until November 1792. In October 1789 the Duke of Orléans was curtly told by Leeds that Louis XVI should not look to the foreign powers 'either with Hope or Apprehension' but should set about putting his own house in order.[11] When Leopold II did begin to intervene in French affairs in the summer of 1791, the British stayed conspicuously aloof. The 'Padua Circular' appealing for international action against the Revolution was given a reply whose formal correctness could not disguise chilly rejection.[12] With majestic condescension, the new foreign secretary, Lord Grenville, observed that the principal powers of Europe appeared not to have learnt the lesson so obvious to the British that no territorial acquisition was worth the costs involved. British policy, he insisted, would continue to be 'the most scrupulous neutrality in the French business'.[13] British diplomats were told not to attend the conference held at Pillnitz between the rulers of Prussia and Austria and the declaration it produced was dismissed as 'equally ill-conceived and undignified'.[14]

No great acumen was required to appreciate that neutrality served Britain's interests best. It did so, moreover, at no cost and with no risk. The intelligent and influential Lord Auckland (*ci-devant* William Eden) summed up the attitude prevailing in government circles very well when he wrote to Grenville: 'I heartily detest and abjure the whole system of the *Democrates* abstractedly considered; but I am not sure that the continued course of their struggles to maintain a disjointed and inefficient Government would not be beneficial to our political interests, and the best security to the permanence of our prosperity.'[15]

Consequently, the deterioration of relations between France and Austria during the winter of 1791–92 was observed with the utmost indifference. There was even some regret at the prospect of Austro-Prussian intervention; as Auckland foresaw, with impressive prophetic insight, 'History shews that offensive leagues against a particular people have seldom succeeded; and for this obvious reason, that the party attacked immediately acquires an union of interests, and the attacking parties have adverse interests of every description.'[16] Not for the first or last time, however, British statesmen proved more adept at predicting the fate of other nations than at understanding their own. Such was the confidence engendered by rapidly expanding prosperity and the impending embroilment of the continental powers in mutually enervating conflict that a vista of untroubled security appeared to stretch as far as the mind's eye could see. Nowhere was this buoyant optimism better expressed than in Pitt's budget speech of 17 February

1792. As the storm clouds gathered over the Continent, the British Isles basked in uninterrupted sunlight:

> I am not, indeed, presumptuous enough to suppose that, when I name fifteen years, I am not naming a period in which events may arise which human foresight cannot reach, and which may baffle all our conjectures. We must not count with certainty on a continuance of our present prosperity during such an interval; but unquestionably there never was a time in the history of this country, when, from the situation of Europe, we might more reasonably expect fifteen years of peace than at the present moment.[17]

Belief in peace in their time by the British was not shaken at all by the outbreak of war between France and the German powers. If ever there were a war in which British interests dictated non-participation, then this was surely it: 'We have nothing here but peace and prosperity at home, and no other concern in the miseries and misfortunes of other countries than what humanity calls for.'[18] So the Austrian invitation to join the counter-revolutionary concert was firmly rejected and a formal declaration of neutrality was issued.[19] The Austrians' disappointment turned to anger when it also emerged that the British were sabotaging their other attempts to enlarge the anti-French coalition. In his capacity as Elector of Hanover, George III declared his own principality neutral and helped to keep the other north German princes out of the war too.[20] Meanwhile, his ministers took prompt and firm action to stifle a bellicose spasm by their Dutch satraps.[21]

Not even the great revolutionary *journée* of 10 August 1792, when the Tuileries palace was stormed by the *sans-culottes* and the monarchy was suspended, could stir the British into taking a closer interest in French affairs. The ambassador, Earl Gower, was recalled on the reasonable ground that the authority to which he was accredited – the monarchy – no longer existed, but it was also stressed that Great Britain remained 'extremely neutral'.[22] In part, this studied indifference was based on the confident belief that the Austro-Prussian invasion force would soon be in Paris restoring order. It was a belief negated by the 'September Massacres' of 2–5 September 1792, when more than a thousand people were slaughtered by the revolutionary crowd, and by the French victory at Valmy on 20 September. Goethe may have believed that the latter event – of which he was an eye-witness – marked a turning-point in the history of the world, but his British contemporaries were unimpressed. Although increasingly alarmed by the Revolution's atrocities in Paris and successes at the front, the government saw no reason to change tack. At the beginning of November it was still rejecting requests that it should intervene in continental affairs – on this occasion requests for assistance from beleaguered Sardinia and Geneva.[23]

The British demonstration that national antipathy was compatible with peaceful coexistence was mirrored by the French. Despite the occasional Anglophobe outburst in the National Assembly, even the most bellicose deputies could appreciate that their main target had to be Austria. When Brissot began his campaign for war in the autumn of 1791, he was careful to exclude Great Britain from his field of fire. In his first major speech, on 20 October, he went out of his way to praise 'the power which has respected our revolution and its emblems most scrupulously'.[24] By the following January he was even advocating an alliance with the old enemy and was predicting it would be easy to secure.[25] As his colleague Condorcet put it, there was now 'a natural community of interest' between two free peoples.[26] Indeed, throughout the first half of 1792 repeated efforts were made to turn this sense of ideological affinity into a formal alliance. Not even the superior gifts of the chief envoy involved – Talleyrand – nor the bait of a West Indian island – Tobago – could achieve that goal. Nor could the eminently cogent and prescient argument that an Austro-Prussian alliance heralded the end of the Holy Roman Empire.[27] Nevertheless, their very employment indicated a wish by the leading revolutionaries to maintain peaceful coexistence.

THE FRENCH CONQUEST OF BELGIUM

What disturbed this harmony so abruptly was the dazzling military success of the revolutionary armies. It was as sudden as it was – apparently – complete. When halted at Valmy on 20 September, the Prussian armies were within 100 miles of Paris. Yet by the end of the month the revolutionary armies were back on the offensive in all theatres: Savoy and Nice they quickly conquered; by the end of October they had occupied much of the left bank of the Rhine and had captured Frankfurt am Main; after their great victory at Jemappes on 6 November, they expelled the Austrians from Belgium. The great surge of pride and confidence which these victories naturally engendered gave a decisive and – for Franco-British relations – fatal twist to revolutionary foreign policy.

Before the nature of that change can be examined, it is necessary to sketch briefly the political changes which had taken place since the fall of the monarchy on 10 August. The King had been replaced by a 'Provisional Executive Council', which turned out to be dominated by the imposing if raffish figure of Danton. So far as the conduct of foreign policy was concerned, the situation was decidedly confused. The new foreign minister, Lebrun, was certainly not its sole controller. Also influential were the diplomatic committee of the (soon to be replaced) Legislative Assembly, Danton and Dumouriez. The last-named had resigned as foreign minister on 14 June, to become minister of war, but almost immediately resigned that office too, to take command of the Army of the North. That did not mean a loss of interest in foreign affairs. On the contrary, both his appetite and opportunity for influence were enhanced by his victories at Valmy and Jemappes. But on the day after the first of those triumphs the new legislature – the National Convention – held its first session. Although its collective political attitude was a good deal more radical than that of its predecessor, its basic structure was not dissimilar. No party commanded an overall majority, so every party was obliged to woo the support of the uncommitted deputies: 'The Plain'. Of the 749 members, Brissot and the Girondins could count on about 200, while Robespierre and 'The Mountain' numbered about 100.[28]

No sooner had the National Convention met than it set about taking control of the executive by establishing the usual committees. In effect they became executive ministries and henceforth the most important policy decisions were taken by them or by the Convention itself.[29] That did not create the same sort of confusion which had characterised relations between the Brissotin-led Legislative Assembly and the Feuillant ministry in the previous year, for Lebrun was close to both Brissot and Dumouriez. He was also subject to the same sort of pressures and stimuli, and it was these which combined to produce a relatively coherent policy. In two easy stages the revolutionaries progressed from a war of prudence to a war of propaganda to a war of imperial expansion.[30]

When pressing for war in the first place, one of the most powerful weapons in the Brissotin arsenal had been the argument that the war would be easy (see p. 108). It had been dented by the failure of the first attempt to invade Belgium at the end of April 1792, but had then been vindicated triumphantly by the events of the autumn. The apparently irresistible progress of French arms in the south, the east and the north made everything seem possible. Moreover, military victory was accompanied by some signs that the great awakening of the oppressed peoples of feudal Europe, which had also been predicted by the Brissotins, was indeed under way. On 19 November news reached the National Convention that supporters of liberty in the German Duchy of Zweibrücken were being persecuted by their prince and were appealing for help. It was also reported that the revolutionary club at Mainz, which had been established after the liberation of the city by the French on 21 October, was also asking for protection. After a highly – and increasingly – emotional debate, the Convention voted through a decree which, in the name of the French people, declared that fraternity and assistance would be given to *all* peoples wishing to regain their liberty. The executive was to issue the necessary orders to generals in the field to protect the people they had liberated against any reprisals from their former despots. The decree was also to be publicised in the local languages throughout the regions in which the French armies were operating.[31]

There is some dispute as to just how premeditated was this massive expansion of revolutionary ambitions. Ever-hostile to the Brissotins, Georges Michon believed the decree of 19 November to be part of their long-term plan to divert the force of the Revolution outwards and to distract the masses from domestic social problems.[32] Examination of the Convention's proceedings suggests rather that it was a genuinely spontaneous response to the news from Germany, encouraged by an excess of oratory and a deficit of deliberation. More appropriate is the verdict of Albert Sorel: 'At Paris the decree of 19 November was nothing more than a pompous parliamentary incident; beyond the frontiers it was a dead letter.'[33] But even if never to be implemented, it was not to be disavowed. The Brissotins were prisoners of their own rhetoric. Urged on by the foreign exiles, one of whom (Clavière) was now in the ministry, their revolutionary vision expanded to encompass the entire Continent: 'We cannot be calm until Europe, all Europe, is in flames', proclaimed Brissot on 26 November.[34]

There was never any prospect that this heady rhetoric would be translated into action, not least because the oppressed subjects of the feudal despots were to prove so resistant to French ideology. What proved much more practical was a policy not of propaganda but of annexation. Even before his victory at Jemappes had made the conquest of Belgium possible, Dumouriez was stating: 'the Rhine should be the sole limit to our country, from Geneva to the sea.'[35] He found strong and influential support back in Paris. Brissot wrote to him on 27 November: 'I can tell you that there is one opinion which is spreading here: namely, that the French Republic must have the Rhine as its frontier. Is public opinion up there [in Belgium] with you in favour of such a reunion? We must get it ready.'[36] Significantly, especially with reference to the likely British reaction, such a frontier would involve the annexation of a substantial slice of the United Provinces as well as all Belgium.

The need to prime the inhabitants of the liberated territories to apply for 'reunion' to France led to the promulgation on 15 December of a decree much more hard-headed than that of 19 November. It was also a response to requests from generals in the field for instructions on how to administer the new territories. The decree itself was a masterly combination of universalist ideology and nationalist *raison d'état*. On the one hand, it ordered the destruction of the old regime and all its works; on the other hand, it made arrangements for the exploitation of local resources to feed the French armies. On the one hand, it arranged for elections to be held, to allow the liberated masses to determine their own future; on the other hand, it took precautions to ensure that the future they chose corresponded with French wishes.[37] Georges Lefebvre delivered the following astringent verdict: 'This famous decree, voted with acclamation on December 15, instituted the dictatorship of revolutionary minorities under the protection of French bayonets, and undertook to secure the fortunes of other peoples, without consulting them, at their expense.'[38] Robespierre was one of the few to realise that the attempt to place the liberated peoples of Europe under French tutelage would only breed counter-revolutionary resistance. When attacking the decree of 15 December, he delivered one more of his memorable epigrams: 'liberty can never be founded by the use of foreign force.'[39] For the time being, not enough deputies of the National Convention were listening. On this issue at least, most of them were still under the sway of the Brissotins and their vision of universal liberation. It was a vision of potent appeal, for it simultaneously promoted revolutionary ideology and French national interests. With French armies victorious everywhere, it was also a vision which seemed eminently realisable.

THE FRENCH THREAT TO THE DUTCH REPUBLIC

While this surge of military success was transforming French plans, changes of comparable dimension were under way in London. The rock on which all British policy was founded was the determination that both parts of the Low Countries – both Belgium and the United Provinces – should be kept out of the hands of France. They were seen as the key to British security, not only in the Channel but also on the sea routes to India (thanks to the Dutch possessions at the Cape of Good Hope and in Ceylon). It was this overriding concern, not to say obsession, which had prompted the intervention in the United Provinces of 1787 and the diplomatic initiative of 1790 which had led to Belgium returning to Habsburg rule after its short-lived revolt. (On these two episodes, see pp. 49, 54). A Belgium ruled by the Habsburgs was held to be the ideal solution, for it created a solid buffer against French expansion to the north. As Grenville told the Sardinian envoy: 'It was England that made the Peace of Utrecht stipulate that the Low Countries might never be relinquished by the House of Austria, so as to oppose a powerful barrier against French designs on Holland. It was England which, to the same end, worked at Reichenbach to preserve them for the House of Austria.'[40] The Austrian ambassador in London was quite right when he reported to Kaunitz in November 1789 that the British court and government were far more concerned about the upheaval in Belgium than they were about the Revolution in France.[41]

Even after the barrier had been restored by the Austrian recapture of Belgium in November 1790, the British remained nervous. They knew that a province which had revolted once might well revolt again, especially as it adjoined a country undergoing a full-blooded revolution and teeming with Belgian exiles. In August 1791 Grenville wrote to Auckland at The Hague:

> Every information I have concurs to shew that the discontents there are gaining ground; and I have pretty strong grounds to believe that the discontented party will seize the first moment of the Emperor's interference in French affairs to raise their standard again, and to connect themselves openly and intimately with the National Assembly. This union of the Netherlands with France is the very thing that this country and the Republic [The United Provinces] have most to apprehend.[42]

If the British were uneasy about Belgium, they were alarmed about the United Provinces. There too, a weak and unpopular regime faced continuing unrest inside the country and continuing agitation by the large colony of exiles at Paris. In March 1790 the Prince of Orange wrote a personal letter to George III, lamenting that the 'Patriot' opposition was stronger than ever before and had been encouraged greatly by the revolutions in Belgium and France. He predicted that the first opportunity would be taken to destroy the existing constitution, to break off the alliance with Great Britain and to restore the United Provinces to 'the yoke of France'.[43] That was special pleading, of course, but the Stadholder's fears were confirmed by Lord Auckland, ambassador at The Hague and the most influential of all the British diplomats.[44] The assertiveness of the Dutch patriots naturally waxed with French military success. By November 1792 Auckland could report: 'Our situation is critical both from within and from without. The patriotic party at Amsterdam has laid aside all reserves, and is become noisy and impudent; and there is scarce a village or an alehouse in this province in which the language is not seditious at the clubs, and frequently with the accession of a travelling Jacobin.'[45]

As French pressure on the main buttress of British security mounted, so did the need and temptation to intervene to prop it up. Yet as late as 6 November Grenville could still insist that neutrality was the best policy:

> With respect to any steps to be taken by this country, I continue fixed in my opinion, or rather I am every day more and more confirmed in it, that both in order to preserve our own domestic quiet, and to secure some other parts at least of Europe free from the miseries of anarchy, this country and Holland ought to remain quiet as long as it is possible to do so, even with some degree of forbearance and tolerance beyond what would in other circumstances have been judged right.[46]

Even as he wrote, Dumouriez's army was routing the Austrians at Jemappes and was opening the way for the conquest of Belgium. Now the pace of events accelerated rapidly in one of those intense but short-winded bursts of activity so characteristic of the period. Almost every day a courier arrived with news of French victories: on 14 November Dumouriez entered Brussels, by the end of the month his troops were hard up against the Dutch frontier. Indeed, technically they had crossed it. On the 16th the Executive Council in Paris had proclaimed the opening of the river Scheldt (closed to international shipping *de facto* since the late sixteenth century and *de jure* since 1648); on the 20th that decision had been confirmed by the National Convention; on the 23rd French gunboats brushed their way past Dutch objections on their way to capture Antwerp. Just to make matters worse, also on 16 November the Executive Council had ordered French generals to pursue the defeated Austrians to wherever they might seek refuge.[47]

With one half of the Low Countries conquered and the other half in imminent danger of conquest, the British could no longer remain passive observers of continental events. No sooner was news of Jemappes in their hands than a declaration was sent to the Dutch government with a firm assurance of British support in the event of foreign invasion or domestic subversion.[48] As Pitt told a Cabinet colleague, the Marquis of Stafford, a war was the last thing Great Britain wanted, but the Dutch had to be supported. Moreover, he added, the best way to avoid conflict was to leave the French in no doubt as to British resolution to honour treaty obligations to an ally.[49] His reasoning was sound, but any chance of success was defeated by the slow pace of international communication. News of this *démarche* did not reach Paris until more than a week later, by which time the decisions to open the Scheldt, to engage in hot pursuit of the enemy and to offer assistance to all foreign peoples seeking to regain their liberty had all been taken and ratified.[50]

For the time being, the French armies remained poised but motionless on the Dutch frontier. So it was the opening of the Scheldt which became the formal bone of contention. Undoubtedly the French action was in breach of a whole string of international treaties reaching back to the Peace of Westphalia of 1648. Yet the British trumpeting about the sanctity of treaties which now followed was more than a little hypocritical. When it had suited them in the past, notably in 1780 and 1784–85, they had not just countenanced the opening of the Scheldt, they had positively encouraged it.[51] Moreover, no one supposed that the Scheldt itself was of much account. The man on the spot, Auckland, told Grenville on 28 November:

> With respect to the affair of the *Escaut* [Scheldt], the conduct of France is offensive, and is certainly meant to be so; and the rights of the [Dutch] Republic are indisputable, and I think it a point likely to awaken the people to a just sense of injury. But I do not believe that the navigation contended for is a point of much real importance: the channel of the river has long been bad for navigation, and it is secretly supposed that the Republic could at any time totally spoil it.[52]

If the intrinsic value of the Scheldt opening was of no consequence, as a symbol of French designs on the United Provinces it had a potent significance. Those designs were real enough. On 20 November Dumouriez wrote to the French envoy at The Hague, de Maulde: 'I count on carrying liberty to the Batavians [Dutch] as I have done to the Belgians; also that the Revolution will take place in Holland so that things will return to the state they were in 1788.'[53] Nor was that the private ambition of a maverick general. Three days later, none other than the foreign minister, Lebrun, told Dumouriez: 'To the glory of having liberated the Belgian Catholics, I hope you will add that of delivering their Batavian brothers from the yoke of the Stadholder.'[54] The British were well aware of these aggressive plans, for Dumouriez's letter to de Maulde had been intercepted by the Dutch and a copy had been sent to London, arriving on 26 November.[55] Through their envoy in London, Chauvelin, the French also announced officially that they regarded the guarantee of the Dutch constitution given by the British in 1788 as a 'manifest outrage' on the inviolable rights of the Dutch nation and consequently as null and void.[56]

It is difficult to see how the British government could have avoided a confrontation. A stark choice had been presented: abandon the Dutch to their fate, or fight. Certainly Pitt and Grenville concluded that the French were trying to force them into declaring war. On hearing of the National Convention's decrees of 20 November, Grenville wrote to Auckland: 'There is, I am afraid, little doubt that the whole is a concerted plan to drive us to extremities.'[57] Orders were issued to increase the number of seamen from 16,000 to 20,000, a bounty was declared for recruits and all 13 guardships were made ready for war service.[58] Retreat was made more difficult by a formal request for assistance from the government of the United Provinces on 29 November.[59]

The ground was also prepared for adhesion to the Austro-Prussian coalition. Shortly after learning of the rout at Jemappes, orders were sent to the British chargé d'affaires at Vienna to make inquiries about Austrian plans.[60] As the Austrians realised, there was acute anxiety in London that they would abandon Belgium as indefensible and switch their main military effort to the Rhineland.[61] As the likelihood of war with France increased, so did British cordiality grow. From being treated with the chilly disdain that came so naturally to Pitt and his even less congenial cousin Grenville, the Austrian ambassador, Count Stadion, now found himself overwhelmed with affectionate attention. So overwhelmed indeed, that on 7 December he took the unusual and expensive step of sending a special courier back to Vienna with a long account of a long interview he had had with Grenville on the previous day. The foreign secretary had told him how much he regretted the mutual animosity which had marked Austro-British relations over the past few years and how much he hoped for improvement. Cordiality, candour and harmony were required, he went on, if the danger presently threatening all European countries with ruin was to be dealt with.[62]

THE HOME FRONT IN GREAT BRITAIN AND IRELAND

Until this point, early December 1792, all the important decisions in Great Britain had been taken by just two men: Pitt and Grenville. Of course they were careful to inform and indeed to consult their king, but it does not appear, that George III altered their policy in any way. Although prone to apoplectic outbursts against the Revolution, his views on what should actually be done corresponded closely with those of his ministers. In September 1792 he was still insisting that there could be no question of intervening in continental affairs; after the events of November he was equally insistent that the French must not be allowed to take control of the Low Countries.[63]

With the backing of the King, Pitt and Grenville might take their country to the brink of war, but in practical terms only Parliament could take the plunge, not least because of its control of taxation. But Parliament was in recess and was not due to reassemble until the middle of January. Its meeting was then brought forward by the government's decision to embody parts of the militia, for by an Act of 1786 the summoning of Parliament was now required within fourteen days of that decision.[64] At once a furious controversy erupted. The radical Whigs believed that the official reason for the mobilisation of the militia – the growing unrest up and down the country – was just a device. What the government really wanted, they believed, was to engineer an early return of Parliament so that they could have an early war with France. Charles James Fox expostulated: 'If they mention danger of *Insurrection,* or rather . . . of *Rebellion,* . . . I shall grow savage, and not think a French *lanterne* too bad for them.'[65]

A very important issue was thus raised, which went well beyond the limits of inter-party conflict. Was the government preparing for war with France to defend legitimate national interests? Or was the government seeking through war an opportunity to split the Whig opposition and to crush the radicals outside Parliament? Or, to use a more modern formulation, was this a case of the primacy of foreign policy (*Primat der Aussenpolitik*) or of domestic policy (*Primat der Innenpolitik*)? The nature, extent and intensity of popular unrest in the British Isles has been the subject of a huge number of books and articles. All this current section can hope to do is to summarise its chief characteristics and relate them to the development of British foreign policy.[66]

It is clear that until 1792 radical political activity outside Parliament was of little consequence, at least so far as the government was concerned. The major outbreak of popular violence had been the 'Church and King' riots *against* radicals at Birmingham in July 1791. George III was more popular than he had ever been: in the spring of 1789, just as the crown was beginning to slip from the head of his French colleague, he received an unprecedented number of loyal addresses from right across the land congratulating him on his recovery from illness.[67] The associations founded to press for political reform were small in size, élitist in composition and decorous in tone. The most important of them, the Society for Constitutional Information (often known simply as 'The Constitutional Society'), was typical in charging its members a guinea on entrance and an annual subscription of five guineas, thus confining its constituency to the wealthy.[68] Average attendance at its meetings was only 30 and only 133 new members joined between April 1791 and May 1794.[69]

During the first half of 1792, however, agitation increased sharply. In November of the previous year, the first of a new kind of political association had been founded at Sheffield. For the first time, a movement for the enfranchisement of working men had been founded *by* working men. No longer was it felt necessary to seek the patronage of a social superior or parliamentary party. Its success was immediate and dramatic: the Sheffield group claimed a membership of over 200 in January 1792, 1,500 in March, 2,400 in May and 2,500 in June, a truly impressive total in a city with a total population of fewer than 30,000.[70]

More important still was the foundation of an equivalent group in London in January 1792 – the London Corresponding Society. This too expanded at a speed which advertised the popularity of its demand for annual parliaments and universal manhood suffrage. With an entrance fee of a shilling and a weekly subscription of just one penny, it was within the reach of every working man. In April 1792 its founder, Thomas Hardy, claimed about 70 members. By November, following a great surge in recruitment in the autumn, there were about 800 committed militants, a general membership of 1,200 and up to 5,000–6,000 'hearers'.[71] The society also had affiliated branches across the length and breadth of the country, from Portsmouth to Edinburgh.[72] Even agricultural centres such as Tewkesbury, Hertford and Sherborne had their own versions,[73] although this will seem barely credible to anyone familiar with that last-named symbol of soporific rural gentility. The emergence of these plebeian groups was accompanied and assisted by a resurgence in the fortunes of the Constitutional Society. Revitalised by the veteran reformer John Horne Tooke, it came to play a crucial role in coordinating the activities of the various extra-parliamentary groups.[74]

Demands for the reform of Parliament were nothing new, of course. During the last few years of the American War, there had been a sustained attempt to expand the franchise and eliminate some of the more obtrusive anomalies of the British parliamentary system. What made this new campaign so much more alarming to the establishment was the increased involvement of the lower classes, the creation of a national network of radical associations – and their avowed association with Tom Paine. One of the earliest projects of the Sheffield Constitutional Society was the publication of a cheap edition of Paine's *The Rights of Man* and all the other radical societies made a point of propagating his views.[75] Partly thanks to their efforts, a truly phenomenal number of copies was sold: perhaps as many as 200,000 by the end of 1792.[76] But the threat of Paine lay as much in what he said as in the huge numbers he said it to. Especially in part two of *The Rights of Man*, published in February 1792, he added to the traditional demands for political change a much more subversive programme of social upheaval. Among other things, he predicted the imminent demise of both the monarchy and the aristocracy.

Like most great propagandists, Paine was a very poor prophet. Yet the authorities could not know that almost two centuries later both the monarchy and the aristocracy would be still comfortably in place. In May 1792 they decided to act: the printer of *The Rights of Man* was prosecuted, Paine was charged with seditious libel and a royal proclamation 'for the preventing of seditious meetings and writings' was issued. Neither the radical challenge nor the government's response should be over-interpreted. If Eric Hobsbawm perhaps overdoes it when he describes Paine's political proposals as 'almost ridiculously moderate', he is quite right that Paine turned out to be just a moderate Girondin when he went to France and was the only member of the National Convention to fight openly against the death sentence on Louis XVI.[77] The plebeian societies which helped to propagate his views studiously eschewed revolutionary methods. Persuasion, not violence, was the only way forward, claimed Thomas Hardy: 'We conceive that the permanency of a reform must be founded on the acquiescence of the public, who, after maturely deliberating on everything proposed, shall have found the plan the most useful and the best that could possibly have been laid down.'[78] In the succinct formulation of Donald Read, the reforming associations were 'a-parliamentary but not *anti*-parliamentary'.[79]

Nor should the government's concern at the events of the first half of 1792 be overestimated. The royal proclamation of 21 May was more precautionary than alarmist and may well have been designed primarily to encourage the split which was currently threatening the Whig opposition.[80] The general opinion of the government was that British public opinion was generally sound, although it might need attention from time to time, to keep it that way. Auckland expressed this attitude well when he wrote to Sir Robert Murray Keith, the British ambassador at Vienna, just four days before the royal proclamation was issued: 'The bulk – under which word I comprise *nineteen-twentieths* of this nation, is contented and decidedly anti-Gallican; and against all levelling or innovating ideas, and duly and fully sensible of their own unexampled prosperity. With such materials, and so vigilant a government, I feel no uneasiness, though the times are *very mad*.'[81]

Real anxiety that continental lunacy would cross the Channel was reawakened in the autumn of 1792, by the oldest *provocateur* of them all: bad weather. Although the harvest of 1789 had been poor, those of 1790 and 1791 had been good and very good respectively, with the result that the price of food fell from 1790 until the middle of 1792.[82] The economy as a whole too was buoyant during the same period.[83] All that changed from the middle of 1792 when what is thought to be a typical British summer put large parts of the country 'in a vortex of mud, clay and water'.[84] The harvest was correspondingly poor and prices rose rapidly. Moreover, this agrarian crisis both coincided with and exacerbated a general recession which led to a fall in trade and a rash of bankruptcies.[85]

For the government it was particularly unfortunate that this downturn in the economy coincided with an upturn in the fortunes of the French Revolution. The news of its salvation by the victory of Valmy reinvigorated and multiplied its British supporters. From one end of the British Isles to the other, radicals took to the streets to demonstrate their joy.[86] The London Corresponding Society more than doubled its membership in a month and its provincial offshoots grew both in number and in size.[87] The political demonstrations combined with a wave of bread riots and strikes to convey the impression of a country on the verge of revolution. As one of Pitt's agents reported at the end of September, 'there never was a period when mischievous persons could find the people more ripe for riot of the most horrid kind'.[88] Representative of the change in attitude this produced among the social élite was the sharp change in the assessment of public opinion made by Anthony Storer, one of Auckland's correspondents. In July 1792 he observed that the 'nonsensical projects' of the French had created general satisfaction with the existing British constitution; just three months later he was detecting a republican mood 'everywhere in the country' and was lamenting the pernicious influence of Paine.[89]

As the rain continued to fall and popular violence continued to rise, the government also became anxious about the deteriorating situation in the Celtic colonies. They had every right to be. As Wolfe Tone recorded in his autobiography, the French Revolution and the propagation of its principles by Paine 'changed in an instant the politics of Ireland'.[90] British politicans such as Henry Dundas, the home secretary, might cheerfully suppose the Irish to be 'too bigoted' to respond to the anti-clerical French,[91] but by the autumn of 1792 there were clear signs that for many their sense of grievance was strong enough to overcome religious scruples. In the course of 1791 the Roman Catholic Committee divided, as a younger and more radical group agitated for cooperation with Protestant dissenters to present a united front to London. A sign of the times was the appointment by the Committee in 1792 of Wolfe Tone, a Protestant lawyer, as their salaried secretary. It was just his ambition to unite all Irishmen to agitate for radical political change, and to that end he had helped to form the United Irishmen the previous year.[92] In the autumn of 1792 conditions similar to those in England brought a similar increase in radical activity. On 17 November the lord lieutenant, the Earl of Westmorland, asked for 11,000 reinforcements and early in the following month his chief secretary reported to London: 'Our situation is become extremely critical. Be assured that it is a matter of deep concern to us all and that it goes to the complete overturning of the Constitution.'[93]

Across the water in Scotland too, discrimination by the Anglican establishment had created special grievances.[94] If Meikle was probably right to assign local causes to the wave of agitation which swept across the country in the autumn, it was strong enough to cause the government real concern.[95] There was also ample evidence of a link with contemporary events in France, whether it was shouts of 'liberty, equality and no king!' at Perth, the erection of liberty trees to celebrate Dumouriez's entry into Brussels, the meeting of a 'General Convention' at Edinburgh or reports from the Highlands that copies of Paine's *The Rights of Man*, translated into Gaelic, were to be found 'in the hands of all the common people'.[96] Nor was all of this imaginative hearsay. No less a person than the home secretary, Henry Dundas, was in Scotland throughout this period and was sending back to Pitt and Grenville reports whose tone by late November was beginning to border on panic: 'If the spirit of liberty and equality continues to spread with the same rapidity it has done since the failure of the Duke of Brunswick . . . it will be in vain for any military that can possibly be spared from this country to quell that spirit which ferments at such a rate that it must break out into open sedition.'[97]

The links between this resurgence of British and Irish agitation and the headquarters of revolution were plain for all to see. The large and noisy colony of expatriate radicals in Paris presented an address to the National Convention on 24 November urging the swift implementation of the Edict of Fraternity passed five days earlier.[98] In September they had been joined by none other than Tom Paine, who had come over to take his seat in the Convention and also to evade his impending trial for seditious libel. Not unreasonably, the Foreign Office concluded that he was engaged in preparing subversive literature for distribution throughout the British Isles.[99] Belief in the international nature of subversion was strengthened by the stream of congratulatory addresses from British societies which flowed across the Channel. This was a common means of communication dating right back to the start of the Revolution, but in the autumn of 1792 the tone became a good deal sharper. An address from the London Corresponding Society contained an overt promise of resistance if Britain should join the counter-revolutionary coalition, while the Society for Constitutional Information looked forward to a British revolution: 'After the example given by France, Revolutions will become easy. Reason is about to make a rapid Progress, and it would not be extraordinary if in a much less space of time than can be imagined the French should send addresses of congratulation to a national convention of England.'[100] Simultaneously, more concrete evidence of solidarity was supplied in the shape of money, arms and ammunition sent over to help the French war effort.[101]

Whether in the form of delegations or addresses, British demonstrations of solidarity were given a warm and well-publicised welcome by the National Convention. More alarming to the government in London was the knowledge that several secret agents had been sent over from Paris to encourage this sense of fraternity with propaganda.[102] Particularly provocative was the reception in November by the official French envoy, Chauvelin, of deputations from the Norwich Revolution Society, the Manchester Constitutional Society, the London Independent Whigs and the London Corresponding Society.[103] Taken in conjunction with the National Convention's Edict of Fraternity, Pitt and his colleagues could only conclude that the French were engaged in a concerted campaign to subvert the British constitution.[104]

Their response gathered momentum as the challenge increased. The royal proclamation against seditious writings of 21 May was followed by reorganisation of the London police in June and the construction of barracks to keep troops isolated from contamination by radicals.[105] In October local authorities were reminded that they could use those troops to maintain public order; in November Treasury solicitors were told to organise a campaign to prosecute seditious libel; in December those solicitors appointed agents in most districts to gather the necessary intelligence.[106]

Given the rudimentary administrative apparatus at its disposal, the government could not have hoped to contain the radical threat by repression alone. Also needed was a campaign to mobilise public opinion behind the monarchy, the traditional constitution and the social establishment. As Grenville wrote to his brother, the Marquis of Buckingham: 'The hands of Government must be strengthened if the country is to be saved; but, above all, the work must not be left to the hands of Government, but every man must put his shoulder to it, according to his rank and station in life, or it will not be done.'[107] The chief chosen instrument was the 'Association for the Preservation of Liberty and Property against Republicans and Levellers' (APLP), founded on 20 November 1792 by the police official John Reeves. Although given an air of spontaneity, it was essentially government-sponsored. Its task was to impede radical meetings and publications, to initiate the prosecution of sedition, to assist the authorities in dealing with riots and to circulate royalist propaganda.[108] Its success was phenomenal, making even the fastest-growing radical societies seem positively sluggish by comparison. By the end of November, there was a branch in almost every parish in London and it was spreading throughout the country at corresponding speed. Within a very short time about 2,000 branches had been founded.[109] It was, quite simply, by far the most successful of all the myriad extra-parliamentary associations founded during the late eighteenth century.[110]

No doubt the powerful support given by the government, the judiciary and the Church (even the SPCK helped to distribute propaganda) accounts in part for the APLP's dramatic growth, but the fact remains that there was a great well of loyalist sentiment waiting to be tapped. As Roy Porter has observed: 'For every bourgeois Friend of the People, there were a dozen friends of property, and a score more who just raised their goblets to trade.'[111] Moreover, for every radical who was inspired by Valmy or Jemappes, there were many more who were alienated by the September Massacres. In May 1792, the liberal reformer Sir Samuel Romilly wrote that, despite everything, the French Revolution was 'the most glorious event, and the happiest for mankind that has ever taken place since human affairs have been recorded'; in September he wrote to a French correspondent: 'one might as well think of establishing a republic of tigers in some forest of Africa as of maintaining a free government among such monsters.'[112] For many, the trial of Louis XVI, which began on 10 December, and his subsequent execution on 21 January 1793, proved the last straw. The most eloquent expression of this ultimate disillusionment was given by William Cowper: 'I will tell you what the French have done. They have made me weep for a King of France, which I never thought to do, and they have made me sick of the very name of liberty, which I never thought to be.'[113] Particularly gratifying for the government was the way in which this loyalist surge drowned party rivalries. At Leicester, for example, a city notorious for its radicalism, there was a public meeting on 22 December of both government supporters and opposition Whigs which agreed on a joint proclamation to support the present form of government and to repress riots.[114]

The relevance of this digression on the domestic political scene in Great Britain should now be apparent. Not only is it relevant, it is crucial to an understanding of the course of British policy between November 1792 and January 1793 (and, as will be seen later, crucial to an understanding of the course of French policy in the same period).

The coincidence of the National Convention's Decree of Fraternity of 19 November with the intensification of radical agitation in Britain convinced Pitt and his colleagues that the French were set on a path of international subversion and, more specifically, war with Great Britain. Consequently, it persuaded them to make a positive response by giving assurances to the Dutch, by protesting in the most forthright manner about the closure of the Scheldt and the 19 November decree and by launching a campaign inside the country to rally loyalist opinion. The immediate and spectacular success of the last of those initiatives then gave emphatic reassurance as to the state of public opinion and banished any fears that the conduct of the war which now seemed inevitable might be paralysed by domestic unrest. If the APLP had failed, if the momentum of the radical societies could not have been checked, the British government might well have had to accept what terms the French would offer over the Low Countries.

In the event, its hand was strengthened sufficiently to allow the maximum policy to be pursued with confidence. Not only the success of the APLP but also the reports which streamed in from this or that local dignitary presented a picture of Francophobe loyalism.[115] On 18 December the under-secretary of state at the Foreign Office, James Bland Burges, wrote to Auckland: 'The spirits of our people are higher than you can imagine. There appears to be but one sentiment throughout the country – that of loyalty to the King – affection to the existing constitution – ardour to support it – and an earnest desire to go to war with France!'[116] But the definitive statement of the British position at this stage came from the foreign secretary himself, written also to Auckland and sent out by the same courier on the same day:

> Nothing can exceed the good dispositions of this country in the present moment. The change within the last three weeks is little less than miraculous. God grant that it may last long enough to enable us to act with that vigour which can alone preserve us. If this disposition flags, and the country relapses into indifference or fear, we shall still be municipalised [revolutionised i.e.]; but if we can maintain the present spirit, it will enable us to talk to France in the tone which British Ministers ought to use under such circumstances as the present, and to crush the seditious disposition here.[117]

Just as it was becoming clear that opinion 'out of doors' was sound, support for the government inside Parliament was also swelling, as the split within the Whig opposition widened beyond the point of no return. This had been a long and complicated process, but if its course can only be summarised, it cannot be neglected, for the outcome exercised an important influence on the government at a crucial stage.[118] The first sign that events in France would prove divisive appeared in Parliament in February 1790, when Fox expressed his mild approval of the Revolution and Burke expressed his vehement rejection.[119] This division caused 'pain inexpressible' (Burke) and 'a concern of mind which it was almost impossible to describe' (Fox) but ended with the former declaring that 'henceforth, his hon. friend and he were separated in politics'.[120]

Yet neither this incident nor the publication of Burke's *Reflections on the Revolution in France* in November 1790, nor the celebrated exchange on 6 May 1791 – when Fox burst into tears in the House of Commons at Burke's announcement that their personal friendship was over too – could divide the opposition as a whole. Burke remained an isolated outsider, spurned by both government and former associates alike. As Pitt commented later, Burke was always right – but six months before anyone else, which for practical purposes was as bad as being six months too late.[121] Such was the force of Fox's personal charm and parliamentary oratory that he experienced little difficulty in 1790 and 1791 in holding the opposition group together. His triumph in the debates on the Ochakov débâcle in March 1791 and the government's acute embarrassment advertised for all his continuing dominant authority.[122]

Behind the façade of unity, however, Burke's dire warnings about the implications of the French Revolution for British politics and society began to erode the foundations of Whig unity. Gradually it became clear that Fox differed from most of his colleagues in his location of the enemy. Still obsessed by the events of 1782–84, he saw George III as a much graver threat to liberty than plebeian agitation. As he wrote to Earl Fitzwilliam on 16 March 1792: 'Our apprehensions are raised by different objects; *you* seem to dread the prevalence of Paine's opinions (which in fact I detest as much as you do) while I am much more afraid of the total annihilation of all principles of liberty and resistance, an event which I am sure you would be as sorry to see as I.'[123] From his country seat at Wentworth Woodhouse, Fitzwilliam was well placed to observe events at Sheffield, the most radical and turbulent of all English cities, and the more he saw the more he was alarmed.[124] As the Revolution in France moved left and as the radical movement in Britain gathered momentum from late 1791 onwards, his anxiety was shared by most other Whig leaders. In effect, the Whigs were splitting into two groups of unequal size, with the majority holding to the traditional ground occupied by Burke and only a minority accompanying Fox into the uncharted territory of support for the Revolution. As Leslie Mitchell has shrewdly observed, the breach between Burke and Fox broke the intellectual back of the Whigs, for henceforth each man could represent a different variety of Whiggery and every Whig would have to choose which of the two was the more representative.[125]

The first clear sign that this choice could not be delayed indefinitely came in April 1792, when a group of young Whig peers and MPs (Grey, Lambton, Tierney, Lauderdale) joined with two veterans (Sheridan and Francis) to found the Association of the Friends of the People, to press for parliamentary reform and to liaise with the extra-parliamentary groups working for the same end. Their initiative evoked angry protests from their more conservative colleagues. One of the most influential, William Windham, expostulated: 'I can consider it as nothing but the first big drops of that storm, which having already deluged France is driving fast to this country.'[126] Pitt responded at once, seeking to turn the rift into a chasm, with an offer to the nominal Whig leader, the Duke of Portland, of a coalition. Angry though they might have been, the Whigs were not yet ready to come to terms with the old enemy. Fox, who had not been party to the foundation of the Association of the Friends of the People and did not join, was able to wave his celebrated 'magic wand' of personal charm and hold the faltering party together.[127] Another approach by Pitt later in the summer was also rejected.

In the event, it was not until 1794 that Portland and his colleagues could bring themselves to form a coalition with Pitt, but a more informal alliance had existed for a long time before that. The timing was of great importance. After the abolition of the monarchy, the September Massacres and the military successes of the Revolution had alarmed the conservative Whigs still further, on 13 November Burke and Windham called on Pitt to tell him that if the government were prepared to take firm action against the French, many Whigs would lend their support. Indeed, it is clear that they were a good deal more eager for war than Pitt or Grenville. This visit came, of course, at a critical moment, just as the British response to the French conquest of Belgium was being considered. As Sir Herbert Butterfield commented: 'The intervention of the opposition reinforced the government, therefore, at what transpired to be the pivotal moment.'[128] Four months later Windham himself wrote of the interview: 'It is not impossible that on that little circumstance much of the subsequent conduct of government, much in consequence of that of the dispositions and plans of foreign powers, and much therefore in the end of the fate of Europe may have turned.'[129]

There was more of the same sort of encouragement for the government to come. When Parliament reassembled at the beginning of December, the Whig leaders decided not to divide the House of Lords on the address of thanks for the King's Speech. They did not want to divide the Commons either, but there Fox held sway and he was not to be persuaded. His insistence on a vote only exposed himself to a humiliating demonstration of the weakness of his position, for his motion was defeated by 290 to 50. Moreover, as the conservative Whig Lord Malmesbury commented, many of those 50 voted for Fox out of a sense of personal loyalty and affection, not because they shared his view of the impending war with France.[130] Although the Duke of Portland could not be induced to dissociate himself formally from Fox, the great majority of Whig peers and MPs lined up behind the government.

Consequently, the division of the opposition was of immense significance in the origins of the war. In March and April 1791 Pitt had been stopped from going to war against Russia over Ochakov largely by the strength of the parliamentary opposition.[131] That crisis had brought his ministry close to defeat and it was not an experience he cared to repeat. If his majority had been similarly fragile in December 1792, he could not possibly have adopted the resolute policy that he did. In the event, with the great majority of both houses squarely behind him, his only political danger lay in not appearing resolute enough. As this parliamentary support was reinforced by opinion out of doors too, he and his government were not just enabled to take a firm line against the French, they were actually obliged to do so.

THE IRRESISTIBLE FORCE MEETS THE IMMOVABLE OBJECT

Meanwhile in France, such political stability was patently absent. Both in the provinces and at Paris, internecine conflict of one kind or another was rife. That did not lead to pessimism about the prospects for war with Great Britain. On the contrary, both in government and the National Convention the belief prevailed that the British would crumble in just the same manner as the Austrians and the Prussians. In part, this confidence derived from a general belief in the invincibility of a revolutionary nation-in-arms (see p. 108), recently reinforced by the victories at Valmy and Jemappes. The foreign minister, Lebrun, wrote to one of his agents in London on 11 November: 'It is very certain that our principles will penetrate everywhere sooner or later of their own accord, precisely because these principles are those of sound reason, for which the largest part of Europe is now ready.'[132] With specific reference to Britain, however, it was lent extra cogency by what appeared to be the imminent collapse of this new enemy as a result of internal revolution.

It seems that no great power can bring itself to believe that a rival regime enjoys popular support. Revolutionary France was no exception. Every incident of unrest in Great Britain and Ireland, every expression of opposition, was puffed up out of all proportion. To return to Burke's image (see p. 132), the grasshoppers' chinks were amplified and the cattle were ignored. All the numerous official and secret agents in London during the autumn of 1792 reported to Lebrun just what he wanted to hear: that Great Britain was on the verge of revolution, that Pitt was about to be dismissed and the Francophile Fox was about to take his place. For example, on 27 November

Chauvelin wrote that there was financial panic in the City, fighting in Ireland and a naval mutiny at Shields.[133] In the words of one of his clandestine colleagues, Noël: 'To the eyes of an outside observer, England offers precisely the same prospect as France did in 1789.'[134] Given the current surge in membership of the radical clubs, the celebrations to mark French victories, the fraternal addresses sent to the National Convention, and so on, such a conclusion was certainly understandable. It was no less erroneous – and fatal: 'Failure to understand the non-revolutionary character of the English reform movement must, indeed, be rated as the fundamental misconception inherent in the Brissotin willingness to extend the war.'[135]

Back in France, these distortions found a ready audience in Lebrun, Brissot, Dumouriez and everyone else concerned with the conduct of foreign policy. On 29 November Lebrun offered the following sanguine assessment: 'If the cabinet of St James adopts a policy of severity and resistance, it will provoke inevitably an insurrection, if not on a national, then at least on a partial scale, including all the towns surrounding the capital. The results would be fatal for the monarchy and the government.' Moreover, that would be just the start, for the situation throughout the British Isles was so combustible that only a spark was needed to ignite England, Scotland and Ireland simultaneously.[136] The complementary obverse of this low opinion of British resistance was a renewed faith in the inexhaustibility of French resources. Now that every Frenchman could be turned into a soldier within six months, now that the French armies could be financed by the Germans, Belgians and Sardinians they had liberated, there seemed no limit to French potential.[137]

These dual convictions of British weakness and French strength prompted Lebrun and his colleagues to opt for a maximalist approach: the annexation of Belgium and the subjugation of the United Provinces. Dumouriez was confident that he could knock out the Dutch in a blitzkrieg so rapid that the British would not have time to respond. Once that had been done, the acquisition of the Dutch navy would make France safe against maritime retaliation, might even open the way to the seizure of the British overseas possessions.[138] Just as the general was dreaming those dreams, in late November, a French diplomat, de Maulde, was at The Hague discussing with Auckland and the Dutch government a general peace plan. His account of the negotiations was so distorted as to convince the French that the British and their Dutch allies were so feeble and nervous that they would do anything to stay out of a war.[139] So full steam ahead could be ordered: the British would almost certainly back down without a fight – as they had done over Ochakov – but if they did not, no matter.[140]

This low opinion of the potential enemy was heartily reciprocated. The British had not expected any serious French resistance to the Austro-Prussian expeditionary force, so the victories of the autumn had come as a great surprise. This setback notwithstanding, it was still expected that France would collapse, more because of internal chaos than allied invasion.[141] The more encouraging news from the German front in December (see p. 156) encouraged the belief that the Prussians and Austrians were now taking the war seriously and that the tide was on the turn. The British were well aware that the French held them in low esteem and so were all the more determined to make a stand. As Grenville wrote to Auckland on 4 December:

> It is clear to me that the French rely, in the present moment, on their intrigues in the interior of both countries [Great Britain and the United Provinces], and that they imagine they have brought us to a condition of inability to resist any demands which they may make. This is above all others a reason for firmness in the present moment, and for resisting, while the power of resistance is yet in our hands.[142]

British confidence was based on the knowledge that the Royal Navy was better prepared for war than at any time in the past.[143] During the ten years of Pitt's administration, the navy had been reformed, refitted and expanded. Between 1783 and 1793 43 major warships – 'ships of the line' – had been built, 10 more were on the stocks or had been ordered and 85 had been repaired.[144] As during the same period the nation's finances had been reorganised on a sound footing, British confidence in their naval superiority was understandable. In the letter to Auckland quoted above, Grenville wrote: 'I have not expressed in my despatch all the security which we feel respecting the comparative state of our preparations with those of France, because it is unwise, in a public paper, so to commit oneself. But to you privately I may say, that our confidence on that head is very great indeed.'[145]

As it turned out, this assessment of relative naval strength was more or less justified. Where the British went badly awry was in their analysis of the French position on the Continent. Just like the Austrians or the Prussians before them, they failed to understand the nature and extent of the forces unleashed by the Revolution. France was patently bankrupt and in a state of political and administrative chaos verging on civil war. So, according to the rules, she should have collapsed and/or made peace. It was too late by the time Pitt and his colleagues came to realise that the revolutionaries had torn up the old regime's rule-book. For the time being, everyone believed with *The Times* that the war would be short.[146] The most authoritative version of government thinking was given by Pitt himself in an interview with Lord Loughborough (a conservative Whig who had just accepted office as lord chancellor) on 20 January 1793:

> Pitt saw it [war] was inevitable, and that the sooner it was begun the better. That we might possess ourselves of the French islands; that the nation now was disposed for war, which might not be the case six weeks hence. That we were in much greater forwardness than the French. They had only six ships

of the line in the Mediterranean – we upwards of twenty; that he had two millions ready, and that he trusted the surplus of the permanent revenue would be 600,000 1. a-year. That the Dutch were quite right, and in earnest; that Russia was willing to go all lengths; that Spain was ready to join, and that all the little Powers only waited our giving the signal. [147]

With each side convinced that the other would collapse and that the war would be short and easy, the outbreak of hostilities could not be long delayed. In both the National Convention and Parliament a gale of bellicose oratory blew their respective members towards a final confrontation. In the former, the proceedings were very much shorter than they had been before the declaration of war against Austria. By December 1792 the Convention had too many other problems to deal with – notably the organisation of the conquests in Belgium and Germany and the trial of the King – to be able to devote much time to this new impending conflict. Moreover, reading the major speeches on the subject, by Kersaint on 1 January and by Brissot on 12 January and 1 February, evokes a strong feeling of *déjà vu*. Although Anglophobia had taken the place of Austrophobia, most of the other arguments for war are very familiar: the British are going to attack us anyway, so we should get our blow in first; they have treated us and our Revolution with outrageous contempt and our national pride demands vengeance; they will be disabled by their huge National Debt; the common people, especially the Irish and the Scots, will rise in our support; the Revolution is opposed only by peers, priests and plutocrats, but it is not they who will be manning the British warships; we need not fear war, only uncertainty, so let us declare it now. [148] There was also a strong dose of nihilism to bring the deputies to their feet: Kersaint reminded them of Cortez burning his boats in full view of his army on the shore of Mexico. [149]

In the British Parliament the debates were much longer and livelier, not least because there was determined opposition to the war from a small but distinguished group of peers and MPs. In the House of Lords, Lansdowne, Lauderdale and Stanhope, in the House of Commons, Grey, Sheridan and Fox all struggled valiantly to prevent war. But the quality of their oratory was more than matched by the government's partisans: Grenville and Loughborough in the Lords, Burke, Windham, Dundas and Pitt in the Commons. [150] As one former supporter of Fox after another rose to declare, with varying degrees of cordiality, support for government policy, war became that much more likely.

Conditions were of course very different from those prevailing in the French legislature. The parliamentary proceedings were much more decorous, the rhetorical style much less demagogic and popular participation was conspicuous by its absence. Yet in many respects the arguments advanced and the prejudices displayed were mirror-images of their French counterparts, even if the mirror had the odd distorting crack. There was the same xenophobia, the same belief in a foreign conspiracy, the same belief in foreign subversion, the same belief in the other's imminent collapse, the same conviction that the war would be short and easy. While the French demanded an end to British control of the United Provinces, the British demanded that that country should never again fall into the hands of France. While the French attacked the English for their oppression of the Irish and the Scots, the British attacked the French for the September Massacres and other instances of domestic tyranny. The parallels must not be overdrawn. None of that terrifying nihilism surfaced in the parliamentary debates and there was what is thought to be a characteristically British obsession with property. As Burke put it, to the accompaniment of vocal approval:

> When the knowledge of these rights was diffused among the multitude, he could not but tremble for the consequences: nor indeed could he hear, without emotions of horror, the application made of them to property in frequent discussions of the French Revolution. It was this kind of application which caused most of the horrors of the French Revolution.[151]

The actual occasions for these debates – the address of thanks for the King's Speech, Fox's motion to send an envoy to France for direct negotiations, Grey's complaint about judicial discrimination against radicals, the Aliens Bill, and so on – were of little significance. What was important, so far as the origins of the war were concerned, was the opportunity presented to the government to make the divisions in the opposition irreconcilable and to demonstrate that the great majority of the propertied classes supported its resolute stand against France.

Meanwhile in France, December had been marked by a sudden change of fortune at the front in Germany and a consequent wavering in Paris. By the beginning of the month a reinforced Prussian army had begun a threatening counter-offensive, which scored an early success with the recapture of Frankfurt am Main on 2 December. The French armies, on the other hand, were being decimated by the return home of tens of thousands of volunteers who believed that the war had been won and had had enough of soldiering. No one supposed that this setback would be more than temporary, but for the time being prudence dictated a respite. Arguing that an immediate attack on the United Provinces would give the British an invaluable lever with which to mobilise public opinion, on 13 December 1792 Lebrun and the Executive Council ordered Dumouriez into winter quarters for the time being – although he was to hold himself ready to march at a moment's notice.[152]

The pause was only momentary. By this time the leaders of both executive and legislature, with Lebrun, Dumouriez and Brissot to the fore, were too publicly committed to be able to give an inch – or rather to be able to be *seen* to give an inch. So while they pursued secret negotiations in London and at The Hague to see whether the British might be induced to abandon the Low Countries without a fight, their public posture remained bellicose. On 19 December Lebrun delivered a highly provocative report to the National Convention on Franco-British relations, in the course of which – among other things – he demanded that Britain should cease its interference in Dutch affairs and threatened an appeal to the British people over the heads of the government.[153] The gist of this statement, suitably edited by Chauvelin, was then presented to Grenville on 27 December.

It elicited four days later a reply that was utterly intransigent, both in tone and substance, and which reflected the government's impregnable position in Parliament and newly won confidence in public opinion. Grenville made four main points: firstly, that Chauvelin was not recognised as an official French envoy, since all official communications with France had been suspended since the *journée* of 10 August. Secondly, the French 'explanation' of the Fraternity Decree of 19 November was rejected, for it had been contradicted by the National Convention's fêting of British fomenters of sedition and by the continued insistence on the right to interfere in the affairs of other countries. Thirdly, the unilateral decision to open the Scheldt was unacceptable, both for itself and for its implied rejection of all treaties which did not suit French interests: 'England never will consent that France shall arrogate the power of annulling at her pleasure, and under the pretence of a pretended natural right, of which she makes herself the only judge, the political system of Europe, established by solemn treaties, and guaranteed by the consent of all the powers.' Fourthly, and here Grenville came to the crux of the matter: 'This government, adhering to the maxims which it has followed for more than a century, will also never see with indifference, that France shall make herself, either directly or indirectly, sovereign of the Low Countries, or general arbitress of the rights and liberties of Europe.'[154]

From that point war was inevitable unless one or other side backed down. For the reasons discussed earlier, such a retreat was neither possible nor desired by either party. During January, as the National Convention busied itself with the trial and execution of the King, the semi-official clandestine negotiations continued, to as little purpose as before. No sooner did the news of the execution of 21 January reach London than Chauvelin was told to leave the country. No sooner did Chauvelin report back to the Executive Committee than the decision was taken to ask the National Convention to declare war. Primed by a dose of vintage Brissot, the deputies duly obliged without any debate on the main issue and with complete unanimity. It was also decided to carry out the earlier threat of a direct appeal to the British people, by means of an address to be composed by Barère, Fabre d'Eglantine – and Tom Paine.[155]

AN IDEOLOGICAL WAR?

As with the war of 1792, the war of 1793 owed little to any irreconcilable conflict between two opposing ideologies. British ministers positively welcomed the Revolution, not because they approved of revolutionary principles, but because they liked the revolutionary practice which had immobilised an old and feared rival. Not even such excesses as the abolition of the monarchy or such atrocities as the September Massacres could move them from a policy of strict neutrality. It was only when French power revived with a vengeance in the autumn of 1792 that neutrality made way for hostility. Such was the importance attached to the Low Countries – 'as necessary a part of this country as Kent', as Burke put it (see p. 47) – that no government that wished to stay in office could relinquish control without a fight. Moreover, for Pitt and his colleagues the region had a special significance. It had been the successful intervention in the United Provinces in September 1787 which had given them their first great diplomatic triumph and had made them correspondingly reluctant to see the prize snatched back by France. Belgium had been the occasion of another notable coup in 1790 when Habsburg authority – now suitably tempered by a pledge to respect the traditional constitution – was restored. No wonder then, that the French invasion of the latter and their threat to the former should have been resisted with such determination.

However unoriginal, the conventional view that it was concern for the Low Countries which turned British policy to active resistance to the Revolution must be confirmed.[156] The rival candidates have only a little to be said for them. Certainly, even before the war began, there was talk of 'compensations' and of the ease with which French West Indian islands could be conquered,[157] but equally certainly this was not a prime objective. As Grenville told Earl Gower in a private letter in August 1791: 'You may rest assured . . . that we are fully persuaded that the islands in the West Indies are not worth to us one year of that invaluable tranquillity which we are now enjoying.'[158] 'Compensations' played for the British the same sort of role as for the Austrians: not sufficient in themselves to justify war, but a welcome sweetener when it became unavoidable for other reasons. There is even less to be said for the Whig view that Pitt went to war to split the opposition.[159] That is a fine example of putting the cart before the horse, for – as was argued above – it was rather the case that Pitt was able to go to war *because* the Whigs were split. With such combative personalities as Fox and Burke, Sheridan and Windham, to do his work for him, for Pitt to have launched a war for this reason would have been an act of overshooting grotesquely incompatible with such a prudent personality.

More complex is the question of the role played by the threat of French subversion. That the resurgence of the radicals in the autumn of 1792, following the French military victories, caused real alarm to the government and to the social élites as a whole is undeniable. Indeed, one historian has written of a 'Great Fear' of men of property.[160] It is equally clear that Pitt and the rest of the government came to the conclusion that the French had launched a campaign to foment a revolution throughout the British Isles.[161] But while the fear and resentment this engendered made for hostility to France, it did not point to *war*. On the contrary, it was when the government was reassured about the state of public opinion that it could pursue a forward policy.

For the French, too, it was the fate of the Low Countries which was decisive. As late as the end of October 1792, Lebrun was still hoping for an *alliance* with Great Britain.[162] The rapid conquest of Belgium, and the knowledge that the United Provinces would drop into their laps like the rotten plum it was, put paid to that scheme. The temptation to avenge the humiliation of 1787 was now irresistible. In the three months which followed, several additional grievances were raised against the British and many hard words were spoken about their treatment of the Irish and the Scots, but no other issue of substance emerged.

In 1787 war had been avoided because the French had backed down, paralysed by bankruptcy and immobilised by lack of will. In 1793 neither side would back down because each believed victory was certain. Once again, it was the mutual miscalculation of their power relationship which took them past hostility and into war. Each over-estimated its own assets and underestimated those of the other; each underestimated its own problems and overestimated those of the other. It turned out that in fact they were more or less evenly balanced, and so the war which was to last less than twelve months (in the view of the British) or was to be over before it began (in the view of the French) dragged on for twenty-two years.

THE WAR BETWEEN FRANCE AND SPAIN

As a postcript, a brief account and analysis of the origins of the war between France and Spain, which broke out on 7 March 1793, will be attempted. With a common frontier, a common dynasty and a long-established alliance, it was natural that the Spanish should have taken a closer interest in what was happening in France than anyone else, except perhaps the Austrians, who were bound by similar geographical and familial ties. In addition, the sense of being the defenders of the true faith against the infidels of the north was still very strong.[163]

Indeed, it is likely that Charles IV was more upset by the National Assembly's attack on the Church than he was by the attack on his Bourbon cousin.[164] Consequently, the Revolution was greeted in Spain by a bevy of prophylactic legislation to prevent the contagion crossing the Pyrenees. More provocative was the hectoring tone adopted by the Spanish government when reacting to events in France. After the Flight to Varennes, the chief minister, Count Floridablanca, sent a most inflammatory note to the National Assembly, castigating its conduct, stressing Charles IV's concern for the fate of Louis XVI and threatening retaliation.[165] Even more trenchant was the language employed in the reply to Louis XVI's notification that he had 'accepted' the new constitution. With a refreshing but imprudent candour, Charles IV stated baldly that he did not believe that the acceptance had been voluntary, nor that the French king was in any sense free. For good measure, Floridablanca told the French ambassador that the other European powers had every right to take action against the Revolution:

> To think that the foreign powers ought not to intervene in these matters because they are the internal affairs of France is a great mistake. . . .War against France, given that this nation has succumbed to anarchy, is no less in conformity with the rights of nations than the action taken against criminals and rebels who usurp authority and seize the property of their fellow-citizens.[166]

Even by the standards of Kaunitz, this was undeniably strong language. Yet while it both reflected and exacerbated the intense ill-will which now marked Franco-Spanish relations, it did not lead to war. Every emotional outburst on the part of the Spanish was counterbalanced by the rational consideration that to translate that instinctive hostility into action was to court disaster. With an unsuccessful war against Morocco still dragging on, with a huge and growing budget deficit and, above all, with Great Britain thought to be waiting to pounce on the unprotected colonies, *raison d'état* demanded peace.[167] These pacific forces were strengthened greatly by the dismissal of Floridablanca in February 1792 and his replacement by the veteran Count Aranda. The new minister at once agreed to receive the envoy from the National Assembly and signalled his determination to remain neutral in the impending Austro-French conflict.[168]

In France, a similar mixture of verbal abuse and practical restraint was adopted. Every now and again, the National Assembly worked itself into a frenzy over the latest insulting note from Madrid or the latest act of discrimination against French citizens living or travelling in Spain, but retaliation never progressed beyond threats.[169] The definitive statement on this first phase of relations between the two countries was given by Ramond on 27 March 1792. In a relatively sober and well-balanced speech, he listed all the various grievances and points of conflict but concluded by arguing that they could be resolved best by negotiation. French commercial interests in the Mediterranean and the fact that war with Austria seemed certain were powerful advocates of peace.[170] The Assembly agreed and the executive was ordered to take the necessary diplomatic initiative.

This period of acrimonious coexistence was brought to a close by the *journée* of 10 August 1792 and the fall of the monarchy. At court, in the government and among the population at large, there was genuine and intense indignation. On 24 August the Council of State decided to join the Austro-Prussian coalition, a decision which was communicated to the other European powers on 4 September.[171] It was just as well that it took the Spanish so long to mobilise (ten months was the estimate of the war minister!),[172] because it gave a chance for second thoughts. When the decision of 24 August had been taken, the Austrians and Prussians were poised for what everybody expected would be a promenade to Paris. Even before the rusty Spanish war-machine had been cranked into first gear, the battle of Valmy had confounded all expectations. With the chance of cheap participation in some easy spoils of victory having vanished, Aranda drew in his horns again and ordered a return to a policy of neutrality.[173] It was a sensible action and it was also one of his last: on 15 November Aranda was obliged to make way for the Queen's lover, the twenty-five-year-old army officer, Manuel de Godoy.

However impressive his amatory credentials, Godoy was wholly inexperienced in political matters. It is doubtful whether that mattered much, whether even the seventy-five-year-old Aranda could have kept Spain out of a war. For now the initiative had passed to France. The same military success which had sent the Spanish back into neutrality had made the revolutionaries much more assertive. Their acceptance of Spanish neutrality could now be bought only at a price: formal recognition of the French Republic.[174] Even though that would have involved a renunciation of the Bourbon claim to the throne of France, it is possible that this might have been swallowed, had not two further events then intervened. The first was the trial and execution of the King, on 21 January 1793; the second was the change in British policy towards the Revolution.

Most historians have seen the former atrocity as decisive in swinging Spain back to a forward policy, this time for good. Georges Lefebvre, for example, wrote: 'To England, Louis' execution served as a pretext; to Spain it was the cause for war.'[175] In the most recent French account of the origins of the war, Jacqueline Chaumié has also stated that 'la mort du roi fut déterminante'.[176] Certainly the execution provoked a vehement reaction from all sections of Spanish society and inspired a huge anti-French demonstration in Madrid.[177] But whether it led inevitably to war is much more open to doubt. The timing of the change in Spanish policy suggests otherwise. It was early in January, long before Louis XVI had been found guilty, let alone guillotined, but just *after* the first British approach for an alliance had arrived, that orders were sent to Cartagena, Cadiz and Corunna to make the fleet ready and a much more aggressive tone was adopted towards the French.[178] The subsequent negotiations with the British were already well advanced when news of the execution reached Madrid.[179] Together with the Royal Navy, which already had a strong force in the Mediterranean (see p. 155), the Spanish believed they could blockade the French coast and bring the war to a swift and successful conclusion by stopping the enemy's all-important grain supplies and by severing her equally vital trade with the Levant.[180]

A similar miscalculation was being made in Paris. Contempt for the Spanish was part of the stock-in-trade of revolutionary orators. Brissot had provided a particularly fine example back in December 1791:

> Just look at this Spanish prince who dares to doubt the liberty of the King and the stability of our constitution! He has a large navy, but no sailors; monks, but no soldiers; mines, but no money; colonies, but no manufactures; banks, but no credit; debts, and no means to pay them: that is the paralytic state of the government of Spain, whose people can only be revived by liberty! (*Applause.*)[181]

Spain was not thought to pose any sort of military threat: even if France had to face the combined might of all the other European powers, the National Guards of the local departments would be able to hold the line of the Pyrenees without difficulty.[182] So when it came to determining policy in the aftermath of Louis XVI's execution and the subsequent expulsion of their envoy, Bourgoing, the French felt able to demand everything. Spain was to disarm completely, while they themselves would keep part of their army intact on the frontier.[183] This sense of overwhelming military superiority also encouraged them to take the initiative in beginning hostilities. On 7 March 1793 Barère presented a report to the National Convention in which he reviewed relations between the two countries since the Revolution and listed French grievances. They were numerous and familiar: conspiracy against the Revolution, encouragement of the *émigrés*, harassment of French citizens, and so on. Another old friend was the argument that the Spanish were going to attack anyway, so the French should launch a pre-emptive strike. Barère's confidence was total, for he had reliable information that the enemy's soldiers and sailors were few and unreliable, his subjects restive, his finances chaotic. Even the old Brissotin belief in a pro-French rising behind the lines put in a last appearance.

Barère's proposal that war be declared on Spain was accepted at once, without debate and unanimously. It was not long before the inaccuracy of their complacent assumptions about the Spanish ability to resist were exposed. Far from leading to a pro-French rising, the war proved hugely popular, even among the non-Castilian peoples of the frontier regions.[184] Its ranks swelled by an impressive number of volunteers, the Spanish army advanced into Roussillon, won a major engagement at Mas d'Eu on 18 May and proceeded to capture a number of important fortresses and towns.[185] From that point, the fortunes of war became more mixed, especially in the north, but when peace was signed at Basle on 22 July 1795 the Spaniards were still able to negotiate the most favourable peace achieved by any opponent of France in the 1790s.[186]

Once more the Revolution had demonstrated its unique disruptive potential by convincing yet another power of its terminal weakness while simultaneously convincing itself of its invincible strength. The history of the conflict between France and Spain between 1789 and 1793 also underlines the need to distinguish between the causes of hostility and the causes of war. Only when both sides are convinced that war will be the most profitable means of resolving their differences can the suspicion and ill-will which characterise the normal relations between states be transformed from verbal recrimination into physical violence. In the case of Spain and France, as in the case of Austria and France, Prussia and France and Great Britain and France, it was defective intelligence and defective understanding on both sides which made that transition possible. By helping to establish radically different criteria for the assessment of mutual assets and weaknesses, ideology played a very important part, therefore, but not by creating irreconcilable differences, rather by creating irretrievable miscalculation.

REFERENCES AND NOTES

1. Derek McKay and H. M. Scott, *The Rise of the Great Powers 1648–1815* (London 1983) p. 45.
2. Oscar Browning (ed.), *Despatches from Paris 1784–1790*, vol. 2: *1788–1790* (London 1910) pp. 250–3. Dorset took the rumours so seriously that he sent a formal denial to the French foreign minister, Montmorin, who in turn forwarded it to the National Assembly for communication to the deputies – *Archives parlementaires de 1787 à 1860. Receuil complet des débates législatifs et politiques des chambres françaises*, 127 vols, (Paris 1879–1913), vol. 8, p. 287.
3. Quoted in Albert Sorel, *L'Europe et la Révolution française*, vol. 2: *La Chute de la royauté* (Paris 1913) p. 42.
4. See, for example, *Archives parlementaires*, vol. 15, p. 518.
5. Ibid., pp. 381, 389.
6. Quoted in Roy Porter, *English Society in the Eighteenth Century* (Harmondsworth 1982) p. 21.
7. William, Lord Auckland, *Journal and Correspondence*, 4 vols, (London 1861–62), vol. 1, p. 402.

8. Edmund Burke, *Reflections on the Revolution in France*, ed. Conor Cruise O'Brien (Harmondsworth 1968) p. 181.

9. *Schadenfreude* cannot be translated by a single English word. It means 'taking pleasure in other people's misfortunes'.

10. Both remarks are quoted in John Ehrman, *The Younger Pitt*, vol. 2: *The Reluctant Transition* (London 1983) p. 4. See also Edmund Burke's more prolix version of the same theme quoted above, p. 79.

11. Oscar Browning (ed.), *The Political Memoranda of Francis Fifth Duke of Leeds* (London 1884) p. 146.

12. J. Holland Rose, *William Pitt and the Great War* (London 1911) p. 3. On the Padua Circular, see above, p. 86.

13. *The Manuscripts of J. B. Fortescue Esq. preserved at Dropmore*, vol. 2, Historical Manuscripts Commission, Fourteenth Report, Appendix, pt V (London 1894) (hereafter referred to as *Fortescue*) p. 171.

14. Ibid., p. 186. This remark was made by the British ambassador at The Hague, Lord Auckland, to his friend and superior, Grenville. On the Declaration of Pillnitz, see above, p. 86. On the British attitude to Pillnitz, see Felix Salomon, *William Pitt der jüngere*, vol. 1, pt 2: *Bis zum Ausgang der Friedensperiode (Februar 1793)* (Leipzig and Berlin 1906), p. 538.

15. *Fortescue*, vol. 2, p. 97. A little later, on 9 September 1791, the Sardinian envoy to London, Count Saint-Martin de Front, observed that: 'The British Cabinet is resolved to stay neutral . . . it finds it very agreeable not to have to do anything to attract French specie and to seize all her trade' – G. Pallain, *La Mission de Talleyrand à Londres en 1792. Correspondance inédite de Talleyrand avec le Département des Affaires étrangères, le général Biron etc.* (Paris 1889) p. xxi.

16. *Fortescue*, vol. 2, p. 167.

17. Quoted in Rose, *William Pitt and the Great War*, p. 32.

18. Lord Grenville to Earl Gower, 19 July 1792: *Fortescue*, vol. 2, p. 294.

19. A. F. Pribram (ed.), *Österreichische Staatsverträge: England*, vol. 2: *1749–1813, Veröffentlichungen der Kommission für neuere Geschichte Österreichs*, vol. 12 (Vienna 1913) p. 204; J. H. Clapham, 'Pitt's first decade', *The Cambridge History of British Foreign Policy*, eds Sir A. W. Ward and G. P. Gooch (Cambridge 1922) p. 213.

20. J. T. Stoker, *William Pitt et la Révolution française, 1789–1793* (Paris 1935) p. 114.

21. Auckland, *Journal and Correspondence*, vol. 2, p. 458; *Fortescue*, vol. 2, pp. 242–3.

22. This last phrase was coined by James Bland Burges, under-secretary of state at the Foreign Office, in a letter to Auckland written on 17 August 1792 – Auckland, *Journal and Correspondence*, vol. 2, p. 433.

23. J. T. Murley, *The Origin and Outbreak of the Anglo-French War of 1793* (Oxford dissertation 1959) p. 189. This first-rate dissertation remains the most helpful monograph on the origins of the war of 1793.

24. *Archives parlementaires*, vol. 34, p. 314.

25. Ibid., vol. 37, p. 470.

26. Ibid., p. 649.

27. Pallain, *La Mission de Talleyrand*, p. 375. Pallain reprints the correspondence relating to Talleyrand's missions of January–March 1792. For a full account of their progress, see Sorel, *L'Europe et la Révolution*

française, vol. 2, pp. 387 and 438–42.

28. François Furet and Denis Richet, *The French Revolution* (London 1970) p. 161. Probably the best reasonably concise account of the political changes of the summer and autumn of 1792 is still to be found in Georges Lefebvre, *The French Revolution: From its Origins to 1793* (London 1962) pp. 232–9, 247, 264, 269–70.

29. Murley, *The Origin and Outbreak of the Anglo-French War of 1793*, p. 139.

30. Jacques Droz, *Histoire diplomatique de 1648 à 1919*, 3rd edn (Paris 1972) p. 189.

31. *Archives parlementaires*, vol. 53, pp. 472–4.

32. Georges Michon, *Robespierre et la guerre révolutionnaire* (Paris 1937) p. 128.

33. Sorel, *L'Europe et la Révolution française*, vol. 3, p. 170.

34. Lefebvre, *The French Revolution*, p. 274.

35. Michon, *Robespierre*, p. 127.

36. Sorel, *L'Europe et la Révolution française*, vol. 3, p. 201.

37. *Archives parlementaires*, vol. 55, pp. 70–6. For a fuller discussion of this decree and its implications, see T. C. W. Blanning, *The French Revolution in Germany. Occupation and Resistance in the Rhineland 1792–1802* (Cambridge 1983) pp. 64–6.

38. Lefebvre, *The French Revolution*, p. 277.

39. Michon, *Robespierre*, p. 132.

40. Pallain, *La Mission de Talleyrand*, p. xxii. For other comments in the same vein, see A. Aspinall (ed.), *The Later Correspondence of George III*, vol. 1: *December 1783 to January 1793* (Cambridge 1962) p. 451; Browning (ed.), *Political Memoranda*, p. 147; Rose, *William Pitt and the Great War*, p. 48; *Fortescue*, vol. 2, pp. 171–2.

41. Vienna, Haus-, Hof- und Staatsarchiv, Staatskanzlei, England, Berichte, Kart. 127, no. 286: Count Rewiczky to Kaunitz, 27 November 1789.

42. *Fortescue*, vol. 2, p. 171.

43. Aspinall, *The Later Correspondence of George III*, vol. 1, pp. 469–70.

44. *Fortescue*, vol. 2, pp. 68–9, 279.

45. Ibid., p. 334.

46. Auckland, *Journal and Correspondence*, vol. 2, p. 464.

47. The events of these weeks can be followed best in Sorel, *L'Europe et la Révolution française*, vol. 3, ch. 3.

48. J. Holland Rose, 'Documents relating to the rupture with France in 1793', *English Historical Review*, **27** (1912) p. 119.

49. Earl Stanhope, *Life of the Right Honourable William Pitt with Extracts from his MS. Papers*, vol. 2 (London 1861) p. 173.

50. This point about defective communications making war more likely has been well made by John Ehrman in *The Younger Pitt*, vol. 2, pp. 208, 241.

51. S. T. Bindoff, *The Scheldt Questions to 1839* (London 1945) pp. 138–9; T. C. W. Blanning, ' "That horrid Electorate" or "Ma patrie germanique"?: George III, Hanover and the *Fürstenbund* of 1785', *The Historical Journal*, **20** (2) (1977) pp. 319–20.

52. *Fortescue*, vol. 2, p. 346.

53. Rose, *William Pitt and the Great War*, p. 76.
54. Sorel, *L'Europe et la Révolution française*, vol. 3, p. 167.
55. Rose, *William Pitt and the Great War*, p. 76; Murley, *The Origin and Outbreak of the Anglo-French War of 1793*, p. 235.
56. Stoker, *William Pitt et la Révolution française*, p. 154; Rose, *William Pitt and the Great War*, p. 84.
57. *Fortescue*, vol. 2, p. 344. Cf. Pitt's observation to Dundas of the previous day (26 November): 'things . . . [are] likely to come to extremities, and in that case we are necessarily committed' – quoted in Maurice Hutt, *Chouannerie and Counter-Revolution. Puisaye, the Princes and the British Government in the 1790s*, 2 vols (Cambridge 1983), vol, 1, p. 102. n. 18.
58. Paul Webb, *The Navy and British Diplomacy 1783–1793* (Cambridge dissertation 1971) pp. 405–6. 'Guardships' were ships of the line kept in commission during peacetime and therefore in an advanced state of readiness – ibid., p. 51, n. 2.
59. Rose, *William Pitt and the Great War*, p. 77.
60. Pribram, *Österreichische Staatsverträge*, p. 205. The development of Austro-British relations during late 1792 and early 1793 can be followed in some detail in the collection of documents published in volume 2 of Alfred Ritter von Vivenot (ed.), *Quellen zur Geschichte der deutschen Kaiserpolitik Österreichs während der französischen Revolutionskriege* (Vienna 1874).
61. Ibid., p. 376.
62. Ibid., pp. 393–4.
63. See his letters to Grenville of 22 September, 25 November and 3 December – *Fortescue*, vol. 2, pp. 317, 339, 351.
64. Ehrman, *The Younger Pitt*, vol. 2, p. 225. Part II of this massive and scholarly biography contains by far the fullest and most authoritative account of British policy during 1792–93 and supersedes all previous work on the period.
65. Ibid., p. 227.
66. Four recent works which all contain much of value are Clive Emsley, *British Society and the French Wars 1793–1815* (London 1979); Malcolm I. Thomis and Peter Holt, *Threats of Revolution in Britain 1789–1848* (London 1977); J. Stevenson, *Popular Disturbances in England 1700–1870* (London 1979) and Albert Goodwin, *The Friends of Liberty. The English Democratic Movement in the Age of the French Revolution* (London 1979). There is a predictably excellent chapter in John Cannon, *Parliamentary Reform 1640–1832* (Cambridge 1973). See also Roy Porter's sparkling *English Society in the Eighteenth Century* for some characteristically sharp insights on the subject.
67. Linda Colley, 'The apotheosis of George III: Loyalty, royalty and the British nation 1760–1820', *Past and Present*, **102** (1984) p. 122. There were 756 addresses, or more than twice the number submitted with regard to the Jew Bill in 1753, the Cider Tax Bill in 1763, the Wilkes affair of 1769, Catholic Relief and Economical Reform in 1780, parliamentary reform in 1783 and in support of Pitt in 1784 (i.e. the most contentious issues of the last twenty-five years) *put together*. This very important article contains a wealth of illustrations of the King's new popularity. Professor Colley dates the turn-round in George's public

esteem to the mid-1780s.

68. Henry Collins, 'The London Corresponding Society', *Democracy and the Labour Movement*, ed. John Saville (London 1954) p. 110.

69. W. A. L. Seaman, *British Democratic Societies in the Period of the French Revolution* (London dissertation 1954) p. 13.

70. Allan W. L. Seaman, 'Reform politics at Sheffield 1791–7', *Transactions of the Hunter Archaeological Society*, **7** (1957) p. 217.

71. Gwyn A. Williams, *Artisans and Sans-Culottes. Popular Movements in France and Britain during the French Revolution* (London 1968) p. 70.

72 Carl B. Cone, *The English Jacobins: Reformers in Late Eighteenth Century England* (New York 1968) *p. 122.*

73. Robert Birley, *The English Jacobins from 1789 to 1802* (Oxford 1942) p. 13.

74. Goodwin, *The Friends of Liberty*, pp. 215–19.

75. Cannon, *Parliamentary Reform*, pp. 119–21.

76. Cone, *The English Jacobins*, p. 105. This must be a very rough guess and may well be too high. E. P. Thompson, whom no one could accuse of underestimating evidence of popular unrest, writes only of 200,000 by 1793–*The Making of the English Working Class* (Harmondsworth 1968) p. 117. John Ehrman is more conservative, suggesting a figure of 200,000 'by 1794' – *The Younger Pitt*, vol. 2, p. 115.

77. E. J. Hobsbawm, 'Tom Paine', *Labouring Men. Studies in the History of Labour* (London 1964) pp. 1–3.

78. Quoted in P. A. Brown, *The French Revolution in English History* (London 1918) p. 133. For other comments on and illustrations of the moderation of the corresponding societies, see ibid., pp. 61–3 and Ian R. Christie, 'Veitch's "The genesis of parliamentary reform" ', *Myth and Reality in Late-Eighteenth Century British Politics and Other Papers* (London 1970) p. 220.

79. Donald Read, *The English Provinces c. 1760–1960: A Study in Influence* (London 1964) p. 45.

80. Herbert Butterfield, 'Charles James Fox and the Whig Opposition in 1792', *Cambridge Historical Journal*, **9** (3) (1949) p. 310. See also pp. 150–1.

81. Sir Robert Murray Keith, *Memoirs and Correspondence (Official and Familiar)*, ed. Mrs A. Gillespie Smyth, 2 vols (London 1849), vol. 2, p. 518. For other comments on the essential reliability of British public opinion by other leading members of the government, see Auckland, *Diary and Correspondence*, vol. 2, pp. 403, 408, 421, 423.

82. Ehrman, *The Younger Pitt*, vol. 2, p. 92; Nicholas Cox, *Aspects of English Radicalism: The Suppression and Re-emergence of the Constitutional Democratic Tradition 1795–1809* (Cambridge dissertation 1971) p. 24, n. 2.

83. Cone, *The English Jacobins*, p. 178.

84. Quoted in Ehrman, *The Younger Pitt*, vol. 2, p. 214.

85. Ibid. Lord Rosebery, *Pitt* (London 1892) p. 118.

86. Murley, *The Origin and Outbreak of the Anglo-French War of 1793*, pp. 57–8.

87. Ehrman, *The Younger Pitt*, vol. 2, p. 215.

88. J. Stevenson, *Disturbances and Public Order in London, 1790–1821*

(Oxford dissertation 1973) p. 193.

89. Auckland, *Journal and Correspondence*, vol. 2, pp. 421, 463.
90. *The Autobiography of Theobald Wolfe Tone 1763–1798*, ed. R. Barry O'Brien, vol. 1 (Dublin 1912) p. 38.
91. *Fortescue*, vol. 2, p. 184.
92. E. M. Johnston, *Ireland in the Eighteenth Century* (Dublin 1974) pp. 45–7.
93. Murley, *The Origin and Outbreak of the Anglo-French War of 1793*, p. 200.
94. Cone, *The English Jacobins*, p. 166.
95. Henry W. Meikle, *Scotland and the French Revolution* (Glasgow 1912) p. 100.
96. Ibid., p. 96; Cone, *The English Jacobins*, p. 166; Auckland, *Diary and Correspondence*, vol. 2, p. 469.
97. Quoted in Butterfield, 'Charles James Fox', pp. 317–18. For other alarmist reports from Dundas, see Cyril Matheson, *The Life of Henry Dundas, First Viscount Melville 1742–1811* (London 1933) p. 169 and Meikle, *Scotland and the French Revolution*, p. 102.
98. Goodwin, *The Friends of Liberty*, p. 250. On the decree of 19 November, see above, p. 136.
99. Auckland, *Journal and Correspondence*, vol. 2, p. 438; *Fortescue*, vol. 2, p. 309.
100. Cone, *The English Jacobins*, p. 135; Collins, 'The London Corresponding Society', p. 114.
101. Clive Emsley, *Public Order in England 1790–1801* (Cambridge dissertation 1970) p. 36; Butterfield, 'Charles James Fox', p. 317.
102. Murley, *The Origin and Outbreak of the Anglo-French War of 1793*, pp. 36, 38–9, 62–3, 68.
103. Ibid., p. 145.
104. Rose, *William Pitt and the Great War*, p. 73; Emsley, *British Society and the French Wars*, p. 15.
105. Emsley, *Public Order in England*, p. 186; Goodwin, *The Friends of Liberty*, p. 236.
106. Matheson, *The Life of Henry Dundas*, p. 171; Eugene C. Black, *The Association: British Extraparliamentary Political Organisation, 1769–1793* (Cambridge, Mass. 1963) p. 239; Brown, *The French Revolution in English History*, p. 85.
107. Richard Grenville, Second Duke of Buckingham and Chandos, *Memoirs of the Court and Cabinets of George III*, vol. 2 (London 1853) p. 228.
108. Black, *The Association*, pp. 237–9.
109. Austin Mitchell, 'The Association Movement of 1792–9', *The Historical Journal*, **4** (1) (1961) pp. 60–3.
110. Black, *The Association*, p. 252. Donald E. Ginter, 'The Loyalist Association Movement of 1792–3 and British public opinion', *The Historical Journal*, **9** (2) (1966), seeks to argue that the Association movement was also in large measure a movement for parliamentary reform. He has a point, but makes far too much of it, presenting as typical what was clearly exceptional.
111. Porter, *English Society in the Eighteenth Century*, p. 89.

112. Brown, *The French Revolution in English History*, p. 89.
113. Ibid. This is also quoted in Cannon, *Parliamentary Reform*, p. 124.
114. A. Temple Patterson, *Radical Leicester: A History of Leicester 1780–1850* (Leicester 1954) p. 71.
115. See, for example, the reports from the Archbishop of Canterbury, Lord Sheffield and the Earl of Carysfort reprinted in Auckland, *Diary and Correspondence*, vol. 2, pp. 478 and 481 and *Fortescue*, vol. 2, p. 354.
116. Quoted in W. T. Laprade, *England and the French Revolution* (Baltimore 1909) p. 123.
117. *Fortescue*, vol. 2, p. 360.
118. Fortunately there are several good studies available, notably L. G. Mitchell, *Charles James Fox and the Disintegration of the Whig Party 1782–94* (Oxford 1971) F. O'Gorman, *The Whig Party and the French Revolution* (London 1967) and Butterfield, 'Charles James Fox'.
119. William Cobbett (ed.), *The Parliamentary History of England from the Earliest Period to the Year 1803*, vol. 28, cols 329–70.
120. Ibid., cols 356, 363, 370.
121. Paul Kelly, 'Strategy and counter-revolution: the journal of Sir Gilbert Elliot, 1–22 September 1793', *English Historical Review*, **387** (1983) p. 345.
122. Mitchell, *Charles James Fox*, pp. 164, 173.
123. Quoted in Butterfield, 'Charles James Fox', p. 296.
124. E. A. Smith, *Whig Principles and Party Politics: Earl Fitzwilliam and the Whig Party 1748–1833* (Manchester 1975) p. 133.
125. Mitchell, *Charles James Fox*, p. 166.
126. William Windham, *The Windham Papers, The Life and Correspondence of the Rt. Hon. William Windham 1750–1810*, vol. 2 (London 1913) p. 101. For Fitzwilliam's equally choleric reaction, see Smith, *Whig Principles and Party Politics*, pp. 137–8.
127. Butterfield, 'Charles James Fox', pp. 307–14.
128. Ibid., p. 321.
129. Ibid.
130. James Harris First Earl of Malmesbury, *Diaries and Correspondence*, vol. 2 (London 1844) p. 476. A day-by-day account of the dispute between Fox and his Whig colleagues can be found in Malmesbury's diary.
131. Ehrman, *Pitt the Younger*, vol. 2, p. 25.
132. Sorel, *L'Europe et la Révolution française*, vol. 3, p. 165.
133. Murley, *The Origin and Outbreak of the Anglo-French War of 1793*, p. 148.
134. Ibid.
135. Goodwin, *The Friends of Liberty*, p. 258.
136. Stoker, *William Pitt et la Révolution française*, p. 139; Sorel, *L'Europe et la Révolution française*, vol. 3, p. 215.
137. M. A. Thiers, *Histoire de la Révolution française*, 14th edn, vol. 3, (Paris 1846) pp. 238–9.
138. Sorel, *L'Europe et la Révolution française*, vol. 3, pp. 174–5.
139. Murley, *The Origin and Outbreak of the Anglo-French War of 1793*, pp. 227–40.
140. Ibid., pp. 290–1; Sorel, *L'Europe et la Révolution française*, vol. 3, p.

272.
141. Auckland, *Journal and Correspondence*, vol. 2, pp. 426, 484; *Fortescue*, vol. 2, p. 329.
142. Ibid., p. 351.
143. Paul Webb, *The Navy and British Diplomacy 1783–1793* (Cambridge dissertation 1971) p. 407.
144. P. L. C. Webb, 'The rebuilding and repair of the fleet, 1783–1793', *Bulletin of the Institute of Historical Research*, **50** (1977) p. 202.
145. *Fortescue*, vol. II, p. 352.
146. Emsley, *British Society and the French Wars*, p. 16.
147. Malmesbury, *Diaries and Correspondence*, pp. 501–2. Admittedly this is hearsay evidence, since Malmesbury was recording what Loughborough said Pitt had said to him.
148. *Archives parlementaires*, vol. 56, pp. 110–17; vol. 57, pp. 16–25; vol. 58, pp. 112–23.
149. Ibid., vol. 56, p. 112.
150. The debates are to be found in Cobbett, *The Parliamentary History of England*, vol. 30, cols 1–460.
151. Ibid., col. 70. All members of his audience could remember the Gordon Riots of 1780 when mob rule had terrorised London for a week and when £100,000 of damage had been done to property (ten times as much as in Paris throughout the French Revolution) – Porter, *English Society in the Eighteenth Century*, p. 116.
152. Murley, *The Origin and Outbreak of the Anglo-French War of 1793*, pp. 274–83. From 14 December onwards Chauvelin and Noël in London were sending back reports on the state of British public opinion which were the reverse of earlier predictions of impending revolution. They were too late, however, to have influenced the decision of 13 December to halt Dumouriez – ibid., pp. 297–8.
153. *Archives parlementaires*, vol. 55, pp. 164–5.
154. Cobbett, *The Parliamentary History of England*, vol. 30, cols 253–6. This is also reprinted in H. W. V. Temperley and L. M. Penson (eds), *Foundations of British Foreign Policy from Pitt (1792) to Salisbury (1902), or Documents Old and New* (Cambridge 1938) pp. 3–8.
155. *Archives parlementaires*, vol. 58, p. 122.
156. Paul Langford, *The Eighteenth Century* (London 1976) p. 212; McKay and Scott, *The Rise of the Great Powers*, p. 283; Ehrman, *The Younger Pitt*, vol. 2, p. 247.
157. Hutt, *Chouannerie and Counter-Revolution*, vol. 1, p. 109.
158. *Fortescue*, vol. 2, p. 181. Perhaps not surprisingly, French historians have stressed British ambitions in the Caribbean, but have not been able to find much evidence to suggest that they contributed to the outbreak of the war – Thiers, *Histoire de la Révolution française*, vol. 3, pp. 231, 237; Lefebvre, *The French Revolution*, p. 281; Droz, *Histoire diplomatique*, p. 193.
159. Henry Richard Lord Holland, *Memoires of the Whig Party during My Time*, ed. Henry Edward Lord Holland, vol. 1 (London 1852) p. 13; Laprade, *England in the French Revolution*, pp. 184–5.
160. Clive Emsley, 'The London "Insurrection" of December 1792: fact, fiction or fantasy?', *The Journal of British Studies* **17** (2) (1978) p. 86.

161. Rosebery, *Pitt*, pp. 166–7.
162. Murley, *The Origin and Outbreak of the Anglo-French War of 1793*, pp. 90–1.
163. Alfredo Martinez Albiach, *Religiosidad hispana y sociedad borbonica* (Burgos 1969) p. 88; T. C. W. Blanning, 'The role of religion in European counter-revolution 1789–1815', *History, Society and the Church: Essays in Honour of Owen Chadwick*, eds Geoffrey Best and Derek Beales (Cambridge 1985) p. 207.
164. Hermann Baumgarten, *Geschichte Spaniens zur Zeit der französischen Revolution* (Berlin 1861) p. 319.
165. Modento Lafuente, *Historia General de España*, vol. 21: *1780–1795* (Madrid 1858) p. 371.
166. Angel Salcedo Ruiz, *La Epoca de Goya. Historia de España y Hispano-América desde el advenimiento de Felipe V hasta la guerra de la Independencia* (Madrid n.d.) pp. 153–4.
167. Baumgarten *Geschichte Spaniens*, pp. 326–8, 349, 397, 405–6.
168. Lafuente, *Historia General de España*, p. 390.
169. For examples, see *Archives parlementaires*, vol. 36, p. 609; vol. 38, pp. 60–1; vol. 39, p. 78.
170. Ibid., vol. 40, pp. 530–3.
171. Lafuente, *Historia General de España*, pp. 393–6.
172. Baumgarten, *Geschichte Spaniens*, p. 450.
173. Lafuente, *Historia General de España*, p. 400.
174. Ibid., p. 401.
175. Lefebvre, *The French Revolution*, p. 283.
176. Jacqueline Chaumié, *Les Relations diplomatiques entre l'Espagne et la France de Varennes à la mort de Louis XVI* (Bordeaux 1957) p. 181. That statement seems unequivocal enough. However, on the following page she adds 'Mais vers le mi-janvier tout changea. Ce fut la prise de position énergique de l'Angleterre contre la Révolution qui entraîna les hésitations de l'Espagne [over continuing a policy of neutrality].' A little later she seems to contradict the earlier observation about the decisive importance of the death of Louis XVI when she adds 'Dans un exposé sur les raisons qui avaient milité pour la guerre, Godoy donnait le motif qui fut certainement déterminant: "La marine française n'est pas assez puissante pour aider l'Espagne contre l'Angleterre" ' or in other words, it was the apparent collapse of French power and the consequent invincibility of the British which propelled the Spanish into war: ibid., pp. 182–4. Despite its promising title, Albert Sorel's article – 'La diplomatie française et l'Espagne de 1792 à 1796', *Revue Historique*, 11 (1879) – contains nothing of value on the origins of the war.
177. Manuel Ferrandis and Caetano Beirao, *Historia contemporanea de España y Portugal* (Barcelona and Madrid 1966) p. 12.
178. Baumgarten, *Geschichte Spaniens*, pp. 429–33.
179. Chaumié, *Les Relations diplomatiques entre l'Espagne et la France*, p. 184.
180. Baumgarten, *Geschichte Spaniens*, p. 406. Baumgarten is curiously inconsistent on this question of timing: although his account of developments in January makes it clear that it was the British approach which was the real turning-point, he then adds that neutrality might have been

maintained if news of the execution of Louis XVI had not arrived.

181. *Archives Parlementaires*, vol. 36, p. 606.
182. Ibid., vol. 59, pp. 694–90.
183. Lafuente, *Historia General de España*, p. 417.
184. This is one point on which all historians can agree. See, for example, Angel Ossorio y Gallardo, *Historia del pensamiento politico catalan durante la guerra de España con la Republica francesa 1793–1795*, new edn (Barcelona 1977) pp. 28–30; 34; Antonio Dominquez Ortiz, *Sociedad y Estado en el siglo XVIII español* (Barcelona 1976) p. 509; Salcedo Ruiz, *La Epoca de Goya*, p. 165.
185. Lafuente, *Histoira General de España*, pp. 421–2.
186. Baumgarten, *Geschichte Spaniens*, p. 566.

Chapter 6
THE ORIGINS OF THE WAR OF THE SECOND COALITION

THE INSTABILITY OF THE PEACE OF CAMPO FORMIO

In the years after 1792 and 1793 the various combatants learned the hard way that the assumptions which had taken them into war were mistaken. Both revolutionary France and the old-regime powers proved to be far more resilient than the other had expected. Five years of intense fighting in Belgium, the United Provinces, Germany, Spain and Italy were needed before a more realistic assessment of mutual strengths and weaknesses could be agreed and an uneasy peace established on the Continent. So brief was the pause which followed, between the Peace of Campo Formio of 17 October 1797 and the beginning of the Russo-Turkish assault on French possessions in the Ionian Islands on 20 September 1798, that it may be doubted whether 'The War of the Second Coalition' was a separate war at all. Such a doubt is reinforced by the continuity of conflict on the high seas, as the war between France and Great Britain sputtered along its spasmodic way without formal interruption. Moreover, fundamental realignment in the maritime theatre had taken place long before Campo Formio, for the French had turned the Dutch and the Spanish from enemies into allies on 16 May 1795 and 18 August 1796 respectively.

Yet although it was evident from the start that the peace of 1797 would prove probably just a truce, the next war had sufficient novel features to justify separate treatment. The massive expansion of French war aims, the extension of hostilities to the Middle East and, above all, the long-awaited intrusion of Russia as an active belligerent all created a new situation. If only because it will allow, among other things, an examination of the position and interests of the last of the major European powers to join the struggle against the Revolution, it is appropriate that the final substantive chapter of this book should deal with a war whose unprecedented geographical scope ranged from Ireland to Syria, from Copenhagen to Malta.

In the first instance, however, it is the relative position of the oldest enemies – Austria and France – which must be examined. It is crucial to an understanding of Austrian policy that subsequent French triumphs should be ignored. Knowledge of Marengo, Hohenlinden, Ulm, Austerlitz and Wagram leads too easily to an implicit assumption of inevitable superiority. Denied the advantage of hindsight, that was not the Austrians' assessment. On the contrary, the five years of fighting between 1792 and 1797 seemed to suggest that a military solution to the problem of revolutionary France was still feasible. If they had lost Belgium after their defeat at Jemappes on 6 November 1792, they had won it back again after their victory at Neerwinden on 16 March 1793. If they had lost it again after their defeat at Fleurus on 26 June 1794, who was to say that they would not win it back again at some future date? If the French had been able to conquer the left bank of the Rhine, they had been repelled every time they tried to cross the river. Even the campaigns of 1796 could be interpreted in more than one way: certainly General Bonaparte had been triumphant in Italy, but in the main German theatre the Archduke Charles had defeated the Rhin-et-Moselle and Sambre-et-Meuse armies and had chased them back over the Rhine again. In short, the revolutionary armies had *not* proved to be the all-conquering irresistible force of Brissotin ante-bellum oratory. Whenever the Austrians had been able to take the field with roughly equal numbers, their superior discipline and training had proved more than a match for revolutionary *élan*.[1] Moreover, the political developments of these years had not been all loss. Prussia's relapse into timorous neutrality by the Peace of Basle of 6 April 1795 left Austria the undisputed leader of the Holy Roman Empire. In the same year, pain at losing Belgium was assuaged by the massive portion of Polish territory acquired in the third partition.

Nor was the decision to sue for peace in the spring of 1798 a one-sided diktat on the part of the French. Although Bonaparte's army was less than 100 miles from Vienna when peace preliminaries were signed at Leoben on 18 April 1797, no final military verdict had been passed. Indeed it had been Bonaparte's anxiety about the vulnerability of his flank, the fragility of his lines of communication and the insecurity of his rear which had prompted him to take the initiative in offering an armistice.[2] This indecisive outcome of the war was reflected in the indecisive outcome of the peace negotiations. When the Peace of Campo Formio was eventually signed, after six months of hard bargaining, the terms were unexpectedly favourable to the Austrians. In return for ceding Belgium, Lombardy and their pieces of territory in western Germany, they were to receive the Archbishopric of Salzburg, Bavaria east of the Inn, Venice and the terra firma up to the Adige and Po rivers and the Venetian territories of Istria, Dalmatia and Cattaro along the Adriatic.[3] For their part, the French received Belgium, the indirect control of Lombardy (already turned into a satellite state as the 'Cisalphine Republic' in July), the Ionian Islands of Venice and the promise of Austrian assistance to gain most of the

left bank of the Rhine when peace was negotiated with the Holy
Roman Empire.

Loud and long were the cries of execration from the rest of Europe
when part of the treaty was made public. That France should make
peace with Austria at the expense of the ancient republic of Venice was
rightly seen as final proof that the Revolution had lost its innocence
and had become just another rapacious exponent of power-politics.
This was old-regime diplomacy *redivivus*, on a par with the partitions
of Poland. The protests would have been still louder if the secret
articles had leaked out, although Austria would now have been the
main target. For by ratifying the treaty, the Emperor Francis II had
abdicated his imperial responsibilities. By agreeing to support the
French bid for the left bank of the Rhine, he had reneged on an
undertaking that peace between France and the Holy Roman Empire
would be negotiated on the basis of the latter's integrity. By agreeing
to accept the Archbishopric of Salzburg as 'compensation' for the loss
of his territories in the west, he gave advance approval to the secularisation of the ecclesiastical states and thus to the elimination of the
Habsburgs' most loyal allies.[4]

A major reason for the instability of the peace was its lack of finality.
Francis II had signed only as head of the House of Habsburg and only
in respect of the territories he ruled in that capacity. Peace between
France and the Holy Roman Empire was to be negotiated separately at
a special congress, which opened at Rastatt on 16 November 1797.
With the vital interests of every one of the 2,000-odd component parts
of the Empire at stake, either as predator or prey, the complexity of
the proceedings and their susceptibility to delaying tactics need hardly
be stressed. More than a year later, the delegates were still absorbed in
rancorous haggling, long after the *de facto* renewal of war had made
their inconsequential efforts redundant. The difficulties inherent in
such an exercise had been exacerbated by the two main protagonists.
Both Austria and France were dissatisfied with the terms secured at
Campo Formio and were anxious to exploit the Rastatt Congress to
improve them.

Disappointment had been especially acute in Paris, where the
Directory deeply regretted Bonaparte's failure to secure Austrian
consent to ceding the left bank of the Rhine in its entirety. With
stubborn tenacity the Austrian negotiators had insisted that the territory to the north of a line running from the confluence of the river
Nette with the Rhine near Koblenz to Venloo on the Meuse should
remain part of the Holy Roman Empire. The reason was plain and had
nothing whatsoever to do with any defence of imperial interests: it was
just this section which included Prussia's Rhenish possessions. Consequently, if Prussia lost no territory, Prussia could claim no compensation on the right bank. Such, indeed, was the Directory's frustration

at not securing Austrian recognition of France's 'natural frontiers' that it would have preferred rejection of Campo Formio and continuation of the war.[5] Although General Bonaparte's unassailable popularity and the domestic instability ruled that out, the Directors could console themselves with the thought that the peace was only a truce and that it would not be difficult to find an excuse to resume the war. Their foreign secretary, Talleyrand, sent them a memorandum on the subject whose candour and insight merit quotation:

> Given the situation of the Republic, which is a *parvenu* power in Europe, which has raised itself in the teeth of the monarchies and on the ruins of several of them, and which rules the continent now by the terror inspired by its principles and its arms, can it not be said that the treaty of Campo Formio and all the other treaties we have signed are nothing more than just military agreements, some more advantageous than others? The dispute which has been lulled for the time being by the surprise and dismay of the vanquished has in no way been finally resolved by the arms which must always be at the ready so long as hatred persists.[6]

At Vienna there was equal dissatisfaction with Campo Formio. It is likely that, had they known that the Tsar Paul I was on the point of offering them diplomatic and military assistance, the Austrians would have chosen to fight on.[7] Like the French, however, they could console themselves with the thought that their decision to accept the peace was not irrevocable. As a senior diplomat, Count Ludwig Cobenzl, observed to his foreign minister, Baron Thugut, just before the treaty was signed: 'We are only concluding a truce which will allow us to re-establish ourselves in Italy more easily than by means of the most successful military campaign; in any case, settling matters in Germany will give us twenty reasons for beginning the war again if we wish to.'[8] No sooner were the terms of the treaty in Thugut's hands than he was putting out the first feelers to the British about a possible revival of the anti-French coalition.[9] For the time being, however, prudence suggested at least a pause in hostilities. Austrian finances had been floundering even before war began in 1792; by 1797 they were being kept afloat only by the printing of increasingly dangerous amounts of paper money.[10]

Any chance that the respite would be more than a brief interlude was destroyed by the unabated expansionist surge of French policy. The Revolution was now eight years old but showed no signs of maturing into less assertive middle age. On the contrary, it had just acquired a fresh infusion of youthful vigour. On 4 September 1797 the *coup d'état* of 'Fructidor' (so-named after the month of the revolutionary calendar in which it occurred) had purged the royalists from the legislative councils and had swung the regime emphatically to the left. Particularly important for the future course of foreign affairs had been the elimination from the executive of the two directors most in favour of peace: Carnot and Barthélemy. Into prison with them went their plans to return France to her old frontiers (*les anciennes limites*) as the necessary price of a lasting peace. Now in the ascendant were the supporters of *les grandes limites*, the triumvirate of La Revellière, Barras and Reubell, committed to retaining all French conquests and, if possible, expanding them further. So Fructidor brought an even more assertive tone to French foreign policy; as Albert Sorel commented: 'The feeling of the "purged" Directory was arrogance. It believed itself to be the master of Europe, just as it was the master of Paris.'[11]

The impact on foreign affairs was immediate. Negotiations with the British, under way at Lille since early July, were broken off abruptly and on 26 October preparations were begun for the invasion of England. If the reluctant acceptance of Campo Formio meant an end to the war with Austria for the time being, it did not prevent further expansion on the Continent. In fact, French influence spread further and faster during the year of 'peace' than it had done during wartime. Top of the rejuvenated Directory's list of desirable acquisitions was the Swiss Confederation, since it controlled the most important passes leading to Italy. On 8 December 1797 Reubell and Bonaparte met the most prominent Swiss radical, Peter Ochs, to concert the 'regeneration' of his country. It was accomplished during the first few months of 1798, as a French army assisted native collaborators to turn their country into the 'Helvetic Republic' and to deal with the revolts which this operation provoked. Two former allied members of the Swiss Confederation, Mulhouse and Geneva, were annexed outright on 28 January and 15 April respectively. The object of this exercise and the satellite status of the new creation was advertised by a treaty of 2 August which granted the French in perpetuity free access to the Alpine passes.[12]

The Swiss take-over was only one part of a more general plan to reinforce French control of western and southern Europe. Taking advantage of the death of a French general in a street-brawl in Rome, the papal states were invaded in February, the Pope was exiled and a 'Roman Republic' proclaimed. The subordinate status of these satellites was well advertised in the same month by events in the Cisalpine Republic. After its legislature had declined to accept a patently disadvantageous treaty with France, it was promptly purged in the best Fructidorian manner and ratification was forced through.[13] Its Dutch equivalent – the Batavian Republic – experienced no fewer than three *coups d'état* during the first half of 1798.[14] The Ligurian Republic (formerly Genoa), meanwhile, was being drained of money and materials.[15] Next door in Piedmont, French control was tightened by military occupation in June, which proved to be the prelude to the abdication of the King at the end of the year and subsequent annexation.[16] In short, the Directory was well on its way to achieving the aim expressed by one of its members, La Revellière: 'to unite Holland,

France, Switzerland, the Cisalpine and Ligurian republics by an uninterrupted continuity of territory . . . a nursery of excellent soldiers and a formidable [strategic] position'.[17]

That aim was grandiose enough, but it was not the limit of French ambitions. There was still Germany to be dealt with, through the negotiations with the representatives of the Holy Roman Empire at the Congress of Rastatt. In the instructions prepared for their own envoys, the directors frankly stated that they had no intention of observing the terms of Campo Formio. They were determined to have the whole of the left bank and also to deny Austria any compensation in Germany.[18] To achieve these objectives they counted on the support of the German secular princes, who stood to gain most from the secularisation and reallocation of the ecclesiastical states. Their task was made easier by the abandoning of the Holy Roman Empire by both of the main German powers. Since the first years of the decade, it had become increasingly apparent that they were interested only in the promotion of their own selfish interests. What they had done to Poland, they might well do to the rest of Germany, so the lesser princes turned to the only alternative source of protection: France.[19] With Austria and Prussia at loggerheads and the other princes deeply suspicious of both, the French negotiators held a central position of enviable strength. They were quick to press home their advantage. On 1 December 1797 Bonaparte, who had called in at Rastatt on his way back from Italy, forced the Austrians to agree to withdraw from the left-bank fortress-town of Mainz by the end of the month, in return for French evacuation of Austria's prize, Venice. After that betrayal of imperial interests, everyone could see that the days of the Holy Roman Empire were numbered. As a German radical, Joseph Görres, contemptuously wrote:

> On 30 December 1797, the day of the handing over of Mainz, at 3 o'clock in the afternoon, there died peacefully and blessedly, at the ripe old age of 955 years, five months and 28 days, as the result of total enervation and a final stroke, completely conscious and comforted by all the holy sacraments, the Holy Roman Empire of ponderous memory.[20]

With a wave of the carrot here, and a brandish of the stick there, the French coaxed and cajoled the congress towards their objective. On 11 March 1798 it agreed to cede the left bank, albeit on certain conditions (which were simply ignored). On 4 April it agreed in principle to the secularisation of the ecclesiastical states for the purpose of compensating the secular princes who would lose their possessions on the left bank.[21] The Directory was now in a position to remodel Germany as it had already remodelled Italy.

BONAPARTE'S EXPEDITION TO EGYPT

The spring of 1798 marked the apex of the Revolution's power. In western, central and southern Europe, France had attained a degree of hegemony undreamed of even by Louis XIV. With her sole remaining enemy, Great Britain, unable to intervene on the Continent and now facing rebellion in Ireland, all seemed set fair. Yet if the peak scaled had been high, the rate of descent was commensurately fast. Within eighteen months the very regime had perished, discredited by military defeat, foreign insurrection and civil war. What turned out to be the terminal crisis of the French Republic stemmed in large measure from the War of the Second Coalition and that war was in similarly large measure a self-inflicted wound. After Fructidor the revamped Directory fell prey to the same sort of over-confidence which had taken their Brissotin predecessors down the slippery slope to perdition.

Of all the mistakes the directors made during 1798, the most serious proved to be the decision taken on 5 March to authorise an expedition to conquer Egypt. This represented the completion of a prolonged development which had reorientated French policy from the Rhine to the Mediterranean. Its most effective exponent had been General Bonaparte, whose imperious demands, lightly disguised as arguments, were supported by the unanswerable fact that he was the only French general currently capable of winning battles. The Directory had intended to use his Italian conquests to secure the left bank of the Rhine but had been outmanœuvred by his independent diplomacy. A central part of Bonaparte's plan, from the moment he began to negotiate with the Austrians in the summer of 1797, was the establishment of French control of the Mediterranean from one end to the other. As he told Thugut: 'The French Republic regards the Mediterranean as its sea and wishes to dominate it.'[22]

A major step towards the implementation of that goal was the partition of Venice and its various possessions between France and Austria at Campo Formio. Part of the French share were the 'Ionian Islands', including Corfu, Zante, Cephalonia and Saint Maura.[23] Such was Bonaparte's eagerness to lay hands on his prize that he sent off General Baraguey d'Hilliers and an expeditionary force without waiting for the definitive peace treaty to be signed at Campo Formio.[24] Reporting to the Directory on 16 August 1797, he wrote:

> The islands of Corfu, Zante and Cephalonia are more important for us than all of Italy put together.
>
> I believe that if we were obliged to make a choice, it would be better to return Italy to the Emperor and to keep the four islands, which are a source of wealth and prosperity for our commerce. The Turkish Empire is collapsing with every day that passes; our possession of these islands will enable us to prop it up, in so far as that is possible, or to take our share of it.

> The time is not far off when we shall have to seize Egypt. The vast
> Ottoman Empire, which is falling apart day-by-day, obliges us to take
> timely precautions to preserve our trade with the Levant.[25]

A month later he repeated these observations on the strategic and
commercial importance of the Ionian Islands in a letter to the foreign
minister, now adding Malta to his list of desirable properties. He also
raised again the need to conquer Egypt, especially if the Cape of Good
Hope had to be ceded to the British at some future peace.[26] As the
minister he was addressing was Talleyrand, he knew that he was
preaching to the converted. On 3 July 1797, just a fortnight before he
succeeded Delacroix at the foreign ministry, Talleyrand had signalled
the direction of his policy by reading to the Institute a paper 'On the
advantages to be derived in the present circumstances from new
colonies'. Among other things, he commended to his audience the
plan presented to Louis XV by Choiseul after the Seven Years War,
which had advocated the seizure of Egypt as compensation for the
colonies lost to the British.[27] So the instructions sent from Paris during
the negotiations leading up to Campo Formio were just what
Bonaparte wanted to hear (not that he would have paid any attention if
they had been the reverse). At all costs, Talleyrand urged, the Ionian
Islands must be kept: 'Nothing is more important than to establish
ourselves on a sound footing in Albania, Greece, Macedonia and the
other provinces of the Turkish Empire in Europe, especially those with
a Mediterranean coastline, and most notably Egypt, which one day
could prove immensely useful for us.'[28]

The reasons for this intense interest in the Levant went beyond the
simple desire to paint an impressive section of the globe blue to
counterbalance the loss of the Caribbean islands. Also at stake were
vital commercial interests, increasingly threatened (so the French
merchants in the Levant claimed) by the depredations of pirates and
the competition from Greeks, Ragusans and Algerians.[29] Another
threat which required attention was the potential danger that the
Austrians would exploit their new acquisitions in the Adriatic to
become a major Mediterranean power.[30] More positive was the wish to
take Egypt, not only a huge market and source of raw materials, but
also the ideal base from which to challenge the British in India once the
isthmus of Suez and the Red Sea had been brought under French
control.[31] This anti-British element was strong; when Bonaparte sailed
from Malta on the last leg of his Egyptian expedition and at last
revealed to his soldiers their final destination, he told them: 'Soldiers!
You are going to undertake a conquest whose effects on civilisation
and the commerce of the world will be incalculable. You will strike the
greatest and most painful stroke possible against England until you can
deal her final deathblow.'[32]

Egypt was certainly an attractive target, but it was not the only part of the world which might have caught the Directory's eye. Louisiana, any of the West Indian islands, the Cape of Good Hope – India itself, possessed similar, if not more striking economic and strategic attractions. What made Egypt so appealing and what prompted the French invasion was the apparent ease with which it could be taken. This was the leitmotiv of Talleyrand's crucial report 'On the conquest of Egypt' to the Directory on 14 February 1798. For a man so naturally intelligent and so knowledgeable about the current state of Europe, he made an astonishing series of miscalculations. The only prediction he made which subsequently proved to be accurate was that Prussia would be uninterested. He was at best half-right when he argued that Austria's attention would be absorbed by German affairs and the territories gained at Campo Formio. Entirely and fatally erroneous was his belief that Turkish consent could be gained, that Russia 'is not dangerous to us' and that: 'England cannot intimidate us. Our war with her is the most favourable circumstance for an invasion of Egypt. Threatened by an imminent invasion of her islands, she will not leave her coasts exposed by coming to oppose our project.' Equally mistaken was the old Brissotin delusion that the irresistible appeal of revolutionary principles would do France's work for her:

> What should reassure us most is the spirit of liberty which happily is propagating itself in all the states of Europe, and which, it seems to me, ought to conquer them entirely within a few years. The rulers of these states will not wish to expose themselves to accelerating its development by a war with France.
>
> So the Executive Directory ought not to fear any obstacle to its taking possession of Egypt.

If the international situation was encouraging, conditions within Egypt itself were positively inviting, Talleyrand went on. The Beys who ruled the country could only count on 7,000–8,000 Mameluke cavalry with no notion of how to fight a modern war: 'I can guarantee that in the opinion of those who know Egypt best the conquest would cost hardly a drop of blood.' A modest force of 20,000–25,000 men, together with five ships of the line and six frigates, would be all that was needed. Moreover, the invaders could count on the support of the local population, who would view them as liberators: 'these people will greet us with rapture; for they have long wished that we would come to deliver them from their oppressors.' With this sort of liberationist effusion, one might suppose oneself back in the National Assembly with Isnard or Brissot. In view of the experiences of the intervening six years, during which the masses from one end of Europe to another had rejected the Revolution and all that it stood for, one must wonder whether Talleyrand was writing what he believed or what he thought the Directory might like to hear. More in keeping with his own well-established priorities was the confident forecast that the expedition would pay for itself and start showing a profit within a very short space of time. The foreign minister summed up under four headings, asserting:

1. That the conquest of Egypt in nothing more than a just reprisal for the wrongs done to us by the Porte and the insults we have had to endure there;
2. That it will be easy and even infallible;
3. That it wil involve only modest expenditure, for which the Republic will soon be reimbursed;
4. Finally, that it presents innumerable advantages for the Republic.[33]

Talleyrand's optimism proved to be mistaken in most respects, but it was not entirely unreasonable. The French position did seem highly advantageous. Since the alliance with Spain of October 1796 and the subsequent British decision to withdraw its fleet to concentrate on warding off invasion, it was natural that the Mediterranean should be regarded as a French lake.[34] By his conquest of Italy, Bonaparte had demonstrated that a land power could expel a maritime power from an ocean by capturing its bases.[35] It was also reasonable to conclude that the Turks would be immobilised by domestic problems. Only recently, on 4 January 1798, a French captain returning from a mission to Turkey had reported to the Directory that the regime there was in its death-throes, its army derisory, its economy in ruins, its finances chaotic. He had also recommended that the French should step in at once to pick up the Greek archipelago and Egypt.[36] In addition to the perennial discontent of the various religious and ethnic minorities, led by the Christian Greeks, it was also well known that the Sultan Selim III faced mounting resistance from the restive janissaries and provincial governors, notably Pasvan Oglu, the Pasha of Vidin.[37] As it was thought inconceivable that the Turks could ever combine with Russia and as any attempt to intervene in Egypt would leave their northern provinces dangerously exposed, it was reasonable to conclude that they would confine their reaction to verbal protests.

On 23 February 1798, just nine days after the submission of Talleyrand's recommendations, General Bonaparte reported on his recent tour of inspection of the preparations being made for the invasion of England. His conclusions were depressing. The naval cover necessary was so unready that there was no prospect of an invasion in the foreseeable future. He recommended, therefore, that the project be abandoned. If the Directory wished to strike a blow against Great Britain, it should send an army to capture Hamburg and Hanover, or an amphibious expedition to the Levant to threaten India. In the meantime, some show of an impending invasion of England should be maintained, to keep the British concentrating on defence of home waters.[38] This dual campaign by their foreign minister and their most successful general carried the day with a majority of the directors. Reubell and La Revellière were opposed, wedded as they were to a continental strategy and nervous about sending abroad the élite of the French army.[39] Their less perceptive colleagues were seduced by the prospect of a cheap, easy and effective campaign which had the additional advantage of removing from France a popular general with political ambitions.[40] On 5 March the necessary authorisation was granted.

Even by Bonaparte's hectic standards, events now developed at breakneck speed. On 19 May 13 ships of the line, 7 frigates, 35 other warships and 280 transports, containing 16,000 seamen, 38,000 soldiers and 187 scientific and artistic experts, left Toulon. On 12 June the expedition captured Malta; on 2 July it captured Alexandria; on 21 July it defeated the Mameluke army at the battle of the Pyramids; on 24 July it entered Cairo. So far, so good: just as Talleyrand had predicted, Egypt had fallen with only brief and ineffectual resistance. But, almost at once, his other assumptions began to prove fatally unfounded.

The first, and probably most decisive, was his assumption about the behaviour of Britain. Even for someone as well acquainted with the country as Talleyrand, it was easy to misread the current situation there. All the intelligence reaching France in 1797–98 pointed to war-weariness, not to say exhaustion. In particular, the mutinies at Spithead and the Nore in April and June 1797 seemed to show how worm-eaten were the 'hearts of oak', the only barrier to foreign invasion. The financial crisis of early 1797, complete with a run on the banks and the abandoning of the gold standard, suggested that the old Brissotin prediction that an economy based on credit could not withstand the pressures of war were at last proving correct.[41] Yet in reality the worst was over by the end of 1797. Fiscal reorganisation raised the necessary funds to continue the struggle, the economy began to expand again and the enrolment of huge numbers of volunteers confirmed that public opinion was still eminently sound.[42] Above all, the political will to fight the war *à outrance* had returned. Just as the Directory was authorising Bonaparte's expedition to Egypt, so Pitt and his colleagues were authorising a return by the Royal Navy to the Mediterranean. This was part of a general plan to revive European resistance to the French and, in particular, to revive the flagging spirits of the Portuguese. It was not a direct response to the Egyptian project; on the contrary, until very late in the day it was believed in London that the preparations at Toulon were aimed at Ireland.[43] No matter what its basis, the decision ensured that Nelson's fleet was not far away when Bonaparte's expedition set sail. After narrowly missing his prey *en route*, Nelson finally ran the French fleet to earth in Aboukir Bay on 1 August and there destroyed it.

The news of Nelson's victory caused a sensation in Europe, earning, among other things, the most distinguished musical celebration ever of a military event – Haydn's 'Nelson Mass'. In more practical if more ephemeral terms, the battle of Aboukir Bay restored British naval supremacy in the Mediterranean, trapped Bonaparte in the Middle East for fifteen fruitless months, exposed the new French colonies to recapture and, above all, gave fresh encouragement to France's potential enemies.

No power was more in need of encouragement than Turkey, whose subsequent conduct disproved another of Talleyrand's optimistic assumptions. It should not be supposed that conflict between the archetypal oriental despotism and revolutionary France was inevitable on ideological grounds. While the theocratic feudalism of the Turks was about as far removed from revolutionary principles as it is possible to imagine, *raison d'état* allowed – or rather commanded – a relatively cordial *modus vivendi:* 'The Ottoman attitude towards the Revolution itself was a curious consequence of self-interest, utter ignorance of European conditions and pure romance.'[44] In January 1792, Ahmed Efendi, the private secretary of Selim III, wrote in his diary: 'May God cause the upheaval in France to spread like syphilis to the enemies of the Empire, hurl them into prolonged conflict with one another, and thus accomplish results beneficial to the Empire, amen.'[45] Not even the news of the execution of Louis XVI severed relations – the Turks were inured to regicide by the high mortality rate of their own sovereigns. As the Terror ravaged France in year II, they continued to ask for, and to receive, military experts to assist with the reorganisation of their armed forces. In return, they sent the French ammunition and other military supplies.[46]

For five years after the outbreak of war in the west, this relative harmony persisted. It was Bonaparte's seizure of the Ionian Islands in the summer of 1797 that first suggested that the Revolution might be relevant – and detrimental – to the Turkish Empire after all. If the Turks were unaware that Bonaparte was promoting a plan for the revival of an independent Greece,[47] they knew he was in touch with the disaffected pashas of Janina and Vidin and that his agents were distributing revolutionary propaganda to their Balkan subjects.[48] When Campo Formio confirmed this French intrusion into the eastern Mediterranean, the reaction in Constantinople was almost as violent as that in Venice. Negotiations on military collaboration were broken off and the French military advisers dismissed.[49]

The news of the invasion of Egypt only served to complete the process of alienation. Quite apart from the strategic implications of its loss, the province had been a major source of food for Constantinople's huge population, a fact which was rubbed home daily by rapidly rising prices. By August they had doubled, so economic privation and social unrest were added to the religious and political arguments for retaliation.[50] Yet a multiple sense of grievance was not sufficient reason for resorting to actual hostilities, as indeed it never was or is. With weak finances, an army in the process of reorganisation and the rebellious pashas to contend with, war was not something to be undertaken lightly. When asked by his senior ministers for an immediate declaration of war, on receiving news of the French invasion, Selim III replied very sensibly: 'What is the point in declaring war when we can undertake nothing against the enemy?'[51] The battle of Aboukir Bay on 1 August changed all that. With the French navy destroyed, Bonaparte's army land-locked and France's new colonies in the Ionian Islands exposed, there was plenty the Turks could now undertake against the enemy.[52] As if that were not sufficient encouragement, on 4 September a Russian squadron dropped anchor off Constantinople with the avowed aim of helping the Turks to combat the threat from the French.

THE RUSSIAN ROAD TO WAR

The Russian road to war had been long and tortuous, more than once turning back on itself. Its meanderings had demonstrated that by itself mutual enmity, however strong, is never enough to lead to actual war. Of all the great powers, Russia was the most strident in condemning the French Revolution; of all the great powers, Russia was the last to go to war against it. In the years after 1789 Catherine the Great displayed none of the neutrality of Britain, the prudence of Austria or the inconsistency of Prussia. She urged armed intervention to restore the old regime and showered money on the émigrés. Nor was this counter-revolutionary ardour feigned for public show; the Tsarina's anger at the revolutionaries' presumption was patently sincere. As she exclaimed to Baron Grimm: 'I am in a terrible rage; I have stamped my feet on reading of these . . . horrors there.'[53] As this outburst was provoked just by the news that Louis XVI had accepted the constitution of September 1791, it can be imagined what reaction such later developments as the abolition of the monarchy and the execution of the King aroused. In fact, the latter atrocity made her physically ill and confined her to bed.[54]

This almost pathological aversion did find some practical expression. After the Flight to Varennes, the French chargé d'affaires was no longer received at court; after the execution of Louis XVI he was expelled, together with all French consuls. Diplomatic relations were broken off de facto in July 1792 and de jure in February 1793. Russians were forbidden to travel to France, French citizens were expelled from Russia, unless they took an oath – in church – abjuring the French Republic and all its works. The commercial teaty of 1787 was suspended until the restoration of 'legal authority' in France, all French imports were prohibited, Russian ships were forbidden to enter French ports and French ships were excluded from Russian ports.[55] Also overtly hostile was a series of treaties concluded with the other old-regime powers. In October 1791 Sweden was promised men, money and ships for an invasion the following year, a project which was aborted by the assassination of Gustavus III at *un ballo in maschera* on 29 March 1792. Although Catherine declined to accede to the Austro-Prussian treaty of 7 February 1792 (see p. 114), she did conclude bilateral alliances with each of them in July of the same year.[56] Perhaps more striking, in view of recent hostility, was the rapid *rapprochement* achieved with Great Britain. In March 1793 not only was a commercial treaty signed but also a convention which sent a large Russian squadron to cruise with the Royal Navy in the North Sea. This naval assistance was renewed by a further treaty in February 1795.[57]

In view of this sustained barrage of hostility, a case could be made for regarding Russia as at war with France from 1793, or even 1792. But, if so, it was only a phoney war. The only instrument which could lend reality to the counter-revolutionary rhetoric was the army, but the 'Russian steam-roller' remained parked in eastern Europe until the end of the decade. Moreover, many of the measures allegedly directed against France had different destinations. The attempt to exclude revolutionary influence was directed more at Russian subjects, and especially at the Poles among them, than against the French. The treaty with Gustavus III was designed primarily to keep Sweden out of the hands of the British and the Prussians.[58] The complex dealings with Austria and Prussia had Poland, not France in view. If only the two other major powers of the east could be embroiled in French affairs, Catherine could deal with the Poles, who had broken away from Russian control after 1787, on her own and at her leisure. As she admitted to her secretary in November 1791: 'I am racking my brains in order to push the courts of Vienna and Berlin into French affairs. . . . There are reasons I cannot talk about; I want to get them involved in that business to have my hands free. I have much unfinished business, and it's necessary for them to be kept busy and out of my way.'[69]

That unfinished business was, of course, Poland. Less than a month after the war in the west had begun, the Russian armies had set about subjugation. During the next three years, all of Catherine's resources were absorbed in arranging the second partition of January 1793, dealing with the revolt of Kosciusko in 1794 and then attending to the third and final partition of 1795. So she rejected Austrian and Prussian demands for military assistance with the cynical and specious argument that, while they were fighting Jacobinism in France, she was waging her own war against it in Poland.[60] Further arguments against sending an army west were the justifiable suspicion that the Swedes and/or Turks would take the opportunity to try another fall and the urgent need for financial recovery after the war of 1787–92.[61] Moreover, after Prussia's withdrawal from the war in April 1795, the way to the west was blocked.[62]

It is also difficult to see what Russia might have gained from a war with France at this stage. In her early memoranda on the Revolution, Catherine had stressed the need to restore France to great-power status, to serve as a counterweight to Great Britain and Prussia, but the revolutionaries had attended to that task more than adequately.[63] Austria and Prussia might hope to barter French conquests for German territory, Great Britain might hope for – and get – French colonies, but there was nothing in the larder to appeal to Russian appetites. Once Poland had been safely gathered in and the frontiers of the three eastern powers were contiguous, the only area allowing Russian expansion in Europe was the south. It was just in that direction that Catherine's incorrigibly rapacious attention began to swivel in 1795. In a secret clause of the treaty of 3 January which initiated the third partition of Poland, the Russians and Austrians agreed that in the event of another war with Turkey the great 'Greek Plan' of 1782 should be revived.[64] In the following year, Catherine and her latest lover, Platon Zubov, embarked on an even more grandiose scheme – the 'Oriental Project', designed to give Russia political and commercial domination of the entire region between Turkey and Tibet. As a first step, an army was assembled in the Caucasus for an invasion of Persia.[65]

It was only at the very end of her long reign that Catherine took her first hesitant steps towards actual war with France. Significantly, her forward move was occasioned by the impending collapse of Austrian resistance in the face of Bonaparte's Italian campaign. With the balance that had proved so beneficial in the past beginning to break down, it was necessary to add a little weight to the anti-French scales. Even so, the Russian response to the Austrian appeal was hedged about with conditions. An army 64,000-strong would be sent west – but only if the Prussians made a contribution of similar size and only if Great Britain provided further subsidies. As Prussia was still sunk in the post-prandial torpor induced by the ingestion of two large slices of Poland, and as 'Pitt's Gold' was now in short supply, it may be doubted whether this expeditionary force would ever have got under way. In any event, it was too late. As General Suvorov was assembling his troops in Podolia, on 17 November 1796 the Tsarina died.[66]

Given what was known about her successor, her forty-two-year-old son Paul I, Russian policy was not expected to change. Strongly influenced by the French *émigrés* who had cultivated the reversionary interest for years, his pronouncements on the Revolution had been even more choleric than those of his mother.[67] On his accession he unleashed a circular to foreign courts pledging all possible opposition to the 'frenzied French Republic' which threatened Europe with the complete destruction of all laws, rights, property, and social order.[68] Yet the same document stated with equal firmness that Russia was exhausted after forty years of virtually incessant warfare and that there could be *no* direct participation in the war against France. General Suvorov's expeditionary force was stood down and the squadron serving with the Royal Navy was recalled.[69] The inaction into which Russia now relapsed may have been malevolently Francophobe, but it was equally clearly inaction.

The reasons for this sharp turn away from a forward policy against revolutionary France have been much debated by Russian historians. Pre-revolutionary scholars, led by Paul's most prolix biographer, Nikolai Shil'der, saw in everything the new Tsar did an instinctive reaction against his detested mother: 'From its very first days the new reign was the negation of the old.'[70] There may well be something in this psychological interpretation. Even a strong and stable personality would have found it difficult to handle the conduct of a mother such as Catherine. Not only had she connived at the murder of Paul's (putative) father but she had also tried to exclude him from the succession, in favour of his own son, Alexander.[71] But, by all accounts, Paul's personality was neither strong nor stable. A popular view of its mercurial quality was well put by Holland Rose: 'The new Tsar Paul, a prey to whims and passions, was the centre of a cyclonic system all his own.'[72]

More recently, Soviet historians have stressed the practical reasons for Paul's restrained foreign policy. They point to the intensity and ubiquity of serf revolts during the period 1796–98, when 278 separate risings affecting 32 provinces (*gubernii*) were logged. On the estate of Prince Golitsyn and Count Apraksin something approaching a civil war was fought out between 16,000 armed serfs and the regular army sent to suppress them.[73] With a new Pugachev rebellion feared, this was no time to be sending the army out of the country – especially as it might return contaminated with the very views it had been sent to eliminate. The continued restiveness of Poland and the neutrality of Prussia were further reasons for staying at home.[74] So was the state of the country's finances. By 1796 the National Debt had reached 215 million roubles and, as the annual income and expenditure were 55.4 and 78.2 million roubles respectively, was set to go on growing.[75]

These were essentially negative reasons for peace. As R. S. Lanin has shown, however, it is possible to interpret Russian policy in a more constructive manner.[76] He argued, with perhaps greater confidence than his evidence permitted, that the new Tsar was seeking to continue what had proved most effective in his mother's system, namely a strategy of 'free hands'. If he could avoid direct involvement in European entanglements and if some sort of balance could be maintained between revolutionary France and the opposition, then Russia would be in a dominant position.[77] If there is little direct support to be found for such a view, it is at least a reasonable inference from what Paul actually did during the first year of his reign.[78]

The first phase was a diplomatic initiative in the spring and summer of 1797 to mediate a general European peace. Recognising that a return to the strict status quo ante bellum was unrealistic, given recent French military success, Paul proposed that France should be allowed to keep Belgium and Liège, but not the left bank of the Rhine. As Russia was a guarantor of the Peace of Teschen, and thus also of the German status quo, he was particularly sensitive about anything affecting the integrity of the Holy Roman Empire. If France had obtained the left bank and the consequential process of compensation and secularisation had been set in motion on the right bank, that integrity would have been not so much compromised as obliterated. So a special envoy, Prince Repnin, was to be sent to Berlin to enlist the support of the Prussians and to make contact with the French.[79] Repnin's mission was aborted before it could begin, because news then arrived that it had been pre-empted by the preliminary Peace of Leoben of 18 April 1797.

Disappointed but undeterred, Paul tried again, first through the regular ambassador in Prussia, Kolichev, and then through another special envoy, Count Panin. Contact was made with the French representative, Caillard, and negotiations began. But by this time the French military position was much too strong to make any assistance from a third party seem attractive. As Caillard reported to Talleyrand, Paul I hoped to use his proffered mediation between France and the Holy Roman Empire to reinforce his status as guarantor of the latter and then to play the same sort of role as that enjoyed by France after 1648. Agreeing with this assessment, the foreign minister sent back instructions not to give an inch.[80] In fact, neither Repnin, nor Kolichev, nor Panin stood a chance. As Avgusta Stanislavskaya has pointed out, Paul I was trying to contain the Revolution with the techniques of old-regime diplomacy and so was doomed to failure. Far from winning 'free hands' for Russia, Paul's mediating policy had succeeded only in giving still more room for manoeuvre to the Directory and Bonaparte.[81]

In the summer and autumn of 1797 the Russians were given three sharp reminders that revolutionary France was more than just another European power. First, the occupation of the Ionian Islands and the arrest of the Russian consul at Zante brought French troops for the first time into a Russian zone of interest. Then the *coup d'état* of Fructidor revitalised the Revolution. Finally, the Peace of Campo Formio confirmed that France was now a major force in the eastern Mediterranean. The fragile negotiations at Berlin could not survive these shocks; in September and October respectively, the Russians and the French ordered them to be broken off.[82]

Until this point Paul's attention had been devoted almost exclusively to the situation in Germany. He had shown his lack of interest in the south by reducing some of his mother's schemes for the region's development.[83] The only indication of a Mediterranean interest had been a convention signed in January 1797 with the ruler of Malta, the Order of the Knights of St John of Jerusalem, by which the Order's old Polish branch was reconstituted as the Grand Priory of Russia.[84] Previous attempts to secure an alliance with the Maltese Knights, to make use of the island's port facilities during maritime wars with the Turks, had been foiled by the predominant French influence. Now that the Revolution had destroyed that influence and left the Knights friendless, the way was open for a renewal of Russian interest. It is possible, as Saul argues, that Paul's interest at this stage was primarily religious,[85] but once Bonaparte had taken over the Ionian Islands, Malta's strategic position made the island a highly desirable prize. In the aftermath of Campo Formio, on 29 November 1797, Paul declared himself to be the Order's protector.[86]

Alarm about French expansion in the Mediterranean was exacerbated greatly by simultaneous rumours about French designs on Poland. Their source was authoritative, for Count Panin had a spy in the French embassy in Berlin, who was intercepting communications between the Directory and Caillard. On 9 January 1798 Panin reported that the Directory had told a delegation of Poles to be patient, that the French would never forget their nation's services to the Revolution and that their day of vengeance would come.[87] Two weeks later Panin could add that the Prussians were being urged by Caillard to allow their Polish territories to be reformed into an independent state, to which would then be added the Russian and Austrian portions.[88] As it was well known that a Polish legion 7,000-strong was serving in the French army and that military units of Polish exiles were being formed in the Danubian Principalities by Oginski, these reports had to be taken seriously.[89] Russian anxiety was eminently reasonable: if the French could set up satellite states in the Netherlands, Switzerland and Italy – which is just what they were currently doing – then why not in Poland?

By early 1798 the Russians had reached the conclusion that the French appetite for territory was simply insatiable. In Germany, Poland and the Mediterranean, this relentless expansionist surge was now posing a serious threat to Russian interests. To fight the war which now seemed inevitable, a campaign was launched early in 1798 to unite all the major powers of Europe in a grand anti-French coalition. It was the fitful progress of this campaign which accounted for Russia's fitful progress to war.[90] It took place in three stages, the timing of which was determined by the degree of assistance that could be expected from the other powers and by the ability of the French to respond. Significantly, the first act of hostility was in the maritime theatre, in support of the British. As the latter were already at war, there could be no question of lack of support; as the Royal Navy had destroyed the Spanish and

Dutch fleets the previous year, the risk involved was minimal. On 3 May 1798 orders were issued for two squadrons of five ships of the line and two frigates each to sail from the Baltic and Archangel respectively, to assist the British blockade of the Dutch coast. A third squadron of the same size was ordered to be fitted out at Reval.[91] All three were on station by the end of August, thus releasing British vessels for service in the Mediterranean.

It was General Bonaparte who prompted the next escalation. The Russians had been aware for some time that a French expeditionary force was being prepared at Toulon and had concluded that it was directed at them. Prince Andrei Razumovsky, the Russian ambassador at Vienna, reported that it was destined for Albania. There it would join forces with the rebellious Pasha of Vidin, Pasvan Oglu, and march on Bessarabia to link up with the Polish exiles assembled there. The next step, of course, would be the incitement of a general insurrection throughout Russian-occupied Poland.[92] Other Russians – the senior diplomat Kochubey, for example – believed that the French fleet would sail straight to the Crimea.[93] Yet another school of thought held that it would stop at Salonica, from where its army would march overland to Poland.[94] Whatever the precise location of the landfall, the threat was deemed obvious. In April 1798 an approach was made to the Turks for an alliance, the Black Sea Fleet was put on a war footing and armies were assembled at Kiev, Odessa and Ochakov.[95]

News that Bonaparte's fleet had taken Malta prompted further defensive measures. An army was despatched to the Turkish frontier and on 5 August Admiral Ushakov was ordered to sea, to cruise off Constantinople and to respond to any Turkish request for help.[96] But the decision to take the offensive, to pass through the straits and attack French possessions in the Mediterranean was not taken until two essential safeguards had made success seem certain. They were: firstly, the news that the French expedition had disembarked in Egypt and so, for the time being at least, was safely out of harm's way; and secondly, the news that the Turks were willing to cooperate.[97] The further news that Nelson had destroyed the French fleet at Aboukir Bay on 1 August allowed the Russians and the Turks to commence their joint operations against the Ionian Islands with real confidence. Unusually in the history of warfare, it proved to be justified. The first island (Cerigo) fell on 5 October 1798, the last (Vido) on 3 March the following year.

AUSTRIA AND FRANCE RESUME HOSTILITIES

With fleets in the North Sea and the Adriatic, Russia was now at war at either end of Europe. Both operations were relatively small scale, however. Before such pinpricks could be supplemented by a sword-thrust to the heart of revolutionary France, agreement would have to be reached with Austria. That proved to be a much more time-consuming and frustrating operation than might have been expected. Certainly the Austrians were thoroughly disillusioned, and at a very early stage, with the Peace of Campo Formio. As the French continued to expand and consolidate their control of the Netherlands, Switzerland, Germany and Italy (see p. 177), the temptation to resume hostilities grew progressively stronger. As early as February 1798, an exasperated Francis II wrote to his brother, the Archduke Charles, that Austria's position was proving even worse in peace than it had been in war and told him to get the army ready for a resumption of the latter as soon as possible.[98]

Such bellicose spasms were restrained by powerful counter-arguments counselling prudence. The wounds sustained during the last conflict were too fresh, the finances too disordered, the army too disorganised, to allow a fresh round to be started with much confidence.[99] The attitude of the Prussians – hated, feared and suspected in equal measures – was dangerously uncertain. Lured by promises of German territory, might they not move from neutrality to outright support of France? The Tsar's anger at Austria's 'betrayal' in concluding Campo Formio was well known, as was his unpredictability. The British government was displaying its customary selfish avarice in demanding the payment of old debts before agreeing to new subsidies. Until the attitude of all these fair-weather friends had been clarified in a satisfactory manner, there was to be no question of Austria risking its neck for the sake of Europe once more. Moreover, there still remained some sort of hope that Austrian objectives could be obtained by peaceful methods. Throughout the first half of 1798 attempts were made to persuade the French to grant more territory in Italy (preferably the Legations), to prevent Prussian expansion in Germany and to give up the plan to secularise the ecclesiastical states of the Holy Roman Empire.[100]

It was not until the summer of 1798 that these anxieties were allayed and these hopes were confounded. Crucial in determining the Austrian attitude were the negotiations conducted at Selz in Alsace between 30 May and 6 July between the new Austrian foreign minister, Count Ludwig Cobenzl, and François de Neufchâteau, who until 9 May had been a member of the Directory.[101] Nominally, they were concerned with an incident in Vienna on 13 April, during which the French ambassador's residence had been stormed by a mob and after which the ambassador (Bernadotte) had left the city. Cobenzl, however, took the opportunity to make one final attempt to reach a negotiated settlement. Finding his opposite number utterly intransigent, after five weeks of sterile and acrimonious recrimination he left the conference convinced that war was now unavoidable.[102]

Just as the prospect of peaceful expansion was being given the *coup de grâce*, the military option was becoming a good deal more attractive. On 9 March 1798 Francis II had written personally to the Tsar, seeking to improve Austro-Russian relations and, in particular, seeking his help in dealing with the potential Prussian menace. Now that Paul was becoming increasingly worried about French designs on Poland (see p. 190), the response was immediate and cordial.[103] Commencing in April 1798, a major Russian initiative was now launched in Berlin to win the Prussians for a grand coalition against France.[104] Paul's suspicion of the Austrians did not vanish overnight, however. Quite rightly, he assumed that the conference at Selz indicated that the Austrians would strike a bargain with the French if the terms were right. It was not until July that he could be persuaded to promise active support for Austria in the event of a new war. By that time, of course, news had arrived that Bonaparte had captured Malta and was on his way east.[105] By that time also, there was reassuring news from Prussia. On the one hand, the Prussians had declined resolutely to join the coalition, a decision which provoked a characteristically intemperate reaction from the Tsar. On the other hand, the Prussians did give a pledge that they would remain neutral when the continental war resumed. They also rebuffed emphatically a French approach for an alliance.[106]

Any remaining anxiety on that score the Austrians may have felt was finally laid to rest by a Russian guarantee that an 'army of observation' would be deployed in Poland to make sure that the Prussians did not change their minds.[107] With the news that Bonaparte had been trapped in Egypt by Nelson's victory at Aboukir Bay on 1 August, there was no danger that Austria's conqueror of the previous year would return to direct the French war effort. In Vienna the mood was now one of aggressive optimism. The more realistic Archduke Charles wrote to Duke Albert of Saxony-Teschen: 'What you tell me about the success people expect from the new war and the belief that it will be easy to gobble up the new republics terrifies me.'[108]

In short, by the autumn of 1798, most of the arguments which had kept the Austrians at truculent peace in the spring had been weakened, if not refuted. On 6 September their plan of campaign was given to the Russians. There was to be no fighting in Germany, for there the French enjoyed a favourable strategic and political position. The main thrust was to be at Switzerland, to take control of the vital Alpine passes. Such a priority had the added advantage of proving that the Russian army would not be employed in making conquests for the Austrians. With Switzerland already destabilised by revolts against French dominance, its conquest was expected to be straightforward. From there, the invasion of the rebellious south-eastern departments of France could be launched. If further British subsidies could be extracted, even Paris would be within the coalition's reach.[109]

But Austria was not to be hurried. The dangers of a winter campaign in the Alps, the never-ending wrangle with the British over subsidies, the wish to see the Russian assistance actually materialise in the shape of an auxiliary force on Austrian soil, perhaps even a last lingering hope that the French would see reason, kept the Archduke Charles's armies stationary. Austria's hand was then forced by an independent initiative in Italy, for on 12 November 1798 the Neapolitan army invaded the Roman Republic. With good reason, the Neapolitans feared that the relentless French expansion which already had absorbed most of the peninsula would engulf them sooner rather than later. With much less good reason, they supposed that their army, together with Nelson's fleet, would be capable of defeating the French.[110] Although at first they carried all before them, taking Rome on 26 November, it was not long before they were fleeing southwards in headlong retreat. By the end of the year, General Championnet was in Naples and the Neapolitan royal family was in exile on Sicily. On 23 January 1799 yet another French satellite state – the Neapolitan Republic (or the 'Parthenopean Republic', as it was known in Paris) – was added to what was already an impressive collection.

In Vienna the response to appeals for help was at first entirely negative. King Ferdinand of Naples had been told firmly in advance that any premature strike would not attract Austrian support.[111] It was on the Russians that the news of this fresh disaster had a galvanising effect. The dazzling success of the combined operations in the Ionian Islands had opened up for Paul I the vista of a Russian-dominated eastern Mediterranean. On 7 November 1798 the Russian Priory of the Order of the Knights of St John had deposed the grand master, von Hompesch, for alleged treason and had elected Paul in his place.[112] So once Malta had been recaptured – not thought to be difficult, now that Nelson had eliminated the French fleet – Russian control of the region would be secure. So far as Italy was concerned, the ideal solution would be the restoration of the old-regime frontiers in their entirety, with the French excluded altogether and Austrian influence confined to the north. The French occupation of Piedmont in November–December 1798 and the Neapolitan invasion of the Roman Republic at the same time indicated that the time had come for action. An alliance was concluded with Naples, General Herman's corps of 11,000, currently stationed on the Dniester, was ordered to Italy with all possible despatch and Admiral Ushakov's fleet was sent from the Ionian Islands to protect the Neapolitan coast.[113] Significantly, Herman's force included units destined for the garrisoning of Malta.

How indignant was the Tsar, therefore, when he learned that the Austrians had disowned the Neapolitans and had declined them assistance in their hour of need. Even someone less paranoid than Paul would have smelt a rat. The familiar spectre of a secret deal between the Austrians and the French rose once more. On 31 December the Russian ambassador at Vienna was told to threaten complete withdrawal of the Russian auxiliary force – now, at long last, actually in winter quarters at Brünn – if the Austrians did not stop dithering.[114] The threat was then sweetened by a promise to multiply the help offered from one to three corps and to appoint General Suvorov as commander-in-chief, as the Austrians had requested.[115] Almost simultaneously came an ultimatum from the French, on 2 January 1799: expel the Russian force or go to war.[116] This combination of push and pull at last took the Austrians over the edge. The armies were ordered to take up position for a spring offensive, although it was still stressed that they should avoid anything which would make it appear that they were striking first.[117]

If the Austrian road to war had been sluggish and hesitant, their opponents had not hurried. Top priority for the French in 1798 had been the successful conclusion of the Congress of Rastatt. If the reorganisation of Germany could only be completed, they reasoned, all Europe north of the Alps could be neutralised and the French war effort could be concentrated on the current weak spot – Italy. It was even thought possible that Austria would not dare to resume hostilities if confronted with a *fait accompli*.[118] It was now that the folly of the Egyptian adventure made itself fully felt. Just when the French needed to concentrate on the settlement of central Europe, they made new enemies for themselves in the east. As Talleyrand's over-optimistic assumptions were progressively disproved, so their European hegemony began to crumble. General Bonaparte told his secretary Bourrienne that, had it not been for the disaster at Aboukir Bay, he would have returned very shortly to France and then would have mobilised such an invasion force at the Channel ports that the British would have been forced to abandon the Mediterranean. Reinforcements could then have been sent to Egypt, and France would have become the mistress of the east.[119]

This musing in the subjunctive mood only served as a further indictment of French miscalculation. The disagreeable reality consisted of a resurgent Great Britain, a hostile Russia and Turkey and an increasingly restive Austria. Closer to home too, problems had begun to accumulate. In May 1798 the *coup d'état* of Floréal, carried out by the Directory to adjust the elections to its liking, had demonstrated the regime's continuing instability. Revolts in Switzerland, Italy, Belgium and Luxemburg demonstrated the continuing instability of the regime's control of the rest of Europe. The fiasco of General Humbert's expedition to Ireland in August signalled the final failure of the attempt to open a second front in the British Isles. With the élite of the French army bottled up in Egypt and the remainder scattered across Europe from the North Sea to the Mediterranean, military resources were spread dangerously thin.

All these weaknesses helped to prevent the confident headlong rush into war which had characterised the events of 1792 and 1793. Yet the news was not all bad. By the end of 1798 the various revolts against French rule in the occupied territories had all been brought under control. With the resources of most of western and southern Europe ready to be exploited through the satellite republics, there could be no long-term problem in financing and supplying the war effort. With the Rhine, the Alpine passes and the major Italian rivers and fortresses in French hands, the strategic position was advantageous, if not impregnable. With Prussia neutral and the important German princes now clients, the northern and north-western flanks were secure. Everyone could see that the members of the coalition which threatened France were deeply divided against each other and would be able to cooperate only ineffectively and briefly. The facile crushing of the Neapolitan attack showed that the revolutionary armies could still carry all before them. Inside France, the new conscription law of 5 September 1798 had resurrected the language of 1793: 'Every Frenchman is a soldier and is obliged to come to the defence of the fatherland. . . .When the fatherland is declared to be in danger, all the French are summoned to its defence.'[120]

All these counterbalancing grounds for optimism ensured that, although war might be delayed, it would not be shirked. Once again, it was the French who took the initiative. At the end of February 1799 their advance guard began to cross the Rhine and a formal declaration of war on Austria was issued on 12 March.[121] In truth, war had become a way of life, even a matter of necessity for the Directory. Only war could keep ambitious generals and disruptive soldiers out of France, only war could keep the armies supplied and paid, only war could justify the repeated abuse of the constitution, only war could bring the regime some badly needed prestige. As Albert Sorel observed: 'War alone assured the existence of the Directory, and war could be sustained only by war itself.'[122] On 2 January 1799, on the eve of the resumption of the continental war, one of the directors, Reubell, told a Prussian diplomat: 'war has become our element . . . the nation has become martial (*guerrière*).'[123] His bellicosity soon rebounded. The victories of the Archduke Charles and Suvorov, together with the numerous popular risings against the French all over Europe, prompted the regime's terminal crisis. By the end of the year the Directory had fallen to a *coup d'état* by General Bonaparte. It was appropriate that a regime which had lived by the sword should be executed by its most successful general. As he himself remarked many years later, as he languished in exile on St Helena: 'The Directory was overpowered by its own weakness; to exist it needed a state of war as other governments need a state of peace.'[124]

THE CRIPPLED COALITION

The origins of the War of the Second Coalition were as complex as the aims of the protagonists. They encompassed such grandiose schemes as Bonaparte's eastern expedition and such tedious pettiness as the German princes' wrangling over territory at the Congress of Rastatt. Yet certain dominant themes can be identified. First and foremost was the unabated expansionism of the Revolution. Perhaps because so many Brissotin survivors had found their way back into government after the *coup d'état* of 9 Thermidor II (27 July 1794), the continuity with the policies of 1792–93 is striking. The rival notions of revolution-in-one-country and/or a return to *les anciennes limites* and peace could never achieve ascendancy in revolutionary councils. Fuelled by their supreme confidence in their own strength and their supreme contempt for their opponents' decadence, they took on the rest of the Continent with reckless abandon. What was new about this later phase of revolutionary expansion was its extension from the old Brissotin targets of the Low Countries and the Rhineland to Switzerland, Italy and Egypt. If the war had gone according to plan, India too would have been added to the list. This adoption of a Mediterranean strategy brought Russia into the war and gave an ominous, if brief, foretaste of the events to come after 1812.

The French appetite for territory was shared by their oldest enemies, albeit on a much more modest scale. By 1798–9 the Austrians were far more acquisitive than they had been in 1792. Then it had been just the prospect of the Bavarian Exchange which had eased their entry into war. Now they had set their sights on hegemony both in Italy and Germany. Critics of Thugut, the main architect of Austrian policy – as numerous as they have been vehement – have also been less than fair. In the short term, certainly his strategy proved to be a disaster. The alliance with the Russians collapsed by the end of 1799 and a fresh wave of military defeats in 1800 brought another unfavourable peace, leaving France more securely in control of Italy and Germany than ever before. Yet in the long term the two prizes *were* obtained – but not before three more wars had brought France to her knees at last. If he should not be taken to task for opposing the French attempt to take control of most of the Continent, Thugut can certainly be criticised for his policy towards the other German states. His unreasoned and unreasonable suspicion of Prussia helped to keep neutral the coalition's most valuable potential ally. His ruthless pursuit of Austrian interests at the expense of the Holy Roman Empire as a whole delivered the most important German princes into the welcoming arms of the French. They were to remain there until 1813.[125] When all efforts have been made to view the Austrians' interests through the Austrians' eyes, one has to conclude that their conduct before and during the war

197

provided another example of the often-cited Habsburg ability to snatch defeat out of the jaws of victory.

Although France's other arch-enemy never did leave the first war, Great Britain played a crucial role in fomenting the second. The decision to send the Royal Navy back into the Mediterranean and Nelson's subsequent victory at Aboukir Bay made the biggest single contribution to the belief that the French could be beaten, without which the continental war could not have resumed. At a time when a French invasion of England was still possible and a French-backed rising in Ireland was probable, this was a decision of considerable courage and commendable foresight. Other aspects of British policy command less admiration. The persistent inability to comprehend that allies might have interests not identical with their own crippled the coalition from the start (see p. 48).[126] The quibbling with the Austrians over past debts, reminiscent in its pettiness of similar wrangles with the Prussians in 1794, went well beyond good housekeeping to become self-defeating miserliness.

The British insistence on treating allies as auxiliaries was well illustrated by their stormy relationship with the Russians. In the autumn of 1799 a joint Russo-British expedition was fighting together in Holland; only a year later, not only had Paul I withdrawn all his forces from the war but had formed a League of Armed Neutrality with an overt anti-British purpose. If he had not been assassinated in March 1801, it is very likely that he would have concluded an actual alliance with France.[127] It need hardly be added that responsibility for the brevity of the relationship did not lie entirely with the British. If more coherent than has been supposed by historians convinced of the Tsar's lunacy, Russian policy during Paul I's short reign was certainly volatile. It was also over-ambitious, with ultimate failure guaranteed. Russian control of Italy and the Mediterranean could only have been achieved with the assistance of Great Britain and Austria, yet neither of those powers would have permitted Russian ascendancy in either area. That was demonstrated all too clearly by the events following the British capture of Malta in September 1800. Breaking an unambiguous agreement dating from December 1798, not only did the British decline to share the administration with their allies but also prevented them setting foot on the island.[128]

Flawed from the start, the second coalition very soon fell apart. The lessons taught by the first had only been partially understood and even more partially implemented. Many more years of defeat and suffering in the hard school of French revolutionary warfare were required before the allies could graduate successfully. Only when it was realised that the limitless aims of France had made redundant Austro-Prussian competition for Germany or Anglo-Russian competition for the Mediterranean, and only when it was realised that the challenge of a revolutionary state could only be met by the reform of one's own, would victory be possible.

REFERENCES AND NOTES

1. Gunther E. Rothenberg, *The Art of Warfare in the Age of Napoleon* (London 1977) pp. 247–8.
2. Felix Markham, *Napoleon* (New York 1963) p. 49.
3. André Fugier, *La Révolution française et l'Empire napoléonien, Histoire des relations internationales,* ed. Pierre Renouvin, vol. 4 (Paris 1954) p. 102.
4. Karl Otmar Freiherr von Aretin, *Heiliges Römisches Reich 1776–1806. Reichsverfassung und Staatssouveränität,* 2 vols, vol. 1 (Wiesbaden 1967) pp. 343–4.
5. Albert Sorel, *L'Europe et la Révolution française,* vol. 5 (Paris 1903) pp. 253–4.
6. Ibid., p. 282.
7. A. J. Michailowski-Danilewski and D. A. Miliutin, *Geschichte des Krieges Russlands mit Frankreich unter der Regierung Kaiser Pauls I im Jahre 1799,* vol. 1 (Munich 1856) pp. 37, 328–9.
8. Sorel, *L'Europe et la Révolution française,* vol. 5, pp. 245–6.
9. Piers Mackesy, *Statesmen at War. The Strategy of Overthrow 1798–1799* (London 1974) p. 9.
10. C. A. Macartney, *The Habsburg Empire 1790–1918* (London 1968) pp. 179–80.
11. Sorel, *L'Europe et la Révolution française,* vol. 5, p. 225. Chapter 6 of this volume contains the fullest account of the implications of Fructidor for foreign policy.
12. Jacques Godechot, *La Grande Nation. L'Expansion révolutionnaire de la France dans le monde, 1789–1799,* 2 vols, vol. 1, (Paris 1956) pp. 236–8.
13. Adalbert Wahl, *Geschichte des europäischen Staatensystems im Zeitalter der französischen Revolution und der Freiheitskriege (1789–1815)* (Munich and Berlin 1912) pp. 95–6.
14. Simon Schama, *Patriots and Liberators. Revolution in the Netherlands 1780–1813* (London 1977) pp. 308, 338, 351–2.
15. Giovanni Assereto, *La repubblica ligure. Lotte politiche e problemi finanziari (1797–1799,* (Turin 1975) p. 121.
16. Jacques Droz, *Histoire diplomatique de 1648 à 1919,* 3rd edn (Paris 1972) p. 215; Fugier, *La Révolution française et l'empire napoléonien,* pp. 116–17.
17. Sorel, *L'Europe et la Révolution française,* vol. 5, p. 286.
18. Ibid., pp. 260–1.
19. Aretin, *Heiliges Römisches Reich,* vol. 1, pp. 343–7.
20. Ibid., p. 349.
21. Ludwig Häusser, *Deutsche Geschichte vom Tode Friedrichs des Großen bis zur Gründung des deutschen Bundes,* 3rd edn, vol. 2 (Berlin 1862) p.

167.

22. Sorel, *L'Europe et la Révolution française,* vol. 5, p. 240.

23. The French also obtained Paxos, Ithaca, Cerigo and the ports of Parga, Preveza, Buttrinto and Vonitza on the coast of southern Albania and northern Empirus – Stanford Jay Shaw, *Between Old and New: The Ottoman Empire under Sultan Selim III, 1789–1807* (Cambridge, Mass. 1971) p. 252.

24. Boris Mouravieff, *L'Alliance russo-turque au milieu des guerres napoléoniennes* (Neufchâtel 1954) p. 13.

25. *Correspondance de Napoléon I, publiée par ordre de l'Empereur Napoléon III,* vol. 3 (Paris 1859) p. 311.

26. Ibid., pp. 391–2.

27. C. de La Jonquière, *L'Expédition d'Egypte, 1798–1801,* vol. 1 (Paris 1900) pp. 151–2.

28. Sorel, *L'Europe et la Révolution française,* vol. 5, p. 218.

29. Thomas Naff, *Ottoman Diplomacy and the Great European Powers 1797–1802* (London dissertation 1960) p. 174.

30. Shafik Ghorbal, *The Beginnings of the Egyptian Question and the Rise of Mehemet Ali* (London 1928) p. 11.

31. Sorel, *L'Europe et la Révolution française,* vol. 5, p. 301.

32. Markham, *Napoleon,* p. 60.

33. La Jonquière, *L'Expédition d'Egypte,* vol. 1, pp. 167–8. La Jonquière reprints the report in its entirety on pp. 154–68.

34. J. Holland Rose, 'The struggle for the Mediterranean in the eighteenth century', *The Indecisiveness of Modern War and Other Essays* (London 1927) pp. 77–8.

35. A. B. Rodger, *The War of the Second Coalition 1798 to 1801: A Strategic Commentary* (Oxford 1964) pp. 7–8.

36. La Jonquière, *L'Expédition d'Egypte,* vol. 1, p. 148.

37. Naff, *Ottoman Diplomacy,* p. 198.

38. The report is reprinted in full in La Jonquiére, *L'Expédition d'Egypte,* vol. 1, pp. 172–6.

39. M. S. Anderson, *The Eastern Question 1774–1923* (London 1966) p. 26.

40. Georges Lefebvre, *The French Revolution,* vol. 2: *From 1793 to 1799* (London and New York 1964) p. 219.

41. For an excellent account of British problems during this period, see ch. 10 of I. R. Christie's *Wars and Revolutions. Britain 1760–1815* (London 1982), appropriately called 'Fight for survival'.

42. Ibid., p. 241; J. Holland Rose, *William Pitt and the Great War* (London 1911) p. 330.

43. Christie *Wars and Revolutions,* p. 242.

44. Shaw, *Between Old and New,* p. 247.

45. Quoted in Bernard Lewis, 'The impact of the French Revolution on Turkey', *Cahiers d'histoire mondiale,* **1** (1) (1953) p. 119.

46. Anderson, *The Eastern Question,* p. 24; Naff, *Ottoman Diplomacy,* pp. 119–21, 125.

47. Paul Pisani, 'L'Expédition russo-turque aux îles ioniennes en 1798–1799', *Revue d'histoire diplomatique,* **2** (1888) p. 197.

48. Shaw, *Between Old and New,* p. 253.

49. Johann Wilhelm Zinkeisen, *Geschichte des osmanischen Reiches in*

Europa, vol. 7 (Gotha 1863) p. 37; Naff, *Ottoman Diplomacy,* p. 143.

50. Anderson, *The Eastern Question,* p. 27.
51. A. D. Novicev, 'Der Einfall der Franzosen in Ägypten und der franz ösisch–türkische Krieg, 1798–1802', *Zeitschrift für Geschichtswissenschaft,* **19** (9) (1971) p. 1140. Novicev cites a Turkish source for this remark.
52. Mackesy, *The Strategy of Overthrow,* p. 42.
53. Isabel de Madariaga, *Russia in the Age of Catherine the Great* (London 1981) p. 428. This new and distinguished biography supersedes all previous work on the reign and contains by far the most detailed and authoritative account of Catherine's relations with the Revolution.
54. Ibid., p. 435.
55. Ibid., pp. 442–3; V. Timiryazev, 'Otnosheniya mezhdu Rossiey i Frantsiey sto let tomu nazad', *Istoricheskiy Vestnik,* **70** (1897) p. 969; Charles de Larivière, *Catherine II et la Révolution française* (Paris 1895) pp. 136–8.
56. Madariaga, *Russia in the Age of Catherine the Great,* p. 433.
57. S. B. Okun, *Istoriya SSSR 1796–1825* (Leningrad 1948) p. 35; Michailowski-Danilewski and Miliutin, *Geschichte des Krieges Russlands,* vol. 1, pp. 7, 11–12.
58. Madariaga, *Russia in the Age of Catherine the Great,* p. 422.
59. Ibid., p. 428.
60. Ibid., p. 433.
61. L. A. Nikiforov, 'Issledovaniya po vneshney politike Rossii XVIII veka', *Itogi i zadachi izucheniya vneshney politiki Rossii. Sovetskaya Istoriografiya* (Moscow 1981) p. 152.
62. Okun, *Istoriya SSSR,* p. 35.
63. Madariaga, *Russia in the Age of Catherine the Great,* p. 422.
64. Avgusta M. Stanislavskaya, *Russko-angliyskie otnosheniya i problemy sredizemnomor'ya (1798–1807)* (Moscow 1962) pp. 53–4. Stanislavskaya argued – rightly, in my view – that Catherine always did take the Greek Plan seriously: ibid., p. 53, n. 188. On the Plan, see above, p. 56. Stanislavskaya's book is the most impressive written by a Soviet historian on this period. It is penetrating, cogent and lively; it is based on a wide range of Russian, French and British sources, although the coverage of the German sources is less complete and the German dimension of Paul's policy has been underestimated. The Marxist-Leninist approach is not unduly obtrusive, once the customary obeisance to Marx, Engels and Lenin has been made in the introduction. However, a nationalist bias is very apparent – the Russian élites may have been feudal exploiters, but they were more effective, braver, less selfish, more idealistic than their foreign counterparts. Sometimes even a nineteenth-century flavour in the style of G. A. Henty's adventure stories enlivens the narrative – 'With Ushakov to the Mediterranean', 'With Suvorov to Italy'.
65. Norman E. Saul, *Russia and the Mediterranean 1797–1807* (Chicago 1970) p. 15.
66. This last episode can be followed best in Michailowski-Danilewski and Miliutin, *Geschichte des Krieges Russlands,* pp. 13–15.
67. Madariaga, *Russia in the Age of Catherine the Great,* p. 572.

68. A. L. Narochnitsky, 'Diplomatiya v gody termidorianskoy reaktsiy i Direktorii (1794–1799)', *Istoriya Diplomatii*, vol. 1 (Moscow 1959) p. 457.

69. Michailowski-Danilewski and Miliutin, *Geschichte des Krieges Russlands*, vol. 1, pp. 17–19; A. S. Trachevsky, *Diplomaticheskiya snosheniya Rossii s Frantsyey v epokhu Napoleona I*, vol. 1 (St Petersburg 1890) p. vi.

70. N. K. Shil'der, *Imperator Pavel Pervyy. Istoriko-biograficheskiy ocherk* (St Petersburg 1901) p. 293. The value of this work, which consists mainly of extracts from contemporary memoirs about trivia, stands in inverse ratio to its bulk – which is huge. Greatly superior is the roughly contemporaneous work by E. S. Shumigorski, *Imperator Pavel I. Zhizn' i Tsarstvovanie* (St Petersburg 1907).

71. Madariaga, *Russia in the Age of Catherine the Great*, pp. 31–2, 572.

72. J. Holland Rose, 'The political reactions of Bonaparte's Eastern Expedition', *English Historical Review*, **44** (1929) p. 48.

73. M. M. Shtrange, *Russkoye obshchestvo i frantsuzkaya revolyutsiya 1789–1794 gg.* (Moscow 1956) pp. 177–8.

74. Okun, *Istoriya SSSR*, pp. 36–7.

75. Saul, *Russia and the Mediterranean*, p. 22. This attractively written and scholarly work contains all manner of important insights and information relevant to the origins of the War of the Second Coalition. There is a useful critical bibliography on Paul I's foreign policy in Clara Jean Tucker, *The Foreign Policy of Tsar Paul I* (Syracuse University dissertation 1966) pp. 339–69.

76. R. S. Lanin, 'Vneshnyaya politika Pavla I v 1796–1798 gg.', *Uchenye zapiski, Leningradskogo Gosudarstvennogo Universiteta, seriya istoricheskikh nauk*, vol. 10 (Leningrad 1941).

77. Ibid., pp. 6–8.

78. Although recommending Lanin's article, Avgusta Stanislavskaya – *Russko-angliyskie otnosheniya*, p. 80, n. 13 – criticises what she regards as the exaggerated degree of coherence and consistency ascribed to Paul's policy, but does not indicate in detail wherein she thinks lay the incoherence and the inconsistency.

79. Lanin, 'Vneshnyaya politika Pavla I', pp. 10–14. Repnin's instructions, dated 28 April 1797, are printed in full in Michailowski-Danilewski and Miliutin, *Geschichte des Krieges Russlands*, pp. 25–34.

80. Trachevsky, *Diplomaticheskiya snosheniya Rossii s Frantsyey*, vol. I, p. viii. The course of Panin's mission can be followed in some detail in A. Brikner, *Materialy dlya zhisneopisaniya Grafa Nikity Petrovicha Panina (1770–1837)*, vol. 2 (St Petersburg 1890) pp. 5–20.

81. Stanislavskaya, *Russko-angliyskie otnosheniya*, pp. 83, 96–7.

82. Michailowski-Danilewski and Miliutin, *Geschichte des Krieges Russlands*, p. 36; Sorel, *L'Europe et la Révolution française*, vol. 5, p. 226.

83. Saul, *Russia and the Mediterranean*, p. 32.

84. Ibid., p. 37.

85. Ibid., pp. 35–6.

86. Lanin, 'Vneshnyaya politika Pavla I', p. 30.

87. Michailowski-Danilewski and Miliutin, *Geschichte des Krieges Russlands*, p. 345.

88. Tucker, *The Foreign Policy of Tsar Paul I*, p. 71.
89. Michailowski-Danilewski and Miliutin, *Geschichte des Krieges Russlands*, p. 345; Shumigorski, *Imperator Pavel I*, p. 143.
90. Tucker argues that the turning-point came in the summer of 1798 when Paul escaped from the influence of both his wife, Maria Fyodorovna, and his favourite, Catherine Nelidova – *The Foreign Policy of Tsar Paul I*, pp. 14–16. Shumigorski – *Imperator Pavel I*, p. 141 – argues, on the contrary, that it was just these two who wooed him away from a policy of non-intervention. Almost all the evidence relating to the influence of this or that faction is unreliable hearsay. As will be seen, there were sound reasons based on *raison d'état* for Russia taking a more positive line against the French.
91. Michailowski-Danilewski and Miliutin, *Geschichte des Krieges Russlands*, vol. 1, p. 57.
92. Ibid., p. 67.
93. V. P. Kochubey to Count S. P. Vorontsov, 23 June 1798 – *Arkhiv Knyazya Vorontsova*, ed. P. Bartenev, vol. 18 (Moscow 1880) p. 140.
94. Stanislavskaya, *Russko-angliyskie otnosheniya*, p. 87.
95. Lanin, *Vneshnyaya politika Pavla I*, pp. 26–8.
96. Saul, *Russia and the Mediterranean*, pp. 62–3.
97. Ibid., pp. 63–5.
98. E. Wertheimer, 'Erzherzog Carl und die zweite Coalition bis zum Frieden von Lunéville, 1798–1801', *Archiv für österreichische Geschichte*, **67** (1886) p. 196.
99. For some forthright comments by Thugut on the internal defects of the Habsburg Monarchy, see his letters to Colloredo of 20 May, 28 June and 11 October 1798 – Alfred Ritter von Vivenot, *Vertrauliche Briefe des Freiherrn von Thugut*, vol. 2 (Vienna 1872) pp. 101, 106, 126.
100. The development of Austrian policy between Campo Formio and the summer of 1798 can be followed in considerable, not to say numbing, detail in Heinrich von Sybel, *Geschichte der Revolutionszeit von 1789 bis 1800,*, 2nd edn, 5 vols, vol. 5 (Frankfurt am Main 1882) bk 5, chs 1–5.
101. Thugut had resigned nominally as foreign minister, to allow himself more time to prepare the Habsburg Monarchy (and especially Italy) for war. This change of personnel did not involve any change of policy and Thugut's influence remained predominant.
102. For contrasting French and German accounts of the Selz conference, see Sorel, *L'Europe et la Révolution française*, vol. 5, pp. 325–7 and Sybel, *Geschichte der Revolutionszeit*, vol. 5, pp. 135–9.
103. Ibid., pp. 92, 100.
104. Lanin, 'Vneshnyaya politika Pavla I', p. 24.
105. Michailowski-Danilewski and Miliutin, *Geschichte des Krieges Russlands*, p. 56.
106. K. T. Heigel, *Deutsche Geschichte vom Tode Friedrichs des Großen bis zur Auflösung des alten Reichs*, vol. 2 (Stuttgart 1899) pp. 311–14; Paul Bailleu, *Preußen und Frankreich von 1795 bis 1807. Diplomatische Correspondenzen*, vol. 1 (Leipzig 1881) pp. xxxvi–xlv.
107. Michailowski-Danilewski and Miliutin, *Geschichte des Krieges Russlands*, p. 56.
108. Wertheimer, 'Erzherzog Carl und die zweite Coalition', p. 197. For

evidence of the change of mood in government circles, see the letter from Thugut to Cobenzl of 19 August 1798 – Alfred Ritter von Vivenot (ed.), *Zur Geschichte des Rastadter Congreßes* (Vienna 1871) pp. 230–4.

109. Hermann Hüffer, *Diplomatische Verhandlungen aus der Zeit der französischen Revolution*, vol. 3: *Der Rastatter Congreß und die zweite Coalition* (Bonn 1879) pp. 89–90.
110. Mackesy, *The Strategy of Overthrow*, p. 56.
111. Heigel, *Deutsche Geschichte*, vol. 2, p. 324.
112. Saul, *Russia and the Mediterranean*, p. 76.
113. Lanin, 'Vneshnyaya politika Pavla I', p. 37.
114. Michailowski-Danilewski and Miliutin, *Geschichte des Krieges Russlands*, vol. 1, p. 95.
115. Shumigorsky, *Imperator Pavel I*, p. 159.
116. Sybel, *Geschichte der Revolutionszeit*, vol. 5, p. 247.
117. Wertheimer, 'Erzherzog Carl und die zweite Coalition', pp. 206–7.
118. Raymond Guyot, *Le Directoire et la paix de l'Europe des traités de Bâle à la deuxième coalition (1795–1799)* (Paris 1912) p. 858.
119. Sybel, *Geschichte der Revolutionszeit*, vol. 5, p. 163.
120. G. Pariset, *La Révolution (1792–1799), Histoire de France contemporaine depuis la Révolution jusqu'à la paix de 1919*, ed. Ernest Lavisse, vol. 2 (Paris 1920) p. 393.
121. Sybel, *Geschichte der Revolutionszeit*, vol. 5, p. 256.
122. Sorel, *L'Europe et la Révolution française*, vol. 5, p. 283.
123. Pariset, *La Révolution*, p. 398.
124. Quoted in Denis Woronoff, *The Thermidorean Regime and the Directory 1794–1799* (Cambridge 1984) p. 167.
125. The most penetrating and best-informed criticism of this aspect of Thugut's policy is to be found in Aretin, *Heiliges Römisches Reich*, vol. 1, ch. 4, pt 9.
126. For Grenville's incorrigible belief that France was – as ever – on the verge of collapse, see Mackesy, *The Strategy of Overthrow*, p. 72.
127. Markham, *Napoleon*, p. 90.
128. Saul, *Russia and the Mediterranean*, p. 145.

CONCLUSION

The major part of this book has been concerned only with the events of a few years. Even if the half-century or so which preceded the outbreak of the revolutionary wars was given brief consideration, the approach has been necessarily microscopic, when set against the whole sweep of human history. Consequently, the macroscopic theories discussed in Chapter 1 have been of little or no assistance. Whether wholly time-less, like those of the psychologists, or with a '10 million year' sweep like those of the ethologists, or even with the more modest time-span of the anthropologists, those theories cannot accommodate the sudden shifts from peace to war and from war to peace. If human nature drove the Austrians and Prussians to make war in 1792, it also kept them at peace in 1791. If the evolutionary process had given the French revo-lutionaries the aggressive instinct and sense of territory which drove them to war in 1792 and 1793, it had also given them the ability to calculate that kept them at peace in 1790 and 1798. If the British élites did use propaganda to carry their subjects into war in 1793, they had remained at peace in 1791. If the primacy of the domestic policy in the shape of serf unrest kept the Russians at peace for most of the 1790s, it did not prevent them going to war in 1798. The inexorable forward march of the forces of production may have ranged all the major European powers against each other at some stage in the 1790s, but they equally kept them at peace for part of the time too.

In short, the theories of non-historical disciplines *may* be able to explain war *per se*, but they cannot explain individual conflicts. To seek a more precise explanatory theory is to risk the charge of super-ficiality: that one's head gets pressed so close to the score that only individual notes, or at best bars, can be encompassed, so that the overall structure and meaning of the music cannot be understood. A tempting reply to that persuasive analogy is that a conductor whose interpretation of the score cannot be reconciled with the notes as actually written and which therefore produces only disjointed rhythms and discordant sounds, ought to be booed off the podium. Yet that

'Viennese' reaction is unnecessarily intolerant. There ought to be room for all kinds of approaches, although to suppose that they can all be accommodated in the course of a single performance is visionary.

At the risk of prolonging this musical metaphor beyond the point of endurance, I shall concede that the reading of the origins of the French revolutionary wars offered in the main part of this book has been very much that of a *Kapellmeister* rather than that of a Maestro. I shall deny, however, that the interpretation was selected first and the music composed last. It was not until the research (if the reading of printed sources and secondary works can be dignified by such a term) was complete that I turned to the theoretical literature. I have indicated in Chapter 1 which parts of it I found most helpful and why. The works of von Clausewitz, Blainey and Howard, in particular, confirmed some conclusions – both general and specific, modified or rejected others, and pointed the way to still more.

Their most illuminating service was to clarify the distinction between reasons for hostility and reasons for war. Relations between states in regular contact with each other, whether as nominal allies or as nominal enemies, are naturally characterised by dissension. As they pursue the same sort of political and economic interests they cannot help but disagree. Even during the most self-conscious periods of cosmopolitanism and free trade, arguments abound. Indeed, the rancorous recriminations which enliven the summit conferences of the Common Market suggest that actual hostility may stand in inverse ratio to nominal amity. Yet it seems improbable that Great Britain will go to war with the rest of the Community to secure a reduction in its financial contribution. Similarly, in the 1790s, of all the great powers, Russia was the most vocally hostile to revolutionary France but was also the last to go to war with it.

This distinction also helps to put ideology in its place. Ideological differences create hostility but they do not necessarily lead to war. In ideological terms, the USA and the USSR are as opposed as it is possible to conceive, yet they have never gone to war against each other. Similarly, in the 1790s revolutionary ideology did not prevent the French from seeking an alliance with Prussia, securing an alliance with Spain or sending military advisers to the Ottoman Turks. Dislike of revolutionary principles and fear of revolutionary contagion certainly played a part in creating such improbable coalitions as that of Austria, Prussia, Great Britain and Spain or that of Austria, Russia, Great Britain and Turkey, but it was not the only, nor indeed the most important adhesive.

During the early stages it was French *weakness*, not revolutionary subversion which attracted the bellicose attention of the German powers. The Prussians, who had less to fear from unrest at home than anyone else, were the most forward because they were the most greedy. It was the prospect of obtaining Jülich and Berg, or another slice of Poland, which excited their interest. When they discovered that the Revolution would not fall over at the first push and then found another way to acquire territory (in the Second Partition of Poland), they made peace and reverted to their old Austrophobe foreign policy. For their part, the Austrians were bound to be more sensitive to the French Revolution *qua* revolution, given the vulnerability of their Belgian provinces and their dynastic links with the French royal family. Yet they too were not so much counter-revolutionary as anti-French. What Leopold II and Kaunitz wanted in France *least* was a revitalised old-regime monarchy ready to cause mayhem in the style of Louis XIV. What they wanted most was a France too weak to challenge Austrian control of the Low Countries, Germany and Italy, but stable enough not to be a source of instability. In short, they wanted to see the new France as a sort of Poland-in-the-west – but with Austria playing the role of Russia. That eminently desirable state of affairs seemed to have been achieved when Louis XVI 'accepted' the new constitution of September 1791. It was when Brissotin pressure threatened to destroy it that a new Austrian initiative was launched which helped to bring war (see p. 102).

Similarly, it was not the wave of revolutionary *ideology* in the autumn of 1792 which prompted Great Britain to move from neutrality to hostility, it was the expansion of revolutionary *power*, into the Low Countries. The 'fraternal decree' of 19 November certainly persuaded the British that the French were launching a determined attempt to subvert all established regimes, but by the end of the year it had become clear that any danger of domestic insurrection had passed. Indeed it was the very soundness of public opinion which encouraged Pitt and his colleagues to choose war as the best means of resolving their differences with the French (see p. 149). The same sort of considerations brought Russia into the war in 1798. By that time revolutionary ideology had been a bone of contention for almost a decade without provoking more than long-term snarling. It was only when French *power* expanded in such a way as to threaten Russian interests in eastern Europe and the eastern Mediterranean that the cold war could become hot.

In short, once it became clear that revolutionary France was a power to be reckoned with, the old European alignments reasserted themselves in a manner that would not have seemed strange to Europe before 1756: France allied to Spain versus Great Britain and Austria plus, occasionally, Russia. The old firms were back in business again. So, however much change the Revolution may have brought to the domestic structures of France, in international terms a better description than revolution would be 'revival': the revival of French power after three-quarters of a century of feeble leadership, misconceived policies and demoralising failure. From this perspective, the really exceptional period in the history of the European states-system was not 1789–1815 but 1756–89, occasioned by the temporary decline of France and the equally temporary rise of Prussia.

The sense that the Revolution marked a return to normality is strengthened by the continuity of attitudes. Certainly the universal principles of national sovereignty, self-determination and international liberation seemed to mark a sharp break with the past. Yet the practice of revolutionary diplomacy was not so different. Within just a year or so of the beginning of the war, the revolutionaries had adopted a policy of *raison d'état* just as narrowly selfish as that of any old regime powers.[1] By 1797 they had left the heady universalist days of 1792 so far behind that they were prepared to partition the independent republic of Venice with – the Habsburgs of all people! Moreover, all along they had shown the traditional attitudes of Austrophobia, Anglophobia and Prussophilia which went back to the opposition to the 'diplomatic revolution' of 1756 and were certainly not created by the Revolution (see p. 120).

Ideology did play an important part in encouraging the powers to resort to warfare in resolving their differences, but it did so, not by creating hostility, but by creating misunderstanding. The French revolutionaries' conviction of the universal validity and absolute superiority of their principles led naturally to a sense of invincibility. If history were on their side and the future beckoned, what human force could withstand for long their inexorable march to victory? This supreme confidence sharpened their vision but narrowed its focus: some things they saw with prophetic clarity, others they overlooked altogether. It enabled them to see beyond the apparent chaos engendered by the Revolution to the real power of a liberated people and, more especially, to the real power of a liberated state. But it also blinded them to the equally real power of their potential enemies. What they thought was the terminal decline of the Habsburg monarchy, for example, turned out to be temporary embarrassment. Revolutionary tunnel-vision magnified old-regime Europe's disabilities but passed by those great reserves of stamina which were to lead to final victory. It was the French Republic that was to prove ephemeral and the ramshackle empires of the east that were to last another century and more. Blissfully unaware that both they and their regime were destined to die young, the Brissotin orators swept the National Assembly to war in a surge of optimistic belief that it would be short and easy.

Ideology performed the same dual function for the other powers of Europe, albeit in reverse order. For these monarchs and their ministers, the power of a state depended on political stability, social order, economic prosperity, sound finances and religious harmony. What they thought they saw in France was civil war, anarchy, pauperisation, bankruptcy and a new religious war. In large measure this selective myopia was due to the creation by their ideology of a set of criteria which were just not applicable to revolutionary France. So, for example, they knew all about the emigration of officers and the mutinies of the rank and file, which apparently had immobilised the French army, but were wholly ignorant of the sources of patriotic enthusiasm and unprecedented numerical strength which the Revolution could tap. Their conservative, aristocratic and hierarchic notions about society in general and warfare in particular made it impossible for them even to conceive that a 'citizen army' could resist, let alone defeat an army of professionals. The ease with which the Prussians and the Austrians had dealt with the Dutch and Belgian insurgents in 1787 and 1790 respectively provided apparently conclusive confirmation of this assumption.

This kind of mutual miscalculation is notoriously common during periods of ideological turmoil, for a conservative's idea of strength is a radical's idea of weakness, and vice versa. It is also common when reliable information is hard to obtain. That is one very important difference which – mercifully – distinguishes the ideological conflict of the late eighteenth century from that of the late twentieth century. It is just because modern intelligence-gathering techniques have become so advanced that the USA and the USSR have been able to assess more or less correctly their power relationship and hence to remain at peace. It was miscalculation based on woefully inadequate intelligence which took the former into a major war in Vietnam and the latter into a minor war in Afghanistan. In the 1790s both sides were groping in the dark, although neither was aware of the fact. The 'Coppelia effect' (see p. 73) convinced each of them that they were seeing one thing when in fact they were seeing quite another. The old regime governments believed much of what their own agents and the French *émigrés* told them about the imminent collapse of the Revolution, not only because that was what they expected and wanted to hear but also because they could know no better. For the same reasons, the French revolutionaries believed *most* of what their own agents and foreign refugees told them about the imminent collapse of the old regimes. If only Kaunitz had known – say – that the Feuillants had been isolated and discredited by the end of 1791, he might never have launched his intimidatory exercise with such counter-productive results (see p. 102). If only Brissot and his supporters had known – say – the true state of public opinion in Germany and the Habsburg dominions, they might have adopted a much less bellicose and provocative tone when dealing with Vienna (see p. 110).

While the Austrians hoped and believed that they could attain their objectives without resorting to actual fighting, the dominant party in the French Legislative Assembly was intent on – desperate for – war. Yet the Brissotins could not have carried the majority, let alone the virtual unanimity, of their fellow-deputies along with them, if Kaunitz had not given them such powerful and timely assistance (see p. 116).[2] The origins of the war of 1792 provide the best possible illustration of the obvious but often-ignored fact that a state cannot go to war all by itself, that it 'takes two to tango'. Nor could they have succeeded without the misguided belief of the court that war would bring counter-revolution.

The task of presenting the clumsy Austrian initiative in its worst possible light and of exposing the treason of the King and Queen was facilitated greatly by the nature of the forum in which they were accomplished. The sheer size of the *manège*, in which the sessions of the Legislative Assembly were held, allowed it to become a permanent political rally, rather than a debating chamber (see p. 112). That, in turn, allowed the Brissotin orators to deploy their superb skills to maximum effect. By tapping such powerful emotions as Austrophobia, nationalism, hatred of the *émigrés*, fear of counter-revolution and (above all) nihilism, they whipped up a frenzy of paranoid aggression among both deputies and spectators. Above all, by creating the conviction that their enemies were terminally decadent but they themselves were invincibly strong, they also created the illusion that victory was certain.

It was in the Legislative Assembly that the crucial decisions were taken. It was there that the final campaign against the Feuillant ministry was launched, which terrorised Louis XVI into appointing ministers eager to take the final steps to war. Yet the Legislative Assembly was not operating in a vacuum. Even more – much more – than the British Parliament, it was subject to all kinds of outside pressures, from Paris especially but also from the French provinces. But this remains one of the great unresearched areas of French revolutionary history. It is just possible that the Brissotins and the Fayettistes acted as they did because they were under pressure from opinion 'out of doors'. Until that hypothesis can be substantiated, however, the reverse relationship remains the more probable. Of course the Brissotins thought they knew – probably correctly – what was best calculated to arouse the revolutionary masses. Yet the evidence suggests that it was they who took the initiative, impelled not by the force of public opinion but by their ambition to seize power and complete the Revolution.

Analysing motives is a notoriously imprecise and hazardous business. Even the individuals or groups of individuals concerned are often unaware of why they are *really* pursuing a certain course of action. Not only is the human capacity for self-deception eternal but politicians, in particular, appear to possess a special talent for believing their own rhetoric. With specific reference to the Brissotins, it is certainly possible that they launched their campaign for war to divert the social radicalism of the revolutionary crowd, to restore monetary stability or to promote more generally the interests of the French bourgeoisie (see p. 71). They certainly did argue that war would promote stability and prosperity. Yet there is nothing in the evidence unearthed so far to suggest that one or other of these socio-economic motives was paramount. Rather it suggests that they were conceived as secondary benefits, welcome but subsidiary to the basic drive for power.

The same observations could be made about the material interests of the other participants. The class character of their policies can certainly be detected. Fear that the example of the Revolution and the force of its principles endangered their social structures did play a part in provoking their hostility to the new regime in France. Yet, as was argued earlier, between an attitude of hostility and a decision to resort to war a great gulf remains. The road to war in 1792, 1793 or 1798 was no linear and inevitable progression, but a meandering, even aimless dawdle, punctuated by diversions and about-turns. Moreover, it is unlikely that it was economic interests which constructed the final bridge. Of course the acquisition of territory would have – and in the case of Prussia and Great Britain actually did – enhance economic resources, but it was power *per se* that was the fundamental concern. Economic interest is certainly one essential component of power, but it does not constitute the totality.

In this concluding chapter I have tried to bring together some of the general observations about the origins of wars in general and of the French revolutionary wars in particular which were developed in the main part of the book. If they, or even some of them, are valid, it may be wondered whether this volume is out of place as the first in a series on the origins of *modern* wars. Yet the French revolutionary wars did constitute the first modern war, not because it represented a conflict between two diametrically opposed ideologies, but because of what it became. By liberating their state in the course of 1792–94, by casting off all inhibitions and maximising their resources, the French revolutionaries waged total war of unprecedented intensity and on an unprecedented scale. Not only did it 'revolutionise the Revolution', it also forced the other European states into emulation, however delayed and partial. After almost a quarter of a century of devastation, exploitation and over-exertion, no part of Europe was untouched: politically, economically, socially, intellectually or culturally. It was not the French Revolution which created the modern world, it was the French revolutionary wars.

REFERENCES AND NOTES

1. For a more extended discussion of this process of degeneration, see ch. 2 of T. C. W. Blanning, *The French Revolution in Germany* (Oxford 1983).
2. The same observation applies, albeit in more muted form, to the tone and substance of Lord Grenville's communications of December 1792 and January 1793 – see p. 157.

FURTHER READING

This brief list is intended only as an introduction to the very extensive literature available. Those books and articles which were found particularly helpful in the preparation of this book are listed in the notes at the end of each chapter.

PRINTED SOURCES

Archives parlementaires de 1787 à 1860, Recueil complet des débats législatifs et politiques des chambres françaises, 127 vols (Paris 1879–1913).

William Cobbett (ed.), *The Parliamentary History of England. From the Earliest Period to the Year 1803*, 36 vols (London 1806–20).

Albert Sorel (ed.), *Recueil des instructions données aux ambassadeurs et ministres de France depuis les traités de Westphalie jusqu'à la Révolution française*, vol. I: *Autriche* (Paris 1884).

F.-A. Aulard, *La Société des Jacobins. Recueil de documents pour l'histoire du Club des Jacobins de Paris*, 6 vols (Paris, 1889–97).

Etienne Dumont, *Souvenirs sur Mirabeau et sur les deux premières assemblées législatives*, ed. J. Bénétruy (Paris 1951).

C. Perroud (ed.), *J.-P. Brissot. Correspondance et papiers précédés d'un avertissement et d'une notice sur sa vie* (Paris 1912).

Charles François Dumouriez, *La vie et les mémoires du général Dumouriez*, 2 vols (Paris 1822).

G. Pallain, *La mission de Talleyrand à Londres en 1792. Correspondance inédite de Talleyrand avec le Département des Affaires étrangères, le général Biron etc.* (Paris 1889).

Correspondance de Napoléon I, publiée par ordre de l'Empereur Napoléon III, vol. 3 (Paris 1859).

A. F. Pribram (ed.), *Österreichische Staatsverträge: England*, vol. 2: *1749–1813, Veröffentlichungen der Kommission für neuere Geschichte Österreichs*, vol. 12 (Vienna 1913).

Alfred Ritter von Vivenot, *Quellen zur Geschichte der deutschen Kaiserpolitik*

Oesterreichs während der französischen Revolution, 1790–1801, 5 vols (Vienna 1874–90).

Alfred Ritter von Arneth (ed.), *Joseph II und Leopold von Toscana. Ihr Briefwechsel von 1781 bis 1790*, 2 vols (Vienna 1872).

Alfred Ritter von Arneth (ed.), *Marie Antoinette, Joseph II und Leopold II. Ihr Briefwechsel* (Leipzig, Paris and Vienna 1866).

Alfred Ritter von Arneth (ed.), *Joseph II und Katharina von Russland. Ihr Briefwechsel* (Vienna 1869).

Alfred Ritter von Arneth and J. Flammermont (eds), *Correspondance secrète du Comte de Mercy-Argenteau avec l'Empereur Joseph II et le Prince de Kaunitz*, 2 vols (Paris 1889–91).

Adolf Beer (ed.), *Joseph II, Leopold II und Kaunitz. Ihr Briefwechsel* (Vienna 1873).

Adolf Beer (ed.), *Leopold II, Franz II und Catharina. Ihre Correspondenz* (Leipzig 1874).

Alfred Ritter von Vivenot (ed.), *Vertrauliche Briefe des Freiherrn von Thugut*, 2 vols (Vienna 1872).

Alfred Ritter von Vivenot, *Zur Geschichte des Rastatter Kongresses* (Vienna 1871).

Paul Bailleu, *Preussen und Frankreich von 1795 bis 1807. Diplomatische Correspondenzen*, vol. 1 (Leipzig 1881).

A. Aspinall (ed.), *The Later Correspondence of George III*, vol. 1: *December 1783 to January 1793* (Cambridge 1962).

Oscar Browning (ed.), *Despatches from Paris, 1784–1790*, 2 vols (London 1910).

Oscar Browning (ed.), *The Political Memoranda of Francis Fifth Duke of Leeds* (London 1884).

The Manuscripts of J. B. Fortescue Esq. preserved at Dropmore, vol. 2, Historical Manuscripts Commission, Fourteenth Report, Appendix, pt v (London 1894) [The Correspondence of Lord Grenville].

William, Lord Auckland, *Journals and Correspondence*, 2 vols (London 1861).

Mrs Gillespie Smyth (ed.), *Memoirs and Correspondence of Sir Robert Murray Keith*, 2 vols (London 1849).

James Harris First Earl of Malmesbury, *Diaries and Correspondence*, vols. 1–2 (London 1844).

J. Holland Rose, 'Documents relating to the rupture with France in 1793', *English Historical Review*, **27** (1912).

A. Brikner, *Materialy dlya zhisneopisaniya Grafa Nikity Petrovicha Panina (1770–1837)*, vol. 2 (St Petersburg 1890).

THE ORIGINS OF GREAT WARS

Carl von Clausewitz, *On War*, eds Michael Howard and Peter Paret (Princeton 1976).

Geoffrey Blainey, *The Causes of War* (Melbourne 1977).

Michael Howard, *The Causes of War* (Oxford 1983).

Goldsworthy Lowes Dickinson, *Causes of International War*, new edn (New

York 1972).

E. F. M. Durbin and John Bowlby, *Personal Aggressiveness and War* (London 1939).

Pryns Hopkins, *The Psychology of Social Movements. A Psycho-Analytic View of Society* (London 1938).

Kenneth N. Waltz, *Man, the State and War: A Theoretical Analysis* (New York 1959).

William Brown, *War and the Psychological Conditions of Peace* (London 1942).

Anthony DeReuck and Julie Knight (eds), *Conflict in Society* (London 1966).

Jerome D. Frank, *Sanity and Survival: Psychological Aspects of War and Peace* (London 1968).

Maurice N. Walsh (ed.), *War and the Human Race* (New York 1971).

Robert Ardrey, *The Territorial Imperative* (London 1967).

Robert Ardrey, *The Hunting Hypothesis* (London 1977).

Konrad Lorenz, *On Aggression* (London 1966).

Ashley Montagu (ed.), *Man and Aggression*, 2nd edn (New York 1973).

J. D. Carthy and F. J. Ebling (eds), *The Natural History of Aggression* (London and New York 1964).

Keith F. Otterbein, 'The anthropology of war', *Handbook of Social and Cultural Anthropology*, ed. John J. Honigmann (Chicago 1973).

Bronislaw Malinowski, 'An anthropological analysis of war', *American Journal of Sociology*, **46** (1941).

Margaret Mead, 'Warfare is only an invention – not a biological necessity', *War: Studies from Psychology, Sociology, Anthropology*, eds Leon Bramson and George W. Goethals (New York 1964).

Dean G. Pruitt and Richard C. Snyder (eds), *Theory and Research on the Causes of War* (Englewood Cliffs, N.J. 1969).

J. David Singer and Associates, *Explaining War. Selected Papers from the Correlates of War Project* (Beverly Hills and London 1979).

Hadley Cantril (ed.), *Tensions that Cause War* (Urbana 1950).

F. H. Hinsley, *Power and the Pursuit of Peace. Theory and Practice in the History of Relations between States* (Cambridge 1963).

Rudolf Goldscheid, *Das Verhältnis der äusseren Politik zur inneren* (Vienna and Leipzig 1914).

Karl Dietrich Bracher, 'Kritische Betrachtungen über den Primat der Aussenpolitik', *Faktoren der politischen Entscheidung. Festgabe für Ernst Fraenkel zum 65. Geburtstag,* eds Gerhard A. Ritter and Gilbert Ziebura (Berlin 1963).

Hans-Ulrich Wehler, 'Moderne Politikgeschichte oder "Grosse Politik der Kabinette"?', *Geschichte und Gesellschaft*, **1** (1975).

Klaus Hildebrand, 'Geschichte oder "Gesellschaftsgeschichte"? Die Notwendigkeit einer politischen Geschichtsschreibung von den internationalen Beziehungen', *Historische Zeitschrift*, **223** (1976).

Hermann Oncken, 'Über die Zusammenhänge zwischen äusserer und innerer Politik', *Vorträge der Gehe-Stiftung,* vol. 9 (Leipzig and Dresden 1919).

Rudolf L. Bindschedler, 'Zum Primat der Aussenpolitik', *Innen- und Aussenpolitik. Primat oder Interdependenz? Festschrift zum 60. Geburtstag von Walther Hofer,* eds Urs Altermatt and Judith Garamvölgyi (Bern 1980).

Karel Kara, 'On the Marxist theory of war and peace', *Journal of Peace*

Research, **5** (1) (1968).

V. Kubalkova and A. A. Cruickshank, *Marxism-Leninism and the Theory of International Relations* (London 1980).

GENERAL

Derek McKay and H. M. Scott, *The Rise of the Great Powers 1648–1815* (London 1983).

William Doyle, *The Old European Order 1660–1800* (Oxford 1978).

Jacques Droz, *Histoire diplomatique de 1648 à 1919*, 3rd edn (Paris 1972).

Albert Sorel, *Europe and the French Revolution*, vol. 1: *The Political Traditions of the Old Regime*, eds Alfred Cobban and J. W. Hunt (London 1969).

Albert Sorel, *L'Europe et la Révolution française*, 8 vols (Paris 1885–1905).

Heinrich von Sybel, *Geschichte der Revolutionszeit von 1789 bis 1800*, 2nd edn, 5 vols (Frankfurt am Main 1882).

Adalbert Wahl, *Geschichte des europäischen Staatensystems im Zeitalter der französischen Revolution und der Freiheitskriege (1789–1815)* (Munich and Berlin 1912).

André Fugier, *La Révolution française et l'Empire napoléonien, Histoire des relations internationales*, ed. Pierre Renouvin, vol. 4 (Paris 1954).

François de Bourgoing, *Histoire diplomatique de l'Europe pendant la Révolution française*, 2 vols (Paris 1865–67).

R. H. Lord, *The Second Partition of Poland* (Cambridge, Mass. 1915).

Leopold von Ranke, *Ursprung und Beginn der Revolutionskriege, 1791 und 1792* (Leipzig 1879).

J. H. Clapham, *The Causes of the War of 1792* (Cambridge 1899).

M. S. Anderson, *The Eastern Question 1774 – 1923* (London 1966).

Piers Mackesy, *Statesmen at War. The Strategy of Overthrow 1798–1799* (London 1974).

FRANCE

Georges Lefebvre, *The French Revolution*, 2 vols (London 1962).

François Furet and Denis Richet, *The French Revolution* (London 1970).

Fernand Braudel and Ernest Labrousse (eds), *Histoire économique et sociale de la France*, vols 2–3 (Paris 1970, 1976).

Jacques Godechot, *La Grande Nation. L'expansion révolutionnaire de la France dans le monde 1789–1799*, 2 vols (Paris 1956).

F. Masson, *Le Département des affaires étrangères pendant la Révolution 1787–1804* (Paris 1877).

Michel Vovelle, *The Fall of the French Monarchy, 1787–1792* (Cambridge 1984).

Pierre Muret, 'L'affaire des princes possessionnés d'Alsace et les origines du conflit entre la Révolution et l'Empire', *Revue d'histoire moderne et contemporaine,* **1** (1899–1900).

Hans Glagau, *Die französische Legislative und der Ursprung der Revolutionskriege 1791–1792, mit einem Anhang politischer Briefe aus dem Wiener K. und K. Haus-, Hof- und Staatsarchiv,* Historische Studien, vol. 1 (Berlin 1896).

Georges Michon, *Essai sur l'histoire du parti Feuillant* (Paris 1924).

Georges Michon, *Robespierre et la guerre révolutionnaire* (Paris 1937).

H.-A. Goetz-Bernstein, *La Diplomatie de la Gironde. Jacques-Pierre Brissot* (Paris 1912).

Albert Mathiez, *La Révolution et les étrangers. Cosmopolitisme et défense nationale* (Paris 1918).

Alphonse Aulard, 'La diplomatie du premier comité de salut public', *Etudes et leçons sur la Révolution française,* 3rd edn, vol. 3 (Paris 1914).

Richard Munthe Brace, 'General Dumouriez and the Girondins 1792–3', *American Historical Review,* **56** (3) (1951).

Felix Markham, *Napoleon* (New York 1963).

C. de la Jonquière, *L'Expédition d'Egypte 1798–1801,* vol. 1 (Paris 1900).

Raymond Guyot, *Le Directoire et la paix de l'Europe des traités de Bâle à la deuxième coalition (1795–1799)* (Paris 1912).

AUSTRIA AND PRUSSIA

Karl Otmar Freiherr von Aretin, *Heiliges Römisches Reich 1776–1806. Reichsverfassung und Staatssouveränität,* 2 vols (Wiesbaden 1967).

Ludwig Häusser, *Deutsche Geschichte vom Tode Friedrichs des Grossen bis zur Gründung des deutschen Bundes,* 3rd edn, 4 vols (Berlin 1861–63).

K. T. Heigel, *Deutsche Geschichte vom Tode Friedrichs des Grossen bis zur Auflösung des alten Reichs,* 2 vols (Stuttgart 1899, 1911).

C. A. Macartney, *The Habsburg Empire 1790–1918* (London 1968).

Andreas Theodor Preuss, *Ewald Friedrich Graf von Hertzberg* (Berlin 1909).

Friedrich Carl Wittichen, *Preussen und die Revolutionen in Belgien und Lüttich 1789–1790* (Göttingen 1905).

Adam Wandruszka, *Leopold II. Erzherzog von Österreich, Grossherzog von Toskana, König von Ungarn und Böhmen, Römischer Kaiser,* 2 vols (Vienna and Munich 1963, 1965).

Kurt Heidrich, *Preussen im Kampfe gegen die französische Revolution bis zur zweiten Teilung Polens* (Stuttgart and Berlin 1908).

Theodor Ludwig, *Die deutschen Reichsstände in Elsass und der Ausbruch der Revolutionskriege* (Strasbourg 1898).

P. Bailleu, 'Zur Vorgeschichte der Revolutionskriege', *Historische Zeitschrift,* **74** (1895).

Kurt Holzapfel, 'Intervention oder Koexistenz: Preussens Stellung zu Frankreich 1789–1792', *Zeitschrift für Geschichtswissenschaft,* **25** (7) (1977).

Reinhold Koser, 'Die preussische Politik von 1786 bis 1806', *Zur preussischen und deutschen Geschichte. Aufsätze und Vorträge* (Stuttgart and Berlin

1921).

Heinrich von Sybel, 'Polens Untergang und der Revolutionskrieg', *Historische Zeitschrift*, **23** (1970).

E. Wertheimer, 'Erzherzog Carl und die zweite Coalition bis zum Frieden von Lunéville, 1798–1801', *Archiv für österreichische Geschichte*, **67** (1886).

Hermann Hüffer, *Diplomatische Verhandlungen aus der Zeit der französischen Revolution*, vol. 3: *Der Rastatter Congress und die zweite Coalition* (Bonn 1879).

GREAT BRITAIN

I. R. Christie, *Wars and Revolutions. Britain 1760–1815* (London 1982).

Paul Langford, *The Eighteenth Century* (London 1976).

John Ehrman, *The Younger Pitt*, 2 vols (London 1969, 1984).

J. Holland Rose, *Life of William Pitt*, 2 vols (London 1911).

Earl Stanhope, *Life of the Right Honourable William Pitt, With Extracts from his MS. Papers*, vols. 1–2 (London 1861).

Felix Salomon, *Wilhelm Pitt der jüngere*, vol. 1, pt 2: *Bis zum Ausgang der Friedensperiode (Februar 1793)* (Leipzig and Berlin 1906).

J. T. Stoker, *William Pitt et la Révolution française, 1789–1793* (Paris 1935).

Roy Porter, *English Society in the Eighteenth Century* (Harmondsworth 1982).

V. T. Harlow, *The Founding of the Second British Empire*, 2 vols (London 1952).

Dietrich Gerhard, *England und der Aufstieg Russlands* (Munich and Berlin 1933).

J. T. Murley, *The Origin and Outbreak of the Anglo-French War of 1793* (Oxford dissertation 1959).

Clive Emsley, *British Society and the French Wars 1793–1815* (London 1979).

Albert Goodwin, *The Friends of Liberty. The English Democratic Movement in the Age of the French Revolution* (London 1979).

Carl. B. Cone, *The English Jacobins: Reformers in Late Eighteenth Century England* (New York 1968).

P. A. Brown, *The French Revolution in English History* (London 1918).

E. M. Johnston, *Ireland in the Eighteenth Century* (Dublin 1974).

Henry W. Meikle, *Scotland and the French Revolution* (Glasgow 1912).

L. G. Mitchell, *Charles James Fox and the Disintegration of the Whig Party 1782–1794* (Oxford 1971).

F. O'Gorman, *The Whig Party and the French Revolution* (London 1967).

Herbert Butterfield, 'Charles James Fox and the Whig Opposition in 1792', *The Historical Journal*, **9** (3) (1949).

SPAIN

Modesto Lafuente, *Historia General de España*, vol. 21: *1780–1795* (Madrid

1858).

Antonio Dominguez Ortiz, *Sociedad y Estad en el siglo XVIII español* (Barcelona 1976).

Vicente Palacio Atard, *La España del siglo XVIII. El siglo de las reformas* (Madrid 1978).

Hermann Baumgarten, *Geschichte Spaniens zur Zeit der französischen Revolution* (Berlin 1861).

Angel Salcedo Ruiz, *La Epoca de Goya. Historia de España y Hispano-América desde el advenimiento de Felipe V hasta la guerra de la Independencia* (Madrid n.d.).

Manuel Ferrandis and Caetano Beirao, *Historia contemporanea de España y Portugal* (Barcelona and Madrid 1966).

Angel Ossorio y Gallardo, *Historia del pensamiento politico catalán durante la guerra de España con la Republica francesa 1793–1795*, new edn (Barcelona 1977).

RUSSIA AND TURKEY

Isabel de Madariaga, *Russia in the Age of Catherine the Great* (London 1981).

S. B. Okun', *Istoriya SSSR 1796–1825* (Leningrad 1948).

Ernst Herrmann, *Geschichte des russischen Staates*, vol. 6: *Russlands auswärtige Beziehungen in den Jahren 1775 bis 1792* (Gotha 1860).

Alexander Brückner, *Katharina die Zweite* (Berlin 1883).

M. M. Shtrange, *Russkoye obshchestvo i frantsuzkaya revolyutsiya 1789–1794 gg.* (Moscow 1956).

A. S. Trachevsky, *Diplomaticheskiya snosheniya Rossii s Frantsyey v epokhu Napoleona I,* vol. 1 (St Petersburg 1890).

A. M. Stanislavskaya, *Russo-angliyskie otnosheniya i problemy sredizemnomor'ya 1798–1807* (Moscow 1962).

Stanford Jay Shaw, *Between Old and New: The Ottoman Empire under Sultan Selim III, 1789–1807* (Cambridge, Mass. 1971).

Norman E. Saul, *Russia and the Mediterranean 1797–1807* (Chicago 1970).

A. J. Michailowski-Danilewski and D. A. Miliutin, *Geschichte des Krieges Russlands mit Frankreich unter der Regierung Kaiser Pauls I im Jahre 1799*, vol. 1 (Munich 1856).

E. S. Shumigorski, *Imperator Pavel I. Zhizn' i Tsarstvovaniye* (St Petersburg 1907).

R. S. Lanin, 'Vneshnyaya politika Pavla I v 1796–1798 gg.', *Uchenye zapiski, seriya istoricheskikh nauk,* vol. 10 (Leningrad 1941).

Boris Mouravieff, *L'Alliance russo-turque au milieu des guerres napoléoniennes* (Neufchâtel 1954).

Bernard Lewis, 'The impact of the French Revolution on Turkey', *Cahier d'histoire mondiale,* **1** (1) (1953).

Johann Wilhelm Zinkeisen, *Geschichte des osmanischen Reiches in Europa,* vol. 7 (Gotha 1863).

A. D. Novicev, 'Der Einfall der Franzosen in Ägypten und der französisch-türkische Krieg 1798–1802', *Zeitschrift für Geschichtswissenschaft,* **19** (9)

(1971).

V. Timiryazev, 'Otnosheniya mezhdu Rossiey i Frantsiey sto let tomu nazad', *Istoricheskiy Vestnik,* **70** (1897).

L. A. Nikiforov, 'Issledovaniya po vneshney politike Rossii XVIII veka', *Itogi i zadachi izucheniya vneshney politiki Rossii. Sovyetskaya Istoriografiya* (Moscow 1981).

INDEX

Index

von, 82
Fischer, Fritz, 17, 19–20, 23
Fitzwilliam, 4th Earl, 150
Floridablanca, Jose Moniño, count of, 61–62, 160
Fortescue, Sir John, 40
Fox, Charles James, 142, 149, 150–2, 155, 158
France see French Revolution: Legislative Assembly; Constituent Assembly; National Convention; Directory
France, old-regime
  decline, 38–9, 41–2
  economic expansion, 46, 55, 58
  foreign policy, 37–8, 41, 55
Francis II, 80, 89, 118, 175, 192–3
Francis, Sir Philip, 150
François de Neufchâteau, Nicolas Louis, 192
Frank, Jerome, D., 7
Frankfurt am Main, 135, 156
Frederick the Great, 28–9, 39–41, 44, 47, 52, 55, 58, 110
Frederick William II, 50, 52–5, 59, 72–3, 78, 81–3, 85–6, 88, 94, 96, 114, 118, 120
French Revolution
  Anglophobia, 51, 131
  Austrophobia, 41, 43, 76, 78, 81, 121, 126
  Declaration of Rights of Man and Citizen, 73
  Estates General, 43
  foreign policy, 36, 60, 62, 70
  international subversion, 85
  national sovereignty, 208
  October Days, 74, 97
  outbreak, 36
  resources, 40
  self-determination, 208
  September Massacres, 134, 151, 156, 158
Freud, Sigmund, 2
Friedman, Herbert, 11

Galicia, 81, 85
Geiss, Imanuel, 17
Geneva, 74, 134, 137, 177
Genoa, 177–8
Gensonné, Armand, 98, 103, 107, 111, 117
George III, 40, 50, 58–9, 66, 134, 139, 142–3, 150, 166
Girondins see Brissotins
Glagau, Hans, 129

Godoy, Manuel de, 161
Goethe, Johann Wolfgang von, 17, 134
Goguelat, François, baron de, 118
Goldscheid, Rudolf, 33
Goltz, count von der, 44, 85, 115
Gordon riots, 170
Gower, Earl, 134, 158
Great Britain see also Pitt, William; George III; Leeds, 5th duke of; Grenville, William Wyndham, lord
  action against radicals, 144, 147–8
  and Belgium, 138–9, 158, 207
  and eighteenth-century wars, 37–8
  and French subversion, 139, 143, 146–7, 149, 156, 159, 207
  and Ireland, 145–6, 152–3, 156, 159, 183, 195, 198
  and old-regime France, 45
  and Prussia, 54, 132, 141, 198
  and Russia, 60, 83, 132, 150, 152–3, 198
  and Scotland, 146, 153, 156, 159
  and Spain, 61, 79, 131, 155, 162
  and the Habsburg Monarchy, 132, 134, 141, 198
  and the United Provinces, 51, 134, 137–42, 149, 153–8, 207
  and the War of the Second Coalition, 183, 198
  economic development, 39
  extra-parliamentary agitation, 143, 144, 147, 153, 167
  Francophobia, 131–2, 149, 156
  hegemony, 36
  loyalism, 143, 145, 148–9, 156, 166
  neutrality, 87, 96, 131–5, 139, 164
  over-confidence, 154–6, 159
  parliament, 142, 151–2, 155–6
  preparations for war, 141
  social unrest, 145, 170
  under-estimate of French strength, 153–4, 156
Grenville, William Wyndham, lord, 133, 138–9, 141–2, 146–7, 149, 151, 154, 157–8
Grey, Charles, 150
Guadet, Marguerite Elie, 111
Gustavus III, 40, 53, 59, 78, 186
Görres, Joseph, 178

Haas, Michael, 16
Habsburg Monarchy, 62
  see also Leopold II; Kaunitz, Wenzel Anton, prince
  abandons Holy Roman Empire, 178, 197

Index

Lenin, V.I., 22–3, 26
Leopold II, 39, 45, 54, 72, 78, 80, 82–3, 86–9, 94, 96, 100, 101–4, 113, 115, 118, 121, 133, 207
Ligurian Republic *see* Genoa
Loménie de Brienne, Etienne Charles, 50, 77
London Corresponding Society, 143, 145, 147
Lord, R.H., 72
Lorenz, Konrad, 9–10
Loughborough, 1st lord, 154–5
Louis XVI, 36, 43, 50, 78–9, 84, 88, 96–7, 99, 101–2, 104–5, 113, 115, 117, 120, 122–3, 133, 144, 160, 207, 210
Lucchesini, Girolamo, marchese di, 82

Madrid, 161
Mainz, 136, 178
Mainz, Friedrich Karl, Elector of, 101
Malinowski, Bronislaw, 13
Malmesbury, 1st lord, 151
Malta, 180, 190–1, 193–4, 198
Mann, Golo, 20
Maria Theresa, 40
Marie Antoinette, 43, 78, 82, 84, 94, 97, 99, 102, 106, 115, 117–18, 121–2, 124, 210
Marx, Karl, 19, 22–3
Masson, F., 116
Maulde, Emmanuel de, 141
Max Franz, Elector of Cologne, 42, 63, 77
Meikle, Henry W., 146
Mercy-Argenteau, Florimond, comte de, 75, 89, 102, 118
Merlin de Douai, Philippe Antoine, 75, 77
Michon, Georges, 71, 106, 137
Miller, James, 17
Mirabeau, Honoré Gabriel Riquetti, marquis de, 76, 131
Mitchell, Leslie, 150
Moltke, Helmuth von, 28
Montagu, Ashley, 11–12, 14–15
Montmorin, Saint Hérem, Armand Marc, comte de, 44, 97
Morris, Desmond, 10, 30
Mountain, The, 136
Mulhouse, 177
Muret, Pierre, 71, 77, 91
Mussolini, Benito, 7

Naples, 194
Napoleon *see* Bonaparte, Napoleon
Narbonne, Louis, comte de, 108–9, 116–17

National Assembly *see* Constituent Assembly; Legislative Assembly
National Convention, 155
    and British radicals, 146–7, 153, 157
    and foreign crusade, 136–8, 152, 162
    and Spain, 160–3
    Anglophobia, 155
    arguments for war, 155
    committees, 136
    conduct of war, 140, 153
    coup d'état of Thermidor, 197
    declaration of war, 157
    decree of 15 December 1792, 137–8
    decree of fraternity, 136–7, 147, 149, 157
    foreign policy, 136
    misunderstanding of situation in Great Britain, 152–3, 155, 159
    trial of Louis XVI, 144, 148, 157, 161, 184, 185
Nationalism, 27
Neapolitan Republic, 194
Necker, Jacques, 116
Nelson, Horatio, lord, 183, 191, 193–4, 198
Nice, 135
Nipperdey, Thomas, 34
Noël, François, 153
Nootka Sound, 61, 68, 79, 131–2

Ochs, Peter, 177
Orléans, Louis Philippe Joseph, duc d', 133
Otterbein, Keith, 14
Ottoman Empire *see* Turkey

Padua Circular, 86, 89, 133
Paine, Tom, 144–6, 157
Panin, Nikita Petrovich, prince, 189–90
Paris, 74
Pastoret, Claude-Emmanuel, 119
Pasvan Oglu, 182, 184, 191
Paul I, 176, 187–90, 193–4, 198
Peace, explanations of, 3–4, 25
Peaces *see* Treaties
Peter the Great, 40
Piedmont, 177, 194
Pillnitz, declaration of, 59, 70, 86–9, 96, 100, 133

Pitt, William, 45–7, 49, 51, 54, 59, 132–3, 140–2, 145–7, 149–52, 154, 158–9, 183, 187
Poland, 36, 38, 42, 44, 53, 55, 59–60, 62, 78, 83–4, 89, 107, 114, 175, 207

224

Index